Praise for *J. H. Oldham and George Bell*

"With his characteristically careful scholarship, deep historical knowledge, and real insight into the personal motives of these two ecumenical pioneers, Keith Clements retrieves and illuminates the foundational dynamics of this formative period of ecumenism. His work also sheds light on the enduring role of the ecumenical movement in world affairs and the prospects for renewal of the fellowship of Christian churches. A singular achievement."

—Ioan Sauca, interim general secretary,
World Council of Churches, Geneva

"As an homage to two among the most influential ecumenists of all time, this book provides insights that need to be studied by generations of ecumenists to come. It is inspirational for the churches today in their search for new ecumenical responses in a post-colonial world."

—Aruna Gnanadason, Chennai, India; formerly director
of World Council of Churches Programme on Women
in Church and Society; author of *With Courage and
Compassion: Women and the Ecumenical Movement* (2020)

"Keith Clements brings his own ecumenical experience to bear in an insightful overview of the work of two of the most influential British ecumenicists of the twentieth century. The final comparative essay is a tour de force, examining not only the legacy of Oldham and Bell but also the development of the ecumenical movement since 1960. In the light of developments such as liberation theology, feminist theology, and post-colonialism Clements makes a convincing case that Oldham and Bell still have much to offer."

—Charlotte Methuen, professor of ecclesiastical
history, University of Glasgow

T0246094

"Clements's fine work values the best in Oldham and Bell without being apologetical. This primer leads the reader into history while it points to challenges we face today, and thus provides a convincing motivation to continue the costly and precious—albeit often precarious—ecumenical and prophetic engagement into the future."
—Rudolf von Sinner, professor of systematic theology and head of postgraduate programme, Pontifical Catholic University of Paraná, Curitiba, Brazil

J. H. OLDHAM
and GEORGE BELL

Shapers of Ecumenical Theology Series
Series Editor: Jesudas M. Athyal

J. H. Oldham
and George Bell

Ecumenical Pioneers

Keith W. Clements

FORTRESS PRESS
MINNEAPOLIS

J. H. OLDHAM AND GEORGE BELL
Ecumenical Pioneers

Oldham extracts
> From *The World and the Gospel* (1916) was printed with permission
> granted by Churches Together in Britain and Ireland.
> "Nationality and Missions" (1920) was printed with permission granted by
> World Council of Churches.
> From *Christianity and the Race Problem* (1924) was printed with
> permission granted by SCM Press.
> From *The Church and Its Function in Society* (1937) was printed with
> permission sought from Allen & Unwin.
> "The Church and the Disorder of Society" (1948) was printed with
> permission granted by SCM Press.

Bell extracts
> The 1934 Ascension Day message was printed with permission granted by
> Fortress Press.
> From *Christianity and World Order* (1940) was printed with permission
> sought from Penguin.
> From *The Church and Humanity* (1946): "Humanity and the Refugee" and
> "If Thine Enemy Hunger" were printed with permissions sought from
> Longmans, Green.
> "The Approach to Christian Unity" (1951) was printed with permission
> granted by Heffers.
> From *The Kingship of Christ* (1954) was printed with permission sought
> from Penguin.

Cover image: WCC Photo Archive and Library of Congress, Bain Collection.
Cover design: Laurie Ingram

Print ISBN: 978-1-5064-7000-9
eBook ISBN: 978-1-5064-7001-6

CONTENTS

SHAPERS OF ECUMENICAL THEOLOGY SERIES

While the history of the modern ecumenical movement is often traced back to the World Missionary Conference in Edinburgh in 1910, it has its roots in lay movements such as the Student Christian Movement (SCM), the Young Women's Christian Association (YWCA), and the Young Men's Christian Association (YMCA), where Christians from different confessions and denominations came together to pray, study the Bible, and share their concerns on social issues. The Faith and Order Commission and the Life and Work Movement arose out of the inspiration of the Edinburgh conference, which showed the possibility of churches working toward unity on other matters. The World Council of Churches (WCC) was born out of bringing the Faith and Order Commission, Life and Work Movement, and the missionary movement together (although the missionary movement formally joined the WCC later at the WCC New Delhi assembly in 1961).

From the beginning, however, there were individuals and initiatives from all over the world that built up the ecumenical movement. At the Edinburgh conference, the most pertinent challenges came from the Chinese and Japanese delegates (there were 17 Asians in a 1,200-delegate meeting). V. S. Azariah of India addressed the overwhelmingly Western audience and said, "You have given your bodies to be burned. We ask for love, give us *friends*," thus setting in motion a process that would make mission truly a movement of the whole inhabited earth, the *oikoumene*.[1] The deliberations at Edinburgh stimulated scholarly interest in non-Western cultures and religions, leading to a long process of discussions that continued at the missionary conferences in Jerusalem (1928), Tambaram (1938), and beyond.

---

[1] For a detailed discussion, see Wesley Ariarajah, "Contribution of Asian Participants to the Edinburgh 1910 Conference," in *Power, Politics and Plurality: Essays by S. Wesley Ariarajah*, ed. Marshal Fernando (Colombo, Sri Lanka: Ecumenical Institute for Study and Dialogue, 2016), 271–84.

In the decades that followed the Edinburgh conference, individuals and initiatives from Asia, Africa, Latin America, and other parts of the world went on to shape the ecumenical movement at various levels. There were also local and regional initiatives, such as base ecumenism in Latin America, Indigenous theologies in Africa, and theologies of marginalized and subaltern people in Asia, as well as the urban-rural mission, interreligious dialogue, and several such trends from around the world. Underlying all these movements was the theological basis of a common understanding about the unity of the churches and the vision of building up a just and participatory community. As the policy statement of WCC puts it, the "ecumenical process which led to the formation of the WCC was not only a response to the gospel imperative of Christian unity. It was also an affirmation of the call to mission and common witness and an expression of common commitment to the search for justice, peace and reconciliation in a chaotic, warring world divided along the lines of race, class and competing national and religious loyalties."[2]

Within this larger context, Fortress Press has undertaken the publication of a series of volumes on the theme, Shapers of Ecumenical Theology. These books will highlight the ecumenical vision of some of the individuals and initiatives that shaped modern ecumenical theology and introduce readers to the formation and development of ecumenical theology in the twentieth century. Each volume will contain a representative selection of key figures and their writings, cutting-edge commentary, and detailed introductory and concluding articles. The focus here is on a guided study of a selection of some pivotal ecumenical figures and their writings. The series has a broad ecumenical reach, and the history of modern ecumenism will be evaluated in the context of postmodernity and postcoloniality. Consequently, these books will not only address the key developments in ecumenical theology during the last century but also include an emphasis on their implications for our times and for the future. The works are expected to be used as textbooks, enabling the students to read the original authors of modern ecumenical

---

[2] "Common Understanding and Vision of the WCC (CUV)," adopted by the Central Committee of the World Council of Churches, September 1997, accessed October 25, 2021, https://www.oikoumene.org/resources/documents/common -understanding-and-vision-of-the-wcc-cuv.

theology. Throughout, key themes and issues that drove ecumenical reflection in the last century will be addressed in the series.

CHRISTIAN UNITY

Apart from the mainline Protestant churches that have traditionally been seen as the primary constituency of ecumenical institutions, modern ecumenical theology was shaped by confessional diversity with an openness to diversity even where differences seemed profound. In this context, the Orthodox confession should perhaps be mentioned first, as fellowship with the Orthodox churches contributed immensely to the self-understanding of the ecumenical movement. Most of the Eastern Orthodox churches that had not joined the WCC in the beginning became part of the council at the New Delhi assembly. Even before the assembly, there were discussions to revise the basis of WCC. In response to the demand of the Eastern Orthodox churches, the Christocentric affirmation in the basis was revised in a Trinitarian setting. The New Delhi assembly also set in motion a long-term study on the theological questions involved in the full integration of the Orthodox communion in the WCC: "Recognizing the central importance given in the Orthodox tradition to the conciliar process in the church of the early centuries, the assembly recommended that a study be undertaken of the councils of the early church and their significance for the ecumenical movement."[3]

Another major Christian group, the Pentecostals, also contributed tremendously to shaping ecumenical theology, especially at the grassroots level and among the most vulnerable sections in Asia, Africa, and Latin America, where Pentecostalism has experienced vigorous growth. The joint consultative group between Pentecostals and the WCC "determined that a study of discipleship and formation would allow the group to move from a convergence agenda—addressing the

---

[3] Konrad Raiser, "Orthodox Contribution to the WCC" (lecture, international symposium on "Orthodox Theology and the Future of Ecumenical Dialogue: Perspectives and Problems," Thessaloniki, Greece, June 3, 2003), http://www.oikoumene .org/en/resources/documents/wcc-programmes/ecumenical-movement-in-the-21st -century/member-churches/special-commission-on-participation-of-orthodox -churches/orthodox-contribution-to-the-wcc.

nature of the church—to a learning agenda in which an exchange of models can strengthen the churches' witness in the world."[4]

The shared vision of ecumenism between the Roman Catholic Church (RCC) and the member churches of WCC too "continues to engage churches and others everywhere in concrete action through its Pilgrimage of Justice and Peace."[5] A joint working group of the WCC and the Vatican was established to monitor, further, and promote the relationship and cooperation between the RCC and the WCC and its member churches. In more recent times, Pope Francis—with his deep sensitivity toward environmental threats and critical views on the international economic order and the plight of the refugees, immigrants, and the poor—has emerged as a willing partner of the ecumenical movement in reshaping the parameters of Christian unity and witness.

There can thus be little doubt that the ecumenical movement, a global effort to realize the biblical vision of the one body of Christ, has been one of the most important developments in Christianity over the past hundred years. Thanks to the ecumenical vision, Catholic, Orthodox, Protestant, and Pentecostal Christians now make common witness to Christ in various parts of the world. Issues that once caused tension among Christians have been resolved through dialogue. Participation in the ecumenical movement has also helped churches of different traditions and cultures forge a broad commitment to reject racism, to stand in solidarity with the poor and the marginalized, to care for the environment, and to strive together for peace. Underlying this endeavor was the vision that the quest for unity is God's will, which has a universal dimension and embraces the human community and all of God's creation: "Church unity is vital to the health of the church and to the future of the human family."[6] Integral to Christian unity is a deep commitment to justice. A commitment to the unity and renewal of the church needs to be held together with an absolute commitment to the reconciliation of

---

[4] "WCC and Pentecostals Discuss Discipleship and Formation in California," WCC, April 11, 2017, https://www.oikoumene.org/en/press-centre/news/wcc-and-pentecostals-discuss-discipleship-and-formation-in-california.

[5] "Pope Francis to Visit World Council of Churches This Summer," WCC, March 2, 2018, http://www.oikoumene.org/en/press-centre/news/pope-francis-to-visit-the-world-council-of-churches-this-summer.

[6] "Common Understanding and Vision."

God's world. As Philip Potter put it in his 1977 address to the WCC Central Committee, "The whole burden of the ecumenical movement is to cooperate with God in making the *oikoumene* an *oikos*, a home, a family of men and women, of young and old, of varied gifts, cultures, possibilities, where openness, trust, love and justice reign."[7]

PERSPECTIVES FROM THE SOUTH

Beyond the confessional unity of the churches and an acknowledgment of God's work in the world, the books in this series will also recognize the shifting center of gravity of world Christianity toward the Global South. We will include here the pioneering role played by the ecumenical movement in challenging a Eurocentric theology and ecclesiology by highlighting the perspectives of the colonized and marginalized people in Asia, Africa, and Latin America. In particular, this series will recognize the pivotal role played by the liberation struggles of oppressed people in shaping ecumenical theology during the last one hundred years. Although base ecumenism, as the "ecumenism of the people," originated in Latin America, it has had important ramifications in other parts of the world as well. As Raimundo C. Barreto Jr. puts it, "Base ecumenism has not only been an important force transforming and revitalizing interchurch and interfaith relations, but it also offers fresh notions of ecumenicity, which are particularly relevant to recent scholarly attempts to re-examine ecumenical relations in the era of world Christianity."[8]

There were also other grassroots theological initiatives that played a role in shaping ecumenical theology. Among those that emerged from Asia, Dalit theology contributed considerably to this process. Dalit theology emerged from the conviction that traditional Christian theology was largely based on the perspectives of the dominant class and caste and, consequently, did not represent the life situations of marginalized communities such as the Dalits: "This non-representative character of traditional theology raised serious

---

[7] Quoted in John Briggs, Mercy Amba Oduyoye, and Georges Tsetsis, eds., *A History of the Ecumenical Movement*, vol. 3, *1968–2000* (Geneva: WCC, 2004), 53.

[8] Raimundo C. Barreto Jr., "Base Ecumenism: Latin American Contributions to Ecumenical Praxis and Theory" (unpublished manuscript, last updated June 15, 2019).

questions about the credibility of the Christian faith when the Indian Church itself became predominantly Dalit in membership."[9]

With one in every four Christians living in sub-Saharan Africa and with a rediscovery of the significance of Indigenous African religions and spirituality in the life of the church, the role of the religions and cultures of that continent for the Christian world is being widely recognized. There are also the realities of Indigenous ecumenical theological expressions, such as Minjung theology from Korea, Burakumin theologies from Japan, the many womanist theologies, the theology of struggle from the Philippines, homeland theology from Taiwan, and so on. This series will recognize the fundamental paradigm shift in the ecumenical agenda from a decisively non-Western perspective.

These books will therefore recognize a growing interest in viewing ecumenical theology from the perspective of the Global South. In particular, they will examine the impact of selected ecumenical theologians on theological formation through a focus on their lives and works and a detailed review of their thoughts as expressions of ecumenical theological engagement with unity and justice. The underlying concern here is that theologizing in Asia, Africa, and Latin America occurs in a context of multireligiosity on the one hand and rampant poverty and social inequality on the other; therefore, religiosity and a commitment to justice and peace are at the center of the ecumenical theology that emerged there.

Theologizing from the Margins

Ecumenism, however, is not something that happens inside the churches; it is about responsible action with regard to "the whole inhabited earth." From the beginning, the ecumenical movement has affirmed that unity is in the struggle for justice. It was the recognition that ecumenism demands a quest for the realization of justice for the sake of unity; it ties together faith and justice. One significant

---

[9] Jesudas M. Athyal, "The Changing Face of the Indian Society . . . and the New Challenges for Dalit Theology" (paper presented at the international consultation on "Dalit Theology and a Theology of the Oppressed," Gurukul Lutheran Theological College, Chennai, India, November 13–15, 2004), https://jmathyal.tripod.com/id1.html.

Shapers of Ecumenical Theology Series

concept of modern ecumenical theology, therefore, is the perspective from the margins. The marginalized are those people who are pushed out of the mainstream to the periphery—those sidelined in the social, political, cultural, and religious life of the dominant society. Ecumenism is a search for the people in the margins, for the most vulnerable sections of society. As D. T. Niles puts it, "The ecumenical vision revealed indeed God's pilgrim people on the center and frontier of the church and the world."[10]

This series of books also recognizes that ecumenical theology will be prophetic in form and content. Prophetic ecumenism will contain both the powerful word to unmask situations of injustice and the powerful word to announce what is possible. As Ninan Koshy states, "Ecumenism should bear witness to this word, as a sign of resistance and at the same time as anticipation of what is hoped. The ecumenical movement can never be silent; bold words are an integral part of ecumenism. The attempt to arrive at consensus can turn to be an abdication of the prophetic duty."[11] These books, we hope, will portray ecumenical theology as the message that will unmask situations of injustice and affirm the message of unity and peace.

Oldham and Bell: Shapers of Ecumenical Theology

It is in this historical and theological background that Fortress Press has initiated the publication of a series of volumes on the theme, "Shapers of Ecumenical Theology." These timely books will highlight the ecumenical vision of key leaders in the movement and suggest its relevance for the contemporary church. Each volume will include a biographical introduction and cutting-edge commentary by well-known scholars in the field, but at the heart of each volume will be significant selections from the writings of the leader or leaders under discussion. Since so much scholarly attention has been given to theologians from North Atlantic countries, this series will emphasize theological voices from other parts of the world.

---

[10] Ninan Koshy, *A History of the Ecumenical Movement in Asia*, vol. 1 (Hong Kong: CCA, APAY, WSCFAP, 2004), 30.

[11] Ninan Koshy, "Ecumenism: Perspectives from the Margins" (lecture, August 14, 2012).

We are happy to publish in the Shapers of Ecumenical Theology series this book by Keith Clements titled *J. H. Oldham and George Bell: Ecumenical Pioneers*. The book introduces the life and thought of two British contemporaries who were decisive in shaping the modern ecumenical movement: the Scottish layman J. H. (Joe) Oldham (1874–1969) and the Anglican bishop George Kennedy Allen Bell (1883–1958). Their careers were rather different but closely related. Oldham was a missionary statesman, the organizing secretary of the 1910 World Missionary Conference, and a pioneering thinker and writer on race and social ethics who set the agenda for the crucial ecumenical conference on church, community, and state at Oxford in 1937. A quiet, skillful diplomat, he was the decisive mind behind the formation of the WCC. Bell, on the other hand, was the public, prophetic voice of the ecumenical fellowship from the 1930s onward, steadfastly leading the churches' support for the Christian opposition to Hitler in Germany, tirelessly working for refugees and all victims of oppression, and after the war, pioneering the work of reconciliation. After the inauguration of the WCC in 1948, he served as the first moderator of its central committee. It was widely believed that he would have become the archbishop of Canterbury but for his courageous and outspoken opposition to the British and American policy of bombing civilian populations during the war.

This book outlines the lives and main engagements of Oldham and Bell in turn and then provides selections of their key writings to illustrate their thinking and impact on ecumenism. A final chapter reflects on their pioneering significance and relevance today. In these concluding words, the author highlights the contemporary relevance of the lives and thought of these two ecumenical pioneers: "In their shaping of the ecumenical life and thought of their time, they opened up new pathways for the future, not all of which we have finished exploring today, and for which adventure and sacrifice are needed no less than yesterday."

As this book is being published, let me acknowledge the support of the Fortress Press team, particularly the president and CEO, Tim Blevins, and the vice president and publisher, Will Bergkamp, in this venture. Fortress Press hopes to partner with ecumenical institutions and publishing houses in a wide range of countries so that the books in this series will be available to people around the world at a locally affordable price. The works in this series will serve as introductory readers, providing a great opportunity for scholars, pastors, students, and lay Christians to come in contact with texts of the pioneers of ecumenical theology. It is our hope and prayer that this series of books will be received well by ecumenical people around the world.

Jesudas M. Athyal
Series editor

The Fanø conference, 1934. George Bell is seated on the front row, tenth from left. J. H. Oldham is on the back row, second left from the open door.
Photo credit: WCC Photo Archive.

INTRODUCTION

A photograph can capture a story in a single moment. It is the end of August 1934 on the Danish island of Fanø. In front of a hotel, facing the camera, are well over a hundred men and women of varying ages and from many different countries, from Europe and North America to the Indian subcontinent and the Far East. Many of them smiling into the sunlight, they have gathered as the Universal Christian Council for Life and Work, founded after the First World War as a means of uniting the churches of the world in working for peace and social justice. Behind the smiles, however, there are serious concerns, for the daily news headlines are about the rise of dictatorships and, yet again, the threat of war. Barely an hour's journey from Fanø lies the border with Germany, where Adolf Hitler has been in power for eighteen months. All the apparatus of a police state is in operation, the oppression of the Jews is spreading fear, and the churches are under brutal pressure to conform to the National Socialist ethos in thought and practice. The Fanø conference is therefore taking place at a dramatic and fateful moment for the future of the world. Firmly on its agenda are two crucial questions. First, should the ecumenical fellowship clearly and decisively side with those Protestants in Germany who have declared themselves to be the "Confessing Church," resisting the Nazi attempt to take over the church? Second, should the council press ahead with its plan to face boldly the challenges ahead, with its proposed world conference on church, community, and state to take place in Oxford in three years' time?

Seated on the front row in the photograph, clad in episcopal cassock, is George Bell, Anglican bishop of Chichester, with his wife, Henrietta, to his right. As the president of Life and Work and chair of its executive committee, he has been carefully but firmly steering the meeting through this challenging agenda. Much less conspicuously, at the back of the group, standing by the open door (as if he has just rushed there from a subcommittee of the conference), is the slim, slightly balding figure of J. H. (Joe) Oldham. A Scottish layman,

1

secretary of the International Missionary Council (IMC), he will be taking charge of the study preparations for the Oxford conference. Like Bell, he has already been much involved with the German situation. Others in the group are significant too—the young German Dietrich Bonhoeffer, for example. But this is the only photograph I know in which the two subjects of this study, Oldham and Bell, both appear, and it aptly captures their distinctiveness: Bell the bishop, by virtue of his prominent position always to the fore, the public and courageous spokesperson of the church; Oldham in the background, the studiously busy lay theologian, planner, organizer, networker, and prolific writer. They had known and greatly respected each other from the time of the First World War, but it was at Fanø that these two British figures were brought together as a team, complementing each other's gifts and insights in a partnership that lasted over the next twenty years, to the immense benefit of the ecumenical movement.

Their importance was recognized both during and immediately after their lifetimes and is engraved on their respective memorials. In the grounds of the Ecumenical Centre in Geneva, home to the World Council of Churches (WCC), stands a sundial bearing this inscription:

TO THE MEMORY OF
JOSEPH H. OLDHAM 1874–1969
MISSIONARY STATESMAN FOREMOST PIONEER OF WCC
FRIEND OF AFRICA

And on a plaque in Chichester Cathedral, we read the following:

GEORGE KENNEDY ALLEN BELL
BISHOP OF CHICHESTER 1929–1958
A TRUE PASTOR
POET AND PATRON OF THE ARTS
CHAMPION OF THE OPPRESSED
AND TIRELESS WORKER FOR
CHRISTIAN UNITY

This book seeks to put flesh on these accurate if skeletal tributes and, in particular, offers an account of their pioneering roles in the ecumenical movement and their relevance today. Since their deaths over fifty years ago, history has moved on, for the churches no less than for other organizations. True, time has not completely erased their memory. Even at a popular level, Bell is remembered as the bishop who opposed the bombing of German cities, while Oldham's description of Christianity as "not primarily a philosophy but a crusade" can still be heard. Fortunately, for a fuller remembrance of them, there is much material, published and unpublished, on which to draw.

My own awareness of both figures and their important place in the ecumenical story began in a general way in the 1960s, when I was a student. By then, Bell had died, and Oldham was in extreme old age, so I never met either of them or heard them speak. But over the following years, I became acquainted with a number of people who had known one or other or both of them personally and whose recollections were very much alive. My first theological teacher and supervisor at Cambridge University, the church historian Alec Vidler, had been a member of Oldham's Moot study group before and during World War II and had assisted him in producing the *Christian News-Letter* and also in setting up the Christian Frontier. In my first pastorate, my senior ministerial partner was Clifford Cleal, who during his time at the social responsibility desk of the British Council of Churches in the 1940s had collaborated with Oldham—"that great man of God," as he called him—and he bequeathed me a small but precious memento in the form of a handwritten note from Oldham. My serious engagement with Oldham began in 1990 thanks to Duncan Forrester of New College, Edinburgh. He was the literary executor of Kathleen Bliss, Oldham's most important coworker from the late 1930s onward, who had made a start on writing his biography but died in 1989. Duncan invited me to take on the task, which eventually saw the light of day in 1999 as *Faith on the Frontier: A Life of J. H. Oldham*. That was a rewarding assignment, for it not only opened to me the extensive archive of Oldham material that Bliss had assembled and is now lodged in the library of New College but enabled me to meet more people who had known him. The ecumenist bishop Oliver Tomkins introduced me to Eric Fenn, Oldham's assistant at the 1937 Oxford conference and secretary of the Moot, for a whole afternoon of vivid memories and insights despite his great age. (Oliver Tomkins had telephoned him with the stern injunction, "You are not to die before Keith Clements has interviewed you!") Others on my list were Lesslie and Helen Newbigin, Daniel Jenkins, David Paton, Marjorie Reeves, Kenneth Grayston, and Bliss's daughter, Deborah Cassidi, with her childhood memories of the Oldham household at Chipstead. Uninvited but hugely welcome was a vigorous phone call from Donald Mackinnon, another sometime member of the Moot, whom I had last heard lecturing in Cambridge thirty years before.

My studies on Bell have arisen mainly out of my research and writing on Bonhoeffer, and there have been fewer direct personal links to Bell that survived the more than sixty years since his death. But again, it was good to have the personal recollections of those who had known him as a pastor, friend, or collaborator—in particular, John Arnold, Eberhard (George) Wedell, Edwin Robertson, Geoffrey Beck, Peter Walker, and Eberhard and Renate Bethge. Added to these names must be that of one who, like me, is of a later generation but whose scholarship and enthusiasm for Bell and his legacy makes him the unrivaled authority on Bell today—namely, Andrew Chandler, to whose work and friendship I am immeasurably indebted and to whose works I gratefully direct readers of this book for more information and insight. It must be understood that in relation to both Oldham and Bell, it has been impossible to do full justice to all their thinking and activity within this one book.

It has been a long time since the 1934 Fanø conference. Yet today, in a fragile and conflictual world, we are still faced with issues akin to those that troubled the participants in the photograph. Oldham and Bell did not always agree, but both believed passionately in the centrality of the church for Christianity and in a truly united fellowship of the *oikoumene*, the whole inhabited earth. With equal passion, they believed that the church could fulfill its calling only in engagement with the world in its need and complexity. Oldham spoke often of adventure; Bell of sacrifice. These pages, I hope, will illustrate the meaning of both words in their stories, which illustrate the value of partnership in diversity.

The book, as might be expected, falls into two main parts, the first dealing with Oldham, the second with Bell. In each part, following the accounts of their respective careers and contributions to the ecumenical movement, a selection of their writings is presented. This may well be considered the most important part of the content, enabling them to speak for themselves. A final chapter considers their lasting legacy.

Writing about figures from a different time and context to our own and, especially, letting them speak in their own words does, of course, present certain issues of language. For example, watchful readers will notice less than perfect consistency in spelling. The extracts from the writings of Bell and Oldham are left just as they appeared at the hands of their original British publishers, while my own chapters and commentary have been put through the "USA English" spellchecker. Some questions of terminology have had to be resolved. For example, in relation to the German Church Struggle of the 1930s, it was common for Anglophone writers (including Bell) at that time to speak of the "Confessional Church" to denote *Die Bekennende Kirche*, which resisted the attempts to Nazify the Protestant Church. Today, the more accurate term "Confessing Church" is the customary usage, but in actual citations from the authors, I have retained the use of the former term. The matter of exclusive and nonexclusive language is more problematic. Citations are reproduced as they appeared, though the careful reader will notice that both Bell and Oldham were not quite as prone to exclusive usage as might be assumed. There is one area where conventional expressions of the former time will certainly jar today—namely, in relation to race or color, the issue in which Oldham particularly was involved. Again, I have not edited out expressions that were in parlance at the time but are not generally acceptable today, confident that neither Oldham himself nor the authors he was quoting intended any derogatory or racist meaning in them and hoping that readers will recognize that it is precisely to the work of people like Oldham that we owe our changed sensitivity to language in this area.

There are two phrases from the former time that I have had no hesitation in adopting. Bliss spoke of Oldham as "a wily prophet." Bell described the calling of the church as that of a "watchman for humanity," thereby providing an apt if unintended description of himself. I have attached these terms to their respective names in the titles of the biographical chapters.

I gratefully acknowledge much-needed help in preparing the book for publication. Jesudas Athyal, Fortress Press acquiring editor (South Asian theology), has been a most helpful and encouraging guide from the time he first contacted me about undertaking the project. In Geneva, Stephen Brown, WCC journals coordinator and editor of the *Ecumenical Review*, helped greatly in locating and supplying material from the early years of the ecumenical movement, and Anne-Emmanuelle Tankam-Tene, the WCC archivist, assisted likewise with the photographs. At a time when physical access to libraries was proving difficult thanks to the Covid-19 pandemic, Michael Brealey, librarian of Bristol Baptist College, provided alternative ways and means. Last but not least, James Bradnock painstakingly scrutinized with a schoolteacher's eye my manuscript for grammatical and typographical failings. Any errors of any kind that remain are my responsibility.

PART I

J. H. OLDHAM

1

J. H. OLDHAM

The Wily Prophet

In the 1870s, the British Empire, that worldwide dominion on which, it was claimed, "the sun never set," was approaching the peak of its power and reach. J. H. (Joe) Oldham was quite literally a child of that empire. He was born in 1874 in Bombay (today's Mumbai), India, the oldest child of George Oldham, an officer in the British Indian Army, and his wife, Lillah. George and Lillah were devotedly evangelical parents, George being a founder of the Bombay Young Men's Christian Association (YMCA) with aspirations to full-time evangelistic work once his military days were over. Devout and disciplined, the Oldham household was also warmly hospitable and, unusually for that time, as open to Indian as to European friends and visitors.

George Oldham retired from the army in 1881, and the family—including four children now—left India and settled at Crieff in Lillah's homeland, Scotland. Joe was nurtured in a typically Scottish middle-class culture where education was taken with great seriousness, together with good taste in the arts and literature and a love of walking the hills, sport (Joe was an adept rugby player), and church. In the Oldhams' case, church meant the (Presbyterian) Free Church of Scotland. George Oldham pursued his lay vocation as an evangelist to great appreciation by the churches and communities he visited. But tragedy struck with the death of Lillah Oldham, and in 1891, George, wishing now to devote his energies to his children's welfare, moved the household to Edinburgh.

OXFORD EVANGELICALISM

Joe excelled at school and in 1892 entered Trinity College at Oxford University to study the subject known (still today) as litterae humaniores, or more popularly, "Greats": the Greek and Latin classics and contemporary philosophy. It was the assumed route for those

9

who aspired to government service or colonial administration, and the latter was evidently the aim of young Oldham. During his first weeks at Oxford, however, something happened to transform his life forever. While George Oldham's evangelicalism was deeply serious, he had not forced it on his children, and Joe had not as yet expressed any marked religious inclination of his own—until one November evening, he was able to write to his father saying that he had given himself "definitely to Jesus Christ." The famous American evangelist and YMCA leader Dwight L. Moody was in Oxford conducting a mission among the students, and Joe Oldham was among those who responded to his challenge to "break with sin." For Oldham, this meant not only an inward change of heart but immersion in the tide of evangelical activity that was then surging through the student world: active membership in the university Christian Union with its earnest Bible study groups, early morning prayer meetings, outdoor gatherings for witness to other students, and attendance at the annual Keswick Convention in the Lake District and national student conferences. All these reinforced the call for total consecration to Christ, a commitment that its devotees saw supremely embodied in overseas missionary service. "The evangelization of the world in this generation" was the watchword of the Student Volunteer Union (SVU), founded in the United States in 1888, and its British version formed in 1891. At the start of his second year at Oxford, Oldham himself signed the SVU membership declaration: "It is my purpose if God permit, to become a foreign missionary."[1]

It was in 1894 that he had another decisive encounter at Oxford. John R. Mott, chairman of the student section of the YMCA in the United States and chairman of the SVU there, was visiting Oxford, and Oldham was deputed by other leaders of the Christian Union to meet him and show him around the colleges. Mott, a Methodist layman, was already the dynamic driving force of the international Christian student scene and its missionary orientation. He was a powerful and inspiring speaker and organizer, possessed of boundless energies in leadership and formidably persuasive in summoning recruits to the cause. His approach was caricatured as "Young man: God has work for you in Shanghai. Here is your ticket." His purpose

---

[1] Cited in Keith Clements, *Faith on the Frontier: A Life of J. H. Oldham* (Edinburgh: T&T Clark, 1999), 23.

in visiting Britain was to further preparations for the meeting in Sweden in 1895 at which would be formed the World Student Christian Federation (WSCF), linking all national intercollegiate unions and dedicated to world evangelization, and he wanted to know what part Oxford could play in this. Oldham was greatly impressed, if somewhat intimidated, by this American who was nine years his senior. In turn, Mott made a mental note of his sharp-minded young Oxford guide, who was coming of age just as Mott's plans were taking shape. Fifteen years later, the two men would be embarking on a close and lasting partnership of crucial importance for the ecumenical movement.

Viewed from today, when "evangelical" and "ecumenical" are often assumed to be divergent if not opposed commitments, it may be surprising that it was out of this international student evangelistic enterprise that so much of the later ecumenical movement sprang. Such surprise, however, manifests a reading back into the 1890–1910 polarizations and polemics largely unknown at that time. Moody, for one, envisaged the YMCA (and its sister, the Young Women's Christian Association [YWCA]) bringing into fellowship young Christians of all traditions and denominations, as did Mott (who would venture even into Orthodox Russia on his recruiting drives). Student Christian unions were not yet self-dividing into "liberal" and "conservative" factions. All believed in winning the world for Christ. As for Oldham himself, his later growth into ecumenical life, leadership, and social thought did not signify a fall from evangelical grace, a forsaking of the evangelistic imperative. In 1942, fifty years after he made the SVU declaration his own and at the height of his engagement with the social order, he could still write, "To save society we have to begin by saving persons. Nothing can supersede, or take the place of, the evangelistic and pastoral ministries of the Church, reinforced by the insights that general and medical psychology can supply."[2] Over the years, no work of his would be more widely read and appreciated than his pocket-sized *Devotional Diary* (1925).[3] He was ever a man of prayer.

---

[2] J. H. Oldham, with H. A. Hodges and P. Mairet, *Real Life Is Meeting*, Christian News-Letter Books 14 (London: Sheldon, 1942), 23.

[3] J. H. Oldham, *A Devotional Diary* (London: SCM Press, 1925).

THE MISSIONARY VOLUNTEER: INDIA

On graduating from Oxford in 1896, Oldham worked for a year in London as the full-time joint general secretary of the SVU and the Inter-Varsity Christian Union, and in 1897, he fulfilled his own missionary pledge by sailing to the land of his birth, having been appointed the Scottish YMCA secretary in Lahore in Punjab (in today's Pakistan). Mott very likely had a hand in his appointment. From the start, Oldham's work in Lahore was marked by tireless industry on behalf of the YMCA members in support of their own missionary task among their fellow Indians: organizing Bible studies, conferences, and a recreational center and reading room. But above all, it was Oldham's capacity for friendship that was most appreciated. Upon arrival at Lahore station, he had been met by S. K. Datta, a student destined to become one of the leading Indian Christians of his time. It was the start of a close and long-lasting friendship. In fact, all Oldham's close friendships in Lahore were with Indians, with one exception. He was presently joined by Mary Fraser, sister of his Oxford friend Alek Fraser and herself a student in modern languages at Oxford. Their wedding took place in Lahore Cathedral, and typically, Oldham's best man was another of his close Indian friends, Surandra Nath Chandu Lal. The key to friendship, Oldham saw, lay in discarding the European sense of self-sufficiency that engendered an air of self-importance and allowing others to offer their own help and friendship. Mary no less than Joe was a child of empire, her father being in the Indian civil service and governor successively of Punjab and Bengal. Perhaps it was the very fact of their common background in imperial rule that made both Joe and Mary especially sensitive to the problems of the Western missions in India. While some YMCA colleagues were attributing the difficulties encountered by missions to Indian religious obstinacy or moral apathy, Oldham wrote very frankly to his fellow missionaries: "If the missionary finds it difficult to make contact and gain a hearing, then he must look to himself to find the reason. The missionary is a foreigner, separated from Indians by barriers of custom, modes of thought and language, by racial prejudice, *and by belonging to a conquering race.*"[4] He studied Urdu. Again, in a paper on "Foreignness: A Hindrance to Evangelism," he

---

[4] Cited in Clements, *Faith on the Frontier*, 50 (emphasis mine).

writes, "A missionary nods in a friendly way to an Indian Christian student. . . . 'He was too proud to shake hands.' The treatment of Indians by many of our countrymen is contemptuous and insulting."[5] Ten years later, at the 1910 World Missionary Conference in Edinburgh, the young Indian and future bishop V. S. Azariah shook many present by his impassioned plea that, notwithstanding all the heroism and sacrificial labors of Western missions, "[Indians] also ask for *love*. Give us FRIENDS."[6] He was in effect asking for more Oldhams. Oldham was already exemplifying what later became, in conscious debt to the personalist thought of Martin Buber, his famous motto, "Real living is meeting." If being ecumenical involves venturing across boundaries and opening oneself to viewing the world and one's own tradition and culture from the other side, then Oldham's ecumenical education was beginning in Lahore.

Oldham endeared himself to his Indian friends and colleagues, but in 1900, both he and Mary were struck down by typhoid. So serious was their debilitation that medical opinion insisted they return to Britain the following year, with no resumption in India for the foreseeable future. Though short, the Indian experience had provided Oldham with much to ponder on the problematic relations of missions to race, culture, and imperial power—issues that would accompany him for the rest of his life and inform his ecumenical perspective.

THEOLOGICAL STUDIES: MISSIONS EDUCATOR

Back in Scotland, the Oldhams made their home in Edinburgh, where Joe undertook a three-year theology degree course at New College, supplemented by a year's study at the University of Halle in Germany. Aided by Mary's tuition, he became accomplished in German and was able to benefit fully from the one who was, for him, the star attraction at Halle: Gustav Warneck (1834–1910), professor of theology of missions. Until Warneck, "missiology" was an almost unknown concept, and his chair at Halle was the first in missions anywhere, but he already had a following in Scotland, and Oldham

---

[5] See Clements, 50.

[6] See Ruth Rouse and Stephen Neill, eds., *A History of the Ecumenical Movement*, vol. 1, *1517–1948* (London: SPCK, 1967), 359.

was treading a not unfamiliar Scottish pilgrim path to Halle. Warneck understood missionary work as requiring three historical phases: the conversion of individuals and the gathering of small churches, the upbuilding of the churches and their leavening influence in the lives of the people, and the Christianizing of the masses involving not only religious but political and social movements.[7] Each phase required study pertaining to the country in question, its social life, language(s), and culture. It was Warneck's particular intellectual contribution, in viewing missions as an object of proper scientific study, to insist on seeing them as part of the wider human, historical scene rather than in pious isolation from secular forces. Particular aspects of Warneck's analyses might be debatable, but the overall impact on Oldham was profound and lasting. It was soon after his return from Halle that Oldham wrote two articles for the *Student Movement*, raising the question of whether it might be the Asian countries that would make something "far grander" of Christianity than the European nations had succeeded in doing for nineteen centuries.[8]

For a time, Oldham considered entering the ministry of the Scottish Free Church, but no invitation from a congregation came, and he was content to remain a church elder and to stay active in the *Student Movement*, for which he wrote a number of aids to Bible study. In 1906, he was appointed full-time study secretary of the Mission Study Council of the United Free Church of Scotland, soon complemented by his appointment as missionary study secretary of the burgeoning Student Christian Movement (SCM) in Britain. Thus Oldham was brought into close collaboration with the very able secretary of the SCM, the Anglican priest Tissington Tatlow. Though on a relatively modest scale, at both the denominational level for the Free Church and the ecumenical level for the SCM, the work of providing guides for study groups on missionary work, organizing summer conferences for young people, and engaging in speaking and writing himself foreshadowed what was to be one of Oldham's major contributions to the ecumenical movement: the establishment of *study* as a central

---

[7] Gustav Warneck, *Modern Missions and Culture: Their Mutual Relations*, trans. Thomas Smith (Edinburgh: James Gremmel, 1888); and Warneck, *Outline of a History of Protestant Missions from the Reformation to the Present Time*, ed. George Robson (Edinburgh: Oliphant, Anderson & Ferrier, 1901).

[8] J. H. Oldham, "Christianity and Asia," *Student Movement* 3, no. 5 (February 1906): 106.

necessity. This has perhaps become so familiar in ecumenical circles as to be taken for granted. Many others made important contributions, but Oldham was arguably the single most important figure in embedding study in the ecumenical movement at the international level, and even at this early stage, he was breaking new ground. Hitherto, reading material supplied by missionary organizations tended to be geared toward promoting the missions as they were and ensuring financial support by their constituencies, comprising hagiographical accounts of missionary heroism or success stories of evangelistic advance. After his encounter with Warneck, Oldham (assisted by George Robson, chairman of the Mission Study Council, who had translated Warneck's *History of Protestant Missions*) was determined to provide genuine education about the factual history, contexts, and challenges of overseas mission. Thus the booklets for the SCM would, for example, focus on Africa one year, China the next, and so forth. The study emphasis continued. In following up the 1910 Edinburgh missionary conference and founding the *International Review of Missions*, in persistently bringing Africa to the attention of both governments and churches in the 1920s, in organizing the program of the 1937 Oxford Life and Work conference, and in helping shape the agenda of the infant World Council of Churches (WCC)—in all this, the presupposition was that pious enthusiasm was not enough; concerted study and evaluation of the meaning of the gospel *and of what was happening in the world* were essential. Here Oldham led by example. He was ever the student and voracious reader until the end of his days, keeping up not just with theology and biblical scholarship but with the sciences (natural, social, and political), philosophy and anthropology, economics, and educational theory, devouring everything from government reports to novels and poetry—and not forgetting newspapers.

THE WATERSHED: EDINBURGH 1910 AND AFTER

Oldham made his wider reputation by his crucial role as secretary of the 1910 World Missionary Conference. The conference was proposed in 1907 at the foreign missions conference of North America, and that same year, an invitation came from Scotland to hold such a conference in 1910. Mott soon had his hand on the tiller, and it was his dynamism and vision that largely shaped what would follow.

Its purpose would be to express and strengthen the cooperation of practical men and women working together for the evangelization of the world. The SVU slogan "The evangelization of the world in this generation" was an evident inspiration, as was the growing sense of need among the missionary societies of North America, Britain, and Europe for closer cooperation in the face of the challenges common to them all. It was at Mott's insistence that Oldham was appointed secretary, and the two years leading up to the conference that took place June 14–23, 1910, were of intense labors for him and his small committee in Edinburgh. A prime task was that of coordinating and gathering the reports of the eight international commissions appointed to prepare material for discussion at the conference, no easy task in that age of steam travel assisted only by the telegraph. It also meant trying to resolve the acute difficulties that even the gathering of information and statistics on the worldwide missionary task could throw up. Anglo-Catholics vigorously opposed, while many evangelicals equally strongly supported calling areas of Latin America or the Middle East "unevangelized" on the grounds that their populations were just "nominally" Roman Catholic or Orthodox. While Mott on his travels acted as a salesman, rousing the interest and enthusiasm of mission boards and churches, in Edinburgh, Oldham and his team worked on product design, down to the last details of the program and hospitality for the 1,200 participants. The result was an impressive success organizationally, notwithstanding that the attendance was overwhelmingly European and American, with very few representatives of the "younger churches" of Africa and Asia. What made this conference different from previous gatherings on mission was, first, that it was composed of official *delegates* of churches and mission boards and so carried a real measure of commitment and accountability; second, it set up a structure, albeit modest, in the form of a continuation committee mandated to implement the resolutions and ongoing commitments made at the conference. It thus merits being described as "the watershed between miscellaneous ecumenical strivings and the integrated ecumenical movement of more recent times."[9] That Oldham played a crucial role was recognized even at the conference itself. When, near the end of the proceedings, having been silent almost throughout the previous nine days, he rose

---

[9] Rouse and Neill, *History of the Ecumenical Movement*, 217.

to make some administrative announcements, the assembly broke into spontaneous and hearty applause. Nor was it surprising that among its first acts, the thirty-five-member Continuation Committee appointed him as its secretary, a full-time post he held until, at length, there came into being in 1921 the International Missionary Council (IMC), of which he continued as secretary until 1938.

The Continuation Committee met three times during 1911-13, in England, in the United States, and at the Hague in the Netherlands. It had been set a colossal task in following up the direction set at Edinburgh for closer missionary cooperation. An executive committee was set up along with nine special committees to work on particular topics. Mott chaired the whole enterprise with his customary drive and skill. The task of coordination and communication between meetings, however, fell largely to Oldham, but he was not thereby reduced to a purely administrative role. No less than Mott, he was driven by an ecumenical vision of cooperation that, in practice, demanded more than some of the Edinburgh constituency perhaps realized. Addressing in 1913 the newly formed Conference of Missionary Societies in Britain and Ireland (CMSBI), Oldham asked "whether there is among the leaders of the missionary movement the loftiness of Christian character, the statesmanship, the largeness of vision, the depth of sympathy, and the faith in God to enable them to achieve a living, rich, effective unity in which the gifts that God has bestowed upon each will find their highest expression and the resources which He had entrusted to His church will be used to the uttermost for the speedy advancement of the Kingdom of God."[10]

Oldham's implicit doubts about the commitment of some churches and missionary bodies to the post-Edinburgh enterprise were not groundless. In 1913, Anglo-Catholics reacted vehemently to the Kikuyu Proposals for a federation of Anglicans, Presbyterians, and other Protestants in East Africa on the basis of agreed acceptance of the Apostles' and Nicene Creeds, with a common membership and acceptance of communion at one another's tables. While this had not been mooted at Edinburgh or in the Continuation Committee, the proposals were interpreted by their opponents as the outcome of Edinburgh, thereby creating unease about all ideas of closer cooperation on the African mission field. But another brake

---

[10] Cited in Clements, *Faith on the Frontier*, 113–14.

on post-Edinburgh hopes was applied by some mission boards themselves who were uneasy that the Continuation Committee appeared
to be too proactive. At its 1913 meeting at the Hague, it was therefore
agreed: "The only committees entitled to determine missionary policy are the Home Boards, the Missions and the Churches concerned.
It believes however that the missionary policy in any particular area
can be rightly determined only in view of the situation of that area as
a whole, and in relation to other work which is being carried on."[11]
If the first sentence was a warning light, the second gave encouragement to Oldham's conviction of the necessity of *common study*, with
which surely none could disagree.

It was out of this conviction that Oldham had already launched
his most important contribution to the immediate post-Edinburgh
agenda, the journal *International Review of Missions* (*IRM*). Still
being published today (by the WCC), it has also proved to be Oldham's longest-lasting material gift to the ecumenical movement,
albeit with its title slightly changed, the singular *Mission* replacing
the plural *Missions*. Scarcely was the Edinburgh conference over
and its official reports delivered to the printers[12] than Oldham was
pondering the idea of a quarterly journal that would include not
only information from the Continuation Committee and articles
from missionaries and administrators but, in the interests of the
scientific study of missions in their contexts, material as scholarly as
found in Warneck's *Allgemeine Missionszeitschrift*. A wide range of
books would be reviewed, and there would be an annual survey
of the state of the worldwide missionary enterprise. Mott, who at
first had envisaged little more than an occasional newsletter, was
duly persuaded by Oldham, who stated his hope that the journal
might "give living and concrete expression to the idea which it is so
vital that the Church should grasp, namely, the unity of the work of
preaching the one gospel of the one God, who sent his only begotten
Son to save the one human race and gather it into one holy fellowship

---

[11] Continuation Committee meeting minutes, the Hague, Netherlands, 1913,
cited in Clements, 116.

[12] J. H. Oldham, ed., *The World Missionary Conference, Edinburgh, 1910*, vols. 1–9
(London: Oliphant, Anderson & Ferrier, 1910). See also W. H. Temple Gairdner,
"Edinburgh 1910": An Account and Interpretation of the World Missionary Conference
(Edinburgh: Oliphant, Anderson & Ferrier, 1910).

and brotherhood."[13] Oldham had committed himself to editing the journal, which he was to do for the next twenty years. The first issue appeared in January 1912.[14] The contents both exemplified Oldham's aims and presaged much that was to come. Article topics included the growth of the church among the Batak of North Sumatra (first of a series on progress in various mission fields), Christianity and Islam, Christianity in Japan, the place of women in the East, and the preparation of missionaries. There was also a report by Mott on the work of the Continuation Committee, plus a stack of book reviews and a bibliography. Thus was forged a vital tool for the shaping of ecumenical theology and missionary cooperation, the first truly international ecumenical journal of the twentieth century. Not only was it an example of "ecumenical studies," but it made clear that serious study was itself an important part of being ecumenical, since it involved the study of the one *oikoumene* to which the church belonged and in which it was called to witness.

WORLD WAR AND WORLD MISSION

The outbreak of the First World War in August 1914 shattered the morale of those churches in the belligerent nations and in many neutral countries too, which had believed that the twentieth century would be an era of unlimited progress in human welfare and, above all, of international peace. But it was the missionary societies who at first felt the blow most keenly. In the first place, the conflict wrought severe disruption, economic and political, to all internationally based activity, of the missions no less than trade. Yet more seriously, the outbreak of war in so-called Christian Europe violated all that the Edinburgh conference had stood for—namely, cooperation at the international level for bringing the gospel to the "non-Christian world." It was not now so evident where the boundaries between Christian and non-Christian worlds lay, as the Christian nations of Europe, often claiming that God was on their side, engaged one another in the bloodiest battles imaginable on their own soil—and

---

[13] J. H. Oldham, letter to John R. Mott, November 19, 1910, cited in Clements, *Faith on the Frontier*, 106.

[14] For a full statement of Oldham's intentions for the journal, see J. H. Oldham, "The Editor's Notes," *International Review of Missions* 1, no. 1 (January 1912): 1–14.

in full view of "non-Christian" peoples on land and sea in Africa, Asia, and the Pacific. The gospel of peace was having to compete with the gospel of nationalism. The ecumenical movement, without as yet having any consolidated organization to support and express its witness, seemed about to be strangled at birth. That this did not happen—that, in fact, the movement begun at Edinburgh survived the crisis, learned from it by carrying out limited but essential tasks and remaining true to the wider vision—was due above all to Mott and Oldham. Mott, being an American citizen, was able to use the benefits of neutrality to travel even to Germany and to be seen as somewhat apart from the stances of the belligerent nations until the entry of the United States into the war in early 1917. Oldham's position was more complicated, both being a British citizen and, as secretary of the Edinburgh Continuation Committee, serving an international body and an international cause. The day after war was declared by Britain, he wrote to Mott that to him, the conflict was an unmitigated disaster, a confirmation "that Christian Europe has departed so far from God and rejected so completely the rule of Christ that a catastrophe of this kind is possible," and that at best, it could be seen as the purifying judgment of God. Contrition, penitence, and humility were required. The hopes and plans of Edinburgh might have to be worked out more slowly than hitherto thought and by other means than had been expected. He continued,

> It is certain, however, that so overwhelming a catastrophe cannot leave us where we were. If the missionary societies set themselves only to make the necessary adjustments on the plane of spiritual experience on which we are at present, nothing great can come out of it. We need to bow in deep humility before God, beseeching Him to show us things of which we had never dreamed, and to make us willing to be led along paths of which at present we have no conception. This surely is something which we must seek for ourselves, and endeavour to help others to seek.[15]

Oldham made clear that notwithstanding the war being a catastrophe, he believed his own country had had no option but to go to arms in defense of international law and to counter the kind of

---

[15] J. H. Oldham, letter to John R. Mott, August 5, 1914, cited in Clements, *Faith on the Frontier*, 122–23.

aggression seen in Germany's invasion of Belgium. He respected but disagreed with the pacifists and with those who saw Germany as wholly demonic and the Kaiser as the antichrist. In 1915, writing one of the series of *Papers in Wartime* organized by William Temple (at that time, vicar of St James's Church, Piccadilly), he declared, "It is not enough to know that Germany is responsible for the war. It is necessary to enquire further how Germany became what she is."[16] Only a transformed church could redeem this fragmented and fragmenting social order. Britain and all of Europe were under divine judgment.

Oldham was therefore calling for and exemplifying a longer, deeper, and wider thoughtfulness in response to the crisis and its causes, revealing the underlying malaise of economic exploitation and racial antagonism. The *IRM* continued its series of surveys and the study of the wider missionary enterprise. Then in October 1915, Oldham was invited by the United Council for Missionary Education to write a book on missions in the light of the war. The result was *The World and the Gospel*, published in 1916, Oldham's most substantial book (220 pages) to date.[17] With passion and rigor, it ranged over theology, the situation in the worldwide mission fields, the state of the churches and society in the West, and the need for spiritual renewal. In one sense, it was a reaffirmation of the Edinburgh vision for a world now shaken by the earthquake of war and a carrying forward of the Continuation Committee's agenda and its methods of fact-finding, analysis, and proposals for future action. But at another level, it was a severe questioning of the assumptions underlying Edinburgh—above all, the belief that given some more cohesion and direction, the churches of the West could manifest the gospel to the whole world: "The Christian protest against the unchristian forces in social and national life must be clearer, sharper and more patent than it has been in the past. It may be that the Church as it was before the war could never have evangelized the world; that its witness had not the penetrating force necessary for so gigantic an undertaking; that before God could

---

[16] J. H. Oldham, "The Witness of the Church in the Present Crisis," in *The Church the Hope of the Future*, Papers for War Time 16, ed. William Temple (Oxford: Oxford University Press, 1915), n.p.

[17] J. H. Oldham, *The World and the Gospel* (London: United Council for Missionary Education, 1916).

answer the prayers of His people some deep-seated evil had to be removed, however terrible the cost."[18]

Oldham inserted his scalpel still more deeply into the British tissue by referring to the alarming results of a recent survey of child poverty in England and commenting that it was doubtful whether a church that was willing to tolerate such a state of things "possessed the moral passion which would enable it to evangelize the world." Moreover, if social ills were to be tackled, there was needed a wholly new Christian attitude to the "secular" world, linking faith and prayer to action in society where God is to be honored in commerce and government no less than in church: "In a far greater degree than has yet been attempted, the Church must learn to hallow the secular life by shedding on its struggles and difficulties the light and healing of God's love."[19]

The World and the Gospel "had the effect of lifting the sights of Christians beyond the horrors of the present to a renewed faith in God's call to mission."[20] Thinking imaginatively in the larger dimensions of space and time enabled Oldham to be both critical and hopeful in wartime. This did not mean that for Oldham, thought supplanted action for the present, for Oldham's actions during the war stand as one of the most remarkable episodes in ecumenical responsibility. The Continuation Committee could no longer function as before and had to become in effect a British-American body managed by Oldham and Mott, thereby jeopardizing relations with the German representatives. While making no apology for his British identity and loyalty, as secretary of the committee (in due course, fused with his role as secretary of the CMSBI), Oldham saw himself as serving all mission organizations associated with Edinburgh, of whatever nationality—the German ones no less than others. The plight of the German missions in British territories (or those soon occupied by the British) in Africa and India particularly was severe. Many German personnel were interned or forcibly repatriated, and the mission properties were threatened with expropriation. The whole German missionary enterprise seemed doomed, and naturally in Germany itself, the mission leaders were incensed and bitter.

---

[18] Oldham, 21. See chapter 2 in this volume for longer extracts.

[19] Oldham, 21.

[20] Kathleen Bliss, cited in Clements, *Faith on the Frontier*, 135.

Where was now the spirit of Edinburgh, of Christian cooperation and peace? Were not Christians "supranational" in purpose and spirit? For Oldham, his obligation was clear: he would do whatever could be done to preserve the German missions and enable their work to continue by some means. Very soon after the outbreak of war, he took steps to create a fund for the German missions and to create a scheme whereby the work of detained or repatriated Germans could be carried on by missionaries of other nationalities, preferably neutral ones. In Germany, this looked like British expropriation by another name. Oldham worked hard to keep up a correspondence with German mission leaders, including Julius Richter and Karl Axenfeld, and prior to 1917, Mott was able to visit them personally. But communication broke down almost completely. It seemed that every move Oldham made on behalf of the German missions was interpreted negatively in Germany, such was the bitterness of war. In fact, later in the war, Oldham worked strenuously, in close concert with Archbishop Randall Davidson and missionary leaders in London, to forestall British colonial expropriation of German mission property. It was probably through such work with Lambeth Palace that Oldham first personally encountered the archbishop's chaplain, George Bell. Oldham's crowning but, at the time, little-noticed achievement came soon after the Armistice, when in 1919, through diplomatic contacts in Paris, he used his prophetic wiliness to ensure that the Treaty of Versailles included a clause guaranteeing religious freedom and the rights of missionaries of all nationalities, German included, to resume and pursue their work in all territories governed by signatories to the treaty. The German missions did indeed eventually resume their work. The vision shown in *The World and the Gospel* had been reflected not in a grandiose program for the postwar world but in surreptitious moves of quiet diplomacy in the direction of reconciliation. It took some time for all this to be realized in Germany, but its significance was registered when in 1933, German Protestant missions were again threatened, this time by the dictatorial regime in Germany itself, and it was to Oldham that the mission leaders then turned for help.

NEW BEGINNINGS: THE INTERNATIONAL MISSIONARY COUNCIL

The immediate postwar years (1919–24) were filled with intense and demanding activity for Oldham, involving much international travel, and no less significantly, with deepening theological reflection on the lessons of the war and responsibilities for the future. The war had highlighted the potency of nationalism rivaling the claim to the universality of the gospel and Christian fellowship. This had led to the near breakdown of relations between Oldham and his Western Continuation Committee colleagues on the one hand and between Oldham and the German mission leaders who had objected to his actions as violating the "supranationality" of missions on the other hand. No less, in part stimulated by the war as one between colonial powers, nationalist movements were now stirring in imperial and colonial territories, notably in India, posing searching questions to the missions on how they would relate to these new movements. For both the so-called Christian nations in the aftermath of war and those now aspiring to independence, missions and churches alike had to face the fundamental theological question of how national identity and loyalty were to be evaluated in relation to the supreme claim of God and loyalty to the universal Christian fellowship. Oldham tackled this question in his paper "Nationality and Missions," with its argument that the reality of nationhood and its positive benefits had to be recognized, but always with the qualification that the kingdom of God had the highest right to loyalty and service, and that only by being subsumed into this larger dominion could the aspirations of nationality be properly fulfilled.[21] The ultimate claim of God and the proper responsibilities of social life were also explored by Oldham in the address "God the Supreme Reality," which he gave in January 1921 to an international student conference in Glasgow hosted by the British SCM.[22] In the audience was a young Dutchman, Willem (Wim) A. Visser't Hooft, who many years later recalled how this

---

[21] J. H. Oldham, "Nationality and Missions," *International Review of Missions* 9, no. 35 (July 1920): 372–83.

[22] J. H. Oldham, "God the Supreme Reality," in *Christ and Human Need: Being Addresses Delivered at a Conference on International and Missionary Questions, Glasgow, January 4th to 9th, 1921*, comp. Student Christian Movement of Great Britain and Ireland (London: SCM Press, 1921), 127–40.

"went to the heart of the matter in a non-emotional, non-rhetorical and utterly convincing way."[23] This was the first encounter of the future first general secretary of the WCC with Oldham.

The aftermath of the war saw major initiatives proposed for the furtherance of Christian unity: in 1920, the letter of appeal from the ecumenical patriarch "unto all the Churches of Christ" to form a league for mutual assistance, dialogue, and the promotion of peace in the world; in the same year, the Lambeth Conference's "Appeal to all Christian People" for reunion; and in 1925, the first preparations for a world conference on Life and Work, which took place in Stockholm, and a preparatory meeting for a world conference on Faith and Order. A prime impulse for such initiatives was the dark experience of division and conflict in the world at large during 1914–18, in which the churches themselves appeared to be complicit, imprisoned in national loyalties rather than embodying the universal peace brought by Christ. For Oldham and the remainder of the Continuation Committee, the priority was to establish, as the long-delayed fruit of the Edinburgh conference, a permanent and truly international missionary organization. After a series of preliminary meetings, beginning at Crans in Switzerland and involving delicate conversations with the still wary (and for some time, still embittered) Germans, there was set up in 1921 at Lake Mohonk, New York, the IMC. Unsurprisingly, Oldham was appointed its secretary, a post he was to hold until 1938.

Oldham shared the aspirations of the various new initiatives toward unity, but for him, as far as the IMC was concerned, the agenda was primarily still to be motivated and shaped by the earlier objectives of *mission*—albeit now with a widening understanding of what mission involved. During his first postwar visit to the United States in 1919–20, Oldham was asked by E. A. Aiken of the Student Volunteer Movement for a summary statement on the goal of Christian missions. What Oldham wrote in response is very revealing of his mind at this critical juncture—when the IMC was still as yet not launched. He begins with a foundational statement: "The goal of Christian missions is to make known to the whole of mankind the gracious and saving acts of God in history, which have their centre and crown in the person and work of Jesus Christ, and which make

---

[23] Willem A. Visser't Hooft, *Memoirs* (Geneva: WCC, 1987), 10.

known His character and His purpose for the world." He proceeds to list the ways in which Christian witness is one not only of word but of life, and therefore, he includes medical missions, philanthropic efforts, industrial and agricultural training, "and Christian education generally as . . . means of forming character in accordance with the Christian view of the meaning and goal of life." His next paragraph, however—at some points echoing Warneck—takes the concept of mission to a new social plane: "A fundamental element in the aim of Christian missions is the establishment of a Christian society. This is essential, first, because the Christian ideal is social, as is shown by the central place of the Kingdom of God in Christ's teaching; and secondly, because the Christian task can never be accomplished by foreigners. The primary object of foreign missionary activity is therefore to establish and to help to train for effective leadership an indigenous Christian Church."[24]

This manifesto is clearly drawing on Oldham's experience over twenty years, right back to his YMCA days in Lahore and his efforts to help train Indians for the task that only they could do in India. The need for an Indigenous church under Indigenous leadership was now uppermost in his mind in his project to establish the National Christian Council in India, where he visited in 1922 and again in 1923—under Indian leadership. It was successful, but only after overcoming resistance from some foreign mission boards (mainly American) that were both wary of losing their autonomy in a unitive structure and reluctant to acknowledge the need for Indian leadership overall. The manifesto continues,

> In so far as the aims of Christian missions need to be modified it would seem to me to be in the direction of a clearer recognition of the demands made by the complexity of modern life. Since the industrial revolution the relations of the individual are no longer as in the preceding age mainly with individuals, but also with large organisations and with highly developed social groups. Under these conditions the attempt to win individuals necessarily involves the attempt to establish the rule of Christ over the whole of life. Moreover, in view of the political and economic relations of the professedly Christian nations with non-Christian peoples it

---

[24] J. H. Oldham, "The Aim of Christian Missions" (unpublished paper), cited in full in Clements, *Faith on the Frontier*, 252.

is necessary for Christian missions, if they are to bear witness to Christ, clearly and publicly to dissociate themselves from selfish and materialistic influences in these contacts and to stand unequivocally for justice and brotherhood in international and inter-racial relations.[25]

This effectively repeats what Oldham had said in *The World and the Gospel* and, with his call for mission to embrace the social dimension and corporate responsibilities of modern human existence, expresses a theme central to his thinking for the rest of his life.

The need "to stand unequivocally for justice and brotherhood in international and inter-racial relations" had already been made real for Oldham in his anguished correspondence with his Indian YMCA friends Datta and K. T. Paul in response to the Amritsar massacre in 1919 and was to be intensified in his leading role in campaigning against enforced African labor in Kenya and, with the CMSBI, making representations to the British Colonial Office on the need for the recognition in colonial policy of the paramountcy of African rights over white settler interests and Indian imported labor. His eyes were further opened to needs and possibilities while visiting the United States and Canada in 1921 for IMC meetings and visiting Black educational institutions in the southern states.

MISSION, RACE, AND AFRICA

The key themes in Oldham's thinking (and action) in the early 1920s were *race relations* and *education*—and the relationship between them in Christian mission. Crucial here were Oldham's encounters, during his visit to the United States 1921, with the southern states and their Black communities. His party visited the Tuskegee Institute in Alabama and other Black educational establishments, and he also went to St. Louis, Indianapolis, and Chicago. He was deeply stirred by his encounters with the Black communities and, above all, by the leadership of their education movements, which were now also receiving students from Africa, one of whom, from Rhodesia, was now on the staff at Tuskegee. Oldham wrote to Lionel Curtis, Oxford academic and founder of the *Round Table* journal, "The

---

[25] Oldham, cited in Clements, 252.

striking thing to me is how all these [African] men have an African consciousness; their loyalty and interest is not Liberian or Rhodesian or Gold Coast, but African. The man to whom I have especially referred is a better educated man than the average missionary. The number of educated Africans at present is small, but they can hold their own with the European just as the Indian can do."[26] Another transformative personal encounter was with the educationist W. E. Hocking, whose *Human Nature and Its Remaking* (1923) offered a view of human personality as plastic and sensible of considerable and creative development, not fixed and determined by inherited and material factors. This was of immense import in challenging the assumed stereotypes of human character, not least racial ones based on dubious biological claims.

Oldham brought together these issues and theological reflections on them in his pioneering 1924 study *Christianity and the Race Problem*.[27] It was his most substantial work, of 280 pages, if for nothing else chiefly known over the years for just one frequently cited sentence: "Christianity is not primarily a philosophy but a crusade."[28] But waging war requires intelligence services as well as weaponry, and what is notable in the book is its combination of fundamental theological principles—humanity as created equal by God with every person invested by God in Christ with worth and the object of God's love—with equal attention to the "facts" as known to the best of contemporary science, psychology, historical research, and studies in economic factors and the ethics of empire. The meanings of equality and inequality, not to mention "race" itself, are dispassionately explored. The whole discussion is set within the overarching historical framework of the expansion of Europe and the reaction against white domination, with India under British rule proving a particularly significant case study, along with Africa, and race relations in the United States. Moreover, Oldham searchingly examines the capacity of Christianity to meet the challenge. Written at a time when race was becoming a hotly debated issue in Europe, the British Empire, and the United States, with so-called biological factors and pseudo-Darwinian theories of survival of the fittest being employed to justify white power

---

[26] See Clements, *Faith on the Frontier*, 176.

[27] J. H. Oldham, *Christianity and the Race Problem* (London: SCM Press, 1924).

[28] Oldham, 26.

and privilege on the global scale, the book was timely and prophetic. In Germany, theories of the "master race" were already gaining currency, while in the United States, not only was racial segregation deeply entrenched sixty years after the Civil War was fought over slavery, but fears of the Asiatic "yellow peril" were being sown.

The book met with a wide and positive response throughout the English-speaking world, running through three editions in a year, and with a particularly warm welcome among Indian reviewers. Nearly a century after its publication, while obviously in some respects dated, the book still stands as a benchmark for engaged theological comment on social, international, and above all, racial issues. It marked the start of a long ecumenical pilgrimage that came to dramatic prominence in 1969 with the WCC's adoption of the Programme to Combat Racism.

In keeping with *Christianity and the Race Problem*, the eight years 1923–31 saw an extraordinarily intense and sustained burst of activity that, following his earlier work on forced labor and the paramountcy of African interests in East Africa, earned Oldham the title "Friend of Africa." It can be treated only in summary fashion here. Appalled by the complacent ignorance of Western governments, in 1924, with the Swiss-born British national Hans Vischer, Oldham founded the London-based International Institute of African Languages and Cultures and served part time as its director. High on his agenda was education in Africa and the role of government, churches, and missions in that provision, for which he campaigned vigorously in the corridors of the British Colonial Office, resulting in the setting up of the government's Permanent Advisory Committee on Education in Africa. He recruited as a close collaborator Edward Lugard, former governor of Nigeria and the chief exponent of the dual mandate theory of enlightened colonialism.[29] Oldham's first visit to Africa in 1926 included stops in South Africa, Tanganyika, and Kenya, and later that year, he participated in the International Conference on Christian Mission in Africa in La Zoute, Belgium. In 1928, even though he was secretary of the IMC (now assisted by William Paton, late of the National Christian Council of India), instead of attending the second World Missionary Conference in Jerusalem,

---

[29] Frederick Lugard, *The Dual Mandate in Tropical Africa* (Edinburgh: William Blackwood, 1922).

he accepted an offer to become a member of the British government's Hilton Young Commission, which visited East and Central Africa to examine firsthand the controversial idea of a closer union among the British territories there. The commission's majority report opposed the proposal on the grounds that it would entrench white settler interest at the expense of the Africans. Oldham wrote profusely on African issues, notably *What Is at Stake in East Africa* (1929), *White and Black in Africa* (1929; a vigorous rejoinder to the patriarch of white South Africa, Jan Smuts), and with his IMC colleague Betty Gibson, *The Remaking of Man in Africa* (1931). Still inspired by the basically optimistic philosophy of Hocking, Oldham saw the key to Africa's future as lying in education; meanwhile, safeguards were needed against manifest injustice wrought by the colonial powers. The study was visionary yet recognized realities on the ground and the art of the possible. It also exposed him to criticism from two sides. Parliamentary opinion sympathetic to white settlers in Africa regarded him as a meddler. More radical critics of colonial policy included Norman Leys, a former medical officer in Kenya. Oldham's campaigning against the atrocities in Kenya notwithstanding, Leys grew increasingly critical of his approach, which Leys regarded as too friendly toward government and paternalistic toward Africans.[30]

New Frontiers: A Theology of Humanity

Oldham combined all this activity with his secretaryship of the IMC (in fact, for a time, part of his salary was paid by the International Institute of African Languages and Cultures), assisted by Paton, who in 1923 had joined him from the National Christian Council of India. As with all Oldham's multifarious concerns, his African involvement involved an extraordinary amount of networking at a personal level, for which he benefited from his membership in the Athenaeum, the most patrician of London clubs favored by bishops and academics. This gave rise to the joke that Oldham's motto was "Find out where power lies and then take it to lunch at the Athenaeum." Not surprisingly, eyebrows were raised in some IMC circles (not least American) at the amount of time and energy he was devoting to what appeared to

---

[30] See J. W. Cell, ed., *By Kenya Possessed: The Correspondence of Norman Leys and J. H. Oldham, 1918–1926* (Chicago: University of Chicago Press, 1976).

be peculiarly British concerns in Africa. Oldham, however, believed that what was at stake in Africa was of universal import. Nevertheless, there must have been surprise when in 1928, the secretary of the IMC elected not to be present at the second World Missionary Conference in Jerusalem in favor of accompanying the Hilton Young Commission to Africa. In fact, by the late 1920s, Oldham's outlook was beginning to change. Without renouncing any of his previous work or denying its importance (though he was now critical of the 1910 Edinburgh conference regarding any substantive contribution to missionary *thought*), he was starting to feel restive with the assumed priorities of the mission boards that governed the IMC and even with the leadership of Mott, whom he still held in the highest personal regard. In 1930, Oldham addressed the Church Missionary Society (CMS) on "The CMS and the Adventure of Today," calling for a radically new start in the missionary movement. He believed the gospel must step into the realities of the lives of Africans, for example, if it is to become real to people. Above all, it must engage with the social complexities besetting people today. It is a mission for laypeople to act out in their daily lives, centered on the needs of the world, not the church. Within the IMC constituency, he felt, the sense of adventure was fading. New frontiers were beckoning. He concludes, "What I have attempted to say to you may be summed up in one word: Listen. Let our attitude . . . be that of listening for God's voice. Let us be ready for change. . . . To those who listen God's whisper will come, and for those who can dare and suffer countless adventures are waiting in the days to come."[31]

New tremors were being felt across the political world, not least in Europe, and fresh currents were flowing in theology and philosophy. Oldham was alert to all these stirrings, and his responses were to prove vital in the new shaping of ecumenical theology. A watershed moment came with the report of the American Laymen's Commission of Inquiry into the work of missionary societies in Asia, *Rethinking Missions* (1932). Led by Hocking, and very much in the spirit of the 1928 Jerusalem conference, the report argued for shifting the goal of missions from the exclusive presentation of Christianity to seeking common ground with other peoples and their faiths. Oldham welcomed the critical inquiry into missions but was less than

---

[31] See Clements, *Faith on the Frontier*, 270.

happy with the report's theological presuppositions—above all, the idea that there is a common basis of agreement between Christians and followers of other religions and that to these common beliefs, further beliefs may be added. He countered, "Christianity, as it has been understood in the past has not to do with man's quest for God, but with God's gift to man. It has been bound up with the belief that God has acted in history. He has spoken to men. It is not our search but God's gift and commission on which everything hinges. . . . The Christian mission . . . stands or falls with the question whether it is a bearer of a Word from God."[32]

Here clearly was someone who was listening to Karl Barth and his theology of God's word addressing humanity in crisis—and thus creating a crisis of its own in calling for a response to God's self-revelation in Christ. This was not a new acquaintance with continental theology, since Oldham's interest had never left him following his studies in Halle (1904–5) and his close relationships with the German mission leaders before, during, and following the First World War. Moreover, in 1926, he had shared in two conferences organized by George Bell, at that time dean of Canterbury Cathedral, of German and British theologians, at Canterbury (1926) and Eisenach (1928). The interest in Barth, however, lay not so much in his being continental but in what he was saying theologically, and likewise with Emil Brunner, whom Oldham visited in Zurich in 1930 and got to know very well. In June of that year, Oldham hosted Barth's first visit to Britain. The IMC was promoting a study of the presentation of the Christian message for the contemporary world and was eager to draw leading Christian thinkers of the caliber of Brunner, Karl Heim, and Paul Tillich. Two meetings of the "Brunner group" took place during 1930–31. Brunner especially appealed to Oldham on account of his stress on faith as a personal encounter with the God who speaks and draws near in grace to the human who receives. Oldham's thirst for Germanic theological thought continued unabated. In May 1932, he must have been one of the few English-speaking readers to have ordered a copy of the young Dietrich Bonhoeffer's *Akt und Sein*, published the previous year but not appearing in English (as *Act and Being*) for another thirty years. What interested Oldham about the

---

[32] Oldham, "Rethinking Missions" (unpublished paper, 1932), cited in Clements, *Faith on the Frontier*, 270.

"theologies of encounter" was their interaction with the contemporary human sciences and the possibilities for a Christian *anthropology* based on the God-created human capacity for personal relationships. This interest in anthropology was bolstered by contemporary personalist philosophies. He had long been acquainted with Buber's seminal *Ich und Du*, but he was also now captivated by Eberhard Grisebach, professor of philosophy and pedagogics at Zurich. Grisebach rejected the idealist form of philosophy, which sought truth in abstract generalizations about knowledge and reality. Reality, especially ethical reality, is not found within the reflective mind but becomes present to the individual in encounters with others, and only in facing and being faced by the other to the point of resistance and contradiction does one come to recognize it. The Russian émigré thinker Nikolai Berdyaev and (later) the Catholic Jacques Maritain also encouraged this personalist interest, which fed into Oldham's view of ecumenism as encounter and dialogue with what is "other." By a sad irony, this strengthening of interest in the interpersonal realm coincided with the growing onset of the affliction that was to beset Oldham for the rest of his life—namely, severe deafness only partly mitigated by the use of a clumsy and not always reliable hearing apparatus that had to accompany him to all his meetings.

Toward Life and Work

For Oldham, this quest for relational anthropology was not a purely academic exercise. It was profoundly related to what was happening in the world and the need for a fresh Christian engagement with society. He was perceiving that the next crucial battle for Christian witness would be not over "religion," whether for Christianity as the one true religion or (as the Jerusalem conference stated) for a united religious front against "secularism," but over a right understanding of humankind—of what constituted truly human existence and the looming threats to it. The Soviet state was brutally imposing mass conformity to its Marxist-Leninist ideology, while fascism was already in power in Italy, threatening in Germany, and alive in movements in France. Such totalitarianisms were so called because they claimed the whole human person, disregarding personal freedom of belief, creativity, and the role of relationships between persons in community. But no less, Oldham believed, the Western

J. H. Oldham, circa 1930.
Photo credit: WCC Photo Archive.

democracies were under threat from the growth of impersonal forces that were present in more and more areas of life, forces over which people felt they had little or no control. The pursuit of economic growth fueled by technological advances was leading to an extending of both corporate and state powers without any examination of the ethical values underlying them. This was the context in which the

Christian voice had to be heard and the question had to be asked: What is now happening to humankind, as created by God for life in community, in relationships measured by freedom and responsibility, as seen in the gospel? But while the issue at heart may have been simple, Oldham realized that the outworking of answers amid the complexities of modern society would require qualities of thought, imagination, and courage beyond anything that the churches had hitherto exhibited in modern times. The question then was, What church-related bodies are available or need to be created to address this challenge?

In 1925, the Life and Work conference in Stockholm had set up a continuation committee that in 1930 reconstituted itself as a permanent body, the Universal Christian Council for Life and Work (hereafter Council for Life and Work). Its main objective was "to perpetuate and strengthen the fellowship between the churches in the application of Christian ethics in the social problems of modern life."[33] In its earliest stages, Oldham was, in fact, somewhat dismissive of the Life and Work Movement, feeling that involvement in it would be a distraction from the IMC scene. By the early 1930s, however, it had grown in strength, with several commissions at work and with a headquarters and research institute in Geneva. Oldham was now sizing it up as a possible vehicle for his newer concerns, especially as a second Life and Work world conference was being envisaged for 1935, at which issues of church and state would be addressed. In view of the global economic crisis, it was decided to postpone this to 1937. An additional attraction was the appointment of George Bell, now bishop of Chichester, as chairman of the executive committee in 1932.[34] Now affecting great interest in the agenda of the Life and Work Movement, Oldham's wiliness took the form of securing his own attendance at a crucial meeting of its council in August 1934 on the Danish island of Fanø.[35] There it was decided that the world conference, now definitely scheduled for Oxford in 1937, should be on the theme "Church, Community, and State," and Oldham was

---

[33] Continuation Committee meeting minutes, Chexbres, Switzerland, 1930, cited in Rouse and Neill, *History of the Ecumenical Movement*, 553.

[34] See chapter 3 in this volume, page 122.

[35] See the introduction in this volume, pages 1–2. On the subtle maneuverings of Oldham in relation to Fanø at this point, see Clements, *Faith on the Frontier*, 275–85.

made chairman of the Committee on Programme for the conference. He was, in effect, now the organizer of the whole program of study before, during, and after Oxford, making it a virtually full-time post on top of his secretaryship of the IMC (in which he was, of course, assisted by Bill Paton). He was now in an unrivaled position for shaping the ecumenical agenda, which he viewed—as did Bell—as in need of facing the hard and complex realities of the contemporary world, armed not with optimistic idealism (a tendency in Life and Work hitherto) but with an astringent yet positive theology along the lines of Barth and Brunner.

Oldham was by now strengthening his friendships and working relationships with a number of staff and leaders in the Geneva-based ecumenical bodies, not least in the youth organizations, whose conferences he was frequently addressing. He and Visser't Hooft, general secretary of the WSCF from 1932 and an enthusiast for Barth, became especially important to each other (rather as young Oldham and older Mott had been from 1908). The American Francis P. Miller, chairman of the WSCF from 1928, shared much of Oldham's theological and philosophical interest (if not always in agreement), which made for lively exchanges and correspondence. With the Faith and Order Commission, emanating from the Lausanne Conference of 1927, however, Oldham had no direct involvement, though knowing well and highly respectful of several of its key players. Temple, for example, had feet in both the Life and Work and Faith and Order camps. Further, although so occupied from 1934 with the planning for Oxford 1937, Oldham was able to devote himself to other ecumenical concerns—two in particular.

A WORLD ECUMENICAL BODY: FIRST STEPS

The first concern was the early exploration of the way toward a world ecumenical organization. This began with a relatively small, completely informal gathering in 1933, suggested by the veteran American Life and Work leader William Adams Brown. Leaders and representatives of the various ecumenical bodies in existence—the IMC, Life and Work, Faith and Order, WSCF, and the World Alliance for International Friendship through the Churches (hereafter World Alliance)—were hosted by Temple, now archbishop of York, at his residence, Bishopthorpe. Both Oldham and Paton attended.

Thereafter, Oldham played a low-profile but central role in furthering discussions, concerned that the "consultative group" that had met at Bishopthorpe should remain just that and nothing more for the time being. His approach was that of careful pragmatism. He wrote to Francis Miller, "The interesting thing is that all the five movements are finding themselves driven back on ultimate problems which are in their essence theological. We are all in the last resort concerned with one and the same problem though each movement approaches it and must continue to approach it from its own distinctive angle. This being so, it becomes increasingly clear that the real problem is how through consultation we can make the best use of the very limited resources at our disposal."[36]

While cautious, Oldham's insistence on starting with the tasks that needed to be done and seeing where those tasks were most appropriately carried out within the already existing bodies probably ensured the eventual outcome of a world council of churches. The process might well have collapsed in utter disagreement had there been a rush to draw up a new blueprint. Even so, world events were soon to inject a degree of urgency into the process.

The German Church Struggle

Oldham's second ecumenical concern during this period was the German Church Struggle. He was in no doubt that in Germany, it was the Confessing Church—as distinct from the Reich church, compromised by the nationalist and racist heresies of the so-called German Christian movement—that merited the support of the ecumenical community. His involvement in that fraught scene, however, was on several levels. First of all, in 1933, in response to pleas from Alphons Koechlin of the Basel Mission and missions leaders in Germany, Oldham sought financial support for the plight of the German missions whose work abroad was being starved of funds by the Nazi government's banning of the export of Reichsmarks and who, at home, were being forced into a single organization controlled by the government-supported Reich church. He visited Nazi Germany twice to consult with the mission staff and, in due course, Confessing Church leaders.

---

[36] J. H. Oldham, letter to Francis Miller, June 8, 1934, cited in full in Clements, *Faith on the Frontier*, 281–82.

Meanwhile, Dietrich Bonhoeffer was pastoring two German congregations in London during 1933–35. Oldham befriended and got to know him well, inviting him to dinner, advising on his efforts for refugees from Nazi Germany, and gleaning much firsthand (and often confidential) information about the German scene. He was also collaborating closely with Bell on the international ecumenical response to the German Church Struggle and was among Bell's advisers on an early draft of his 1934 Ascension Day message to the Life and Work community.[37] Oldham was also brought into the discussions at the Fanø conference, at which the Council for Life and Work declared its solidarity with the Confessing Church. Onward from the conference, Life and Work was much more sympathetic than was Faith and Order to the claim of the Confessing Church, in opposition to the Reich church, to represent the Evangelical Church of Germany at the ecumenical table. Oldham and Bell were at one on that issue, and together they formed a crucial conduit between the Confessing Christians and the ecumenical movement (aided by the fact that Oldham was well versed in German, which Bell was not). Oldham underlined where his theological sympathies lay when addressing a student audience in 1935 on "The Christian World Community." He asked rhetorically what more momentous question can there be for a person than "Whether there is a living Word which he may hear, which he may trust, which he can obey?"—unmistakable Barthian echoes from the 1934 Theological Declaration of Barmen, the founding charter of the Confessing Church.

Church, Community, and State: Oxford 1937

The conference on "Church, Community, and State," which met at Oxford in July 1937, is widely recognized as one of the defining events in the twentieth-century ecumenical story and a crucial landmark in the formation of the WCC. Equally, Oldham is described as "the chief architect and outstanding exponent of the Oxford project."[38] Oldham, of course, did not work alone. From the time of his appointment as chairman of Life and Work's advisory commission on research at Fanø in August 1934, he had able members of the advisory commission in assistance, including notables like John Baillie (Scotland), Brunner

---

37 See pages 165–67 in this volume.

38 Rouse and Neill, *History of the Ecumenical Movement*, 584.

and Visser't Hooft (Switzerland), V. A. Demant and Leonard Hodgson (England), Wilhelm Menn (Germany), and Henry P. van Dusen (United States), plus the staff at the research institute in Geneva, Hans Schönfeld and Nils Ehrenström. He was also determined to recruit assistant staff of his own from the younger ecumenical enthusiasts. Having failed to persuade Lesslie Newbigin, who was determined to go to India, he was joined by another young Presbyterian, Eric Fenn, former secretary of the British SCM.

Oldham's first move, characteristically, was to set out the significance of the conference theme in the contemporary world situation, its theological basis, and the tasks therewith laid upon the churches. His booklet *Church, Community and State: A World Issue* appeared in early 1935 with a preface by Brown and an introduction by Bell. It was a manifesto not just for the conference itself but for what Oldham envisaged as a long-term program of study and engagement for years to come, within which Oxford 1937 would be a vital component but neither the sum total nor the end. Oldham also prepared a similar background booklet, *The Question of the Church in the World of Today*, on similar lines for the IMC conference to take place in Tambaram, India, in 1938. The prime issue to be faced at Oxford, he believed, was the growth of the modern state, which was assuming responsibilities over so many areas of life. The dangers of the extremities of the totalitarian states were obvious, but there were, Oldham believed, dangers also in democratic societies where a philosophy of life and a pattern of living contrary to Christian understanding were being imposed:

> It is when Christian people are unaware that their faith is being undermined that the greater harm may be done. The question for the church is whether the common life and culture in which modern people are increasingly bound together will be inspired by Christian or pagan conceptions of the meaning and purpose of life. The deeper meaning of totalitarian claims will be missed if they fail to open our eyes to a state of things which is found in every country. . . . Only as the Christian Gospel is brought into a close relation to the realities and actual problems of the world to-day can we expect mankind to recognize in it a living word of judgment and redemption.[39]

---

[39] J. H. Oldham, *The Question of the Church in the World of Today* (London: Edinburgh House for IMC, 1936).

Preparatory group for the 1937 Oxford conference, meeting at Bishopthorpe, the residence of the archbishop of York, William Temple. *Front row from left:* third, J. H. Oldham; fourth, William Temple; fifth, Willem A. Visser't Hooft; sixth, Reinhold Niebuhr.
Photo credit: WCC Photo Archive.

The Oxford conference would achieve its purpose only if it became the expression of a church that is a community of persons with hearts kindled by the flame of evangelism, who find life's fulfillment in responsibility to their fellows in mutual respect, service, and love and who draw inspiration from the God who reveals himself as their Father.

To facilitate the international preparation of the study program for Oxford, regional and national advisory groups were formed. Nine subject areas in three groupings were proposed for research. In the first grouping, there was the church and its function in society, church and community, and church and state. The second grouping had the church, community, and state in relation to education; economic order; and the universal church and the world of nations. The third grouping had the theological foundations of the Christian understanding of man, the kingdom of God and history, and Christian faith and the common life. There was here not only a continuation of some earlier Life and Work studies but also a narrower focus than some wished—labor, employment, and social welfare, for example, were relatively marginalized. But Oldham insisted on making hard choices between the doubtless important and the most critical priorities, especially given the churches' scarce resources. For each subject, a team of writers was assembled, both theologians and lay experts in the fields, to prepare study papers. The theologians included eminences like Brunner, Reinhold Niebuhr, C. H. Dodd, Temple, Martin Dibelius, Paul Tillich, and Stefan Zankov. The writers were selected not because they were notably "ecumenical" but because of the particular contribution they could make to the area in question. Nor were all professional theologians—the American diplomat and government advisor John Foster Dulles, for example. Not all the 250 papers produced finally saw the light of day, but the critics and commentators upon them came from wide circles of interest: scientists, political and social thinkers, industrialists, educationists, and literati as well as theologians. It was the most extensive and intensive ecumenical study program devised thus far.

But the path to Oxford did not run smooth. Not only were there major logistical problems to overcome and issues of representation (Oldham insisted on a substantial lay presence as well as youth participation), but differences emerged over the emphasis of the proposed program. In particular, there was resentment in the United States toward what appeared to be a focus on mainly European concerns, together with Oldham's predilection for the neo-orthodox theology and for Brunner in particular. Van Dusen of Union Seminary, New York, told Oldham that in rejecting what he called the secular view of man, Brunner was effectively dismissing what was central to much American theology. Oldham politely but firmly defended Brunner's corner and promised van Dusen some slight modifications of Brunner's paper and further explanations that would surely suffice. Van Dusen and his fellow American R. L. Calhoun were not easily mollified and still asked for a more comprehensive view of the human being to be aired than Brunner could supply. Nor were the Americans happy at Oldham's repeated insistence on the long view of the program, extending well after Oxford, not least because of the dampening effect this would have on obtaining funding for it. The American misgivings were to run virtually up to the conference itself. Moreover, at the final pre-Oxford meeting of the Council for Life and Work, at Chamby, Switzerland, in August 1936, complaints were made about the seeming heaviness of the conference material and program, while William Adams Brown complained both to

Oldham himself and to others about what he felt to be Oldham's undue influence and high-handedness on all matters relating to the conference (Oldham, in turn, complained about Brown being "difficult" throughout the meeting). Some deft footwork by Oldham in the corridors at Chamby helped defuse the misgivings, and he devised a system whereby members of the council could be involved in overseeing the final stages of preparation. There was also some reduction made in the program by merging some areas of study.

The only preparatory material published before the conference was volume 1, *The Church and Its Function in Society*, written jointly by Oldham and Visser't Hooft.[40] It was significant that Oldham willingly wrote in partnership with the secretary of the WSCF, twenty-six years his junior. Oldham had been renewing and strengthening his links with the student Christian bodies since the late 1920s, not least because there, he found people who perforce took the long view and were committed "to a task to which they can give their entire lives."[41] With the SCM in Britain, he said, he had felt more at home than in most gatherings of seniors—a barb aimed at the cautious ethos of even the Council for Life and Work. At any rate, Oldham's contribution to volume 1, taking as its heading the title of the book as a whole, was widely agreed to be first-class. It constitutes a summary of the holistic understanding of the church and its mission that had marked his thinking since the First World War: the distinction and interrelations between the church as an institution and the church as a community of faith, between the givenness of the gospel of grace and the ethics that are a response to that grace, and between the church as a community of worship and the church as active in love, evangelization, mercy, and witness. But in terms of the conference theme, its chief value lies in the later sections on the nature of secular society and the role of the Christian and the church within it. Substantial excerpts are included in chapter 2 of this book. Suffice it to say, there is much realism on the nature of institutional life and the "laws of things" that have to be recognized, yet also an insistence on the possibility and necessity of ethical guidance in secular affairs

---

[40] Willem A. Visser't Hooft and J. H. Oldham, *The Church and Its Function in Society*, Church, Community and State 1 (London: Allen & Unwin, 1937).

[41] J. H. Oldham, letter to Henry P. van Dusen, April 1926, cited in Clements, *Faith on the Frontier*, 320.

and, above all, on the role of the laity for expressing the gospel and Christian ethics within the world. Seminal suggestions are made for the kind of support and structures needed to develop lay ministries. There is also a richer understanding of ethics applicable to the complexities of secular life—notably, the concept of "middle axioms" as a means of translating the imperatives of love and social justice into specific responsibilities in particular cases.

The conference did indeed take place July 12–26, 1937, with 425 delegates from 120 churches in forty countries.[42] The great majority were from Europe and North America, with participants also from Australia, China, the Dutch East Indies (today, Indonesia), India, Japan, Korea, Mexico, New Zealand, the Philippines, South Africa, and South America. The plight of the German churches was felt, paradoxically, by their complete absence due to the refusal of travel documents by the Nazi authorities. Mott presided over the plenary sessions, which were addressed by speakers as varied as the archbishop of Canterbury, Cosmo Gordon Lang; Oldham himself; van Dusen; Stefan Zankov; Brunner; the poet T. S. Eliot; and Niebuhr. The real intensity of the gathering lay in the discussions within the various sections and their reports: *Church and Community, Church and State, Economic Order, Education,* and *The Universal Church and the World of Nations.* Whatever else, there had been serious grappling thus far in ecumenical history with the most challenging crises of the day. The spirit of the conference was summed up in its "Message to the Christian Churches," largely the work of Temple, which includes the memorable utterance, "We do not call the world to be like ourselves, for we are already too like the world. Only as we ourselves repent, both as individuals and as corporate bodies, can the Church call men to repentance. The call to ourselves and to the world is to Christ."[43] It concludes, "The world is anxious and bewildered and full of pain and fear. We are troubled and yet we do not despair. Our hope is anchored in the living God. . . . The Church can be of good cheer; it hears its Lord saying, 'I have overcome the world.'"[44]

---

[42] For the official report, see J. H. Oldham, ed., *The Churches Survey Their Task: The Report of the Conference at Oxford, July 1937, on Church, Community and State* (London: Allen & Unwin, 1937).

[43] Oldham, 57.

[44] Oldham, 63.

Oxford 1937 was arguably the ecumenical movement's greatest moment of self-discovery in the decade leading up to the Second World War. "Let the church be the church" was a slogan popularly associated with Oxford. It does not appear in any of the official statements or reports of the conference, but it does convey what was affirmed there. In face of the actual conflicts already taking place (not least between Japan and China, Italy and Ethiopia, and in Spain), the danger of wider war, and the threatened collapse of civilizations, it had declared the kingdom of God and, therewith, where the church was called to stand. The section report *The Universal Church and the World of Nations*, for example, sets out with abundant clarity the Christian commitment to peace and justice in the context of nationhood and nationalism, which still speaks pertinently well beyond the context of 1937. There could not be a greater contrast with the way the churches had largely been caught up in the partisanship of 1914–18, and this became apparent when world war did break out again in September 1939. The ecumenical fellowship largely remained intact, and Oxford bequeathed a rich store of wisdom to encourage and give direction to the Christian witness in society, which would be taken up again after that conflict. But if Oxford 1937 was a decisive moment for the ecumenical movement, then equally, it could be said to be the crowning, though not the last, achievement of Oldham's ecumenical life.

FURTHER STEPS: THE WORLD COUNCIL OF CHURCHES

Following the meetings of the consultative group representing the various bodies (Life and Work, Faith and Order, IMC, and WSCF) at Bishopthorpe (1933) and Paris (1934), Oldham continued to be closely involved in the discussions exploring the way toward a world ecumenical organization. The group met again at Princeton in late 1935. This meeting was chaired by Temple, by then acknowledged as the main driving force of the whole enterprise, who suggested that "the time had come for an interdenominational, international council representing all the Churches, with committees to carry on various projects now forming the objectives of the distinct world movements."[45] The meeting recommended that the consultative

---

[45] See Rouse and Neill, *History of the Ecumenical Movement*, 701.

group be given regular status and that at their next meetings, the world organizations should take suitable actions to make the existing cooperation more effective. Oldham's pragmatic approach was gaining ground, and new opportunities were opening up. Indeed, says Visser't Hooft, "the man who translated these opportunities into specific and concrete proposals was Dr J. H. Oldham."[46] Oldham himself seized the opportunity of the 1936 Chamby meeting of the Council for Life and Work—though he was heavily occupied, as we have seen, with the preparations for Oxford 1937—and presented a paper on the critical significance of the Oxford conference and the Edinburgh Faith and Order conference (August 3–18) being held so close together in time. He regarded this juxtaposition as what today would be spoken of as a *kairos* moment:

> The holding of the ecumenical conferences in 1937 provides an opportunity which will not recur for many years, of having the whole future of the ecumenical movement examined afresh. . . . In the historical crisis in which the Church finds itself there is need of facing these questions with the greatest deliberation and of bringing to bear on them the best statesmanship that the Church can command. The best means of doing this would seem to be the appointment in consultation with the other ecumenical movements of a committee which would meet prior to the conferences at Oxford and Edinburgh and present a report to the conferences.[47]

This is essentially what did happen in 1937. As proposed by Bell, who was chairman of the Chamby meeting, and agreed soon after by the committee of Faith and Order (and also by the IMC and World Alliance), a commission of thirty-five representatives nominated by the consultative group, met at Westfield College in London just prior to the Oxford conference and reported to both the Oxford and Edinburgh conferences. The report to both was brief yet carefully phrased and, under the heading "A World Council of Churches" (the phrase was coined by the American Samuel McCrea Cavert), stated that with "a view to facilitating the more effective action of the Christian Church in the modern world," the Life and Work and

---

[46] Willem A. Visser't Hooft, "The Genesis of the World Council of Churches," in Rouse and Neill, 701.
[47] Cited in Visser't Hooft, 701–2.

Faith and Order movements should be more closely related in a body representative of the churches and "caring for the interests of each movement."[48] There would be a general assembly of representatives of the churches meeting over five years and a central council of approximately sixty members, which—as far as possible and at Oldham's repeated call—would be one-third laymen or laywomen. Oxford and Edinburgh would each appoint seven members to a constituent committee to complete the details and bring the scheme into existence. Thus was the basic ground plan of the WCC laid down.

Both conferences endorsed the plan. At Edinburgh, however, some in Faith and Order feared that in the proposed WCC, the agenda of Life and Work would predominate to Faith and Order's disadvantage, and Oldham was deeply disappointed that whereas Life and Work willingly allowed itself to be subsumed into the new body, Faith and Order decided to keep its own continuation committee in being, a stance Oldham described as "wanting to be married but remaining single."[49] Be that as it may, Oldham's forethought and careful advocacy had succeeded overall, and he worked hard to ensure that the new body would maintain the study agenda of the Oxford conference. The joint constituent committee arranged for a provisional conference in Utrecht, Netherlands, on May 9–13, 1938, with invitations to the churches, to settle the actual constitution of the WCC, in the preparations for which Oldham was much involved (too much so, at the expense of H. L. Henriod in Geneva, thought Brown). At Utrecht, Temple was in the chair. A new provisional committee was appointed, and one of its first acts was to invite Visser't Hooft to be the first general secretary of the WCC in formation. For two years or more, he had been seen as a likely candidate, but doubts had been expressed, especially in the United States, on account of his relative youth (aged thirty-eight) and his strongly Barthian theological orientation. It was Oldham who in personal correspondence had largely answered these hesitations, and it was Temple who finally drove through any lingering doubts on the Provisional Committee.

---

[48] "A World Council of Churches," in Oldham, *Churches Survey Their Task*, 279.

[49] J. H. Oldham, letter to Willem A. Visser't Hooft, April 26, 1938, cited in Clements, *Faith on the Frontier*, 345.

ECUMENISM, BRITAIN, AND GENEVA, 1938–1948:
THE RESPONSIBLE SOCIETY

Oldham still found much work to do, quite apart from his involvement with the WCC, whose inaugural assembly was delayed by the
Second World War until 1948. From 1938 on, much of his energy
was concentrated on ecumenical work in Britain, which he envisaged as carrying on the WCC agenda—that of the Oxford 1937
conference in particular. In early 1938, he set up the Council on the
Christian Faith and the Common Life (CCFCL) as an ecumenical
instrument for social thought and action. For a variety of reasons,
not least financial, this did not prove viable in the longer term, and
in 1942, it was subsumed under the newly formed British Council
of Churches. More creative and of more lasting value were three
smaller-scale projects. The "Moot" was a discussion group comprising
some twenty members in total but with a core regular participation of
about fifteen, meeting over a weekend three times a year from early
1938, throughout the war, and until November 1947, with a number
of occasional guest invitees including Niebuhr. It included clergy and
theologians John Baillie and A. R. Vidler but was predominately lay,
with philosophers H. A. Hodges, Adolf Löwe, and Michael Polanyi;
literary figures like John Middleton Murry and T. S. Eliot; and educationists like Walter Oakeshott and Walter Moberly. The prize intellectual recruit, and the most influential (apart from Oldham) in
setting the course of the group's discussions, was the sociologist Karl
Mannheim, like Adolf Löwe a refugee of Jewish background from
Nazi Germany. The Moot's deliberations were long, at times tortuous,
but doggedly grappling with the issue of how British society, if it was
not to succumb to a kind of totalitarianism of its own, could sustain
elements of freedom and creativity in the face of a creeping regime
of purely material economic interests and technological application.[50]
Closely related to the Moot was the *Christian News-Letter*, which
Oldham founded with the help of Moot members and the approval
of church leaders, in October 1939, just over a month after the outbreak of war. It was a fortnightly pamphlet of news and comments
on current events, both domestic and international, with a good deal
of social analysis and thoughtful theological discussion. There were

[50] See Keith Clements, ed., *The Moot Papers: Faith, Freedom and Society 1938–1944*
(London: T&T Clark, 2010).

regular supplements by contributors of diverse religious and political outlooks, but they were united in their view that the current world crisis and Britain's part in it required Christian perspectives to be brought to bear. As time went on, attention progressively focused on the prospects of a postwar social order. The newsletter proved widely popular, with a subscriber circulation of up to ten thousand copies a time, with a readership of many more as it was distributed and shared well beyond churchly circles, not least among the armed services, and with citations in other periodicals. Allied to it was a series of Christian News-Letter books, which aired further some of the topics discussed in the Moot and the newsletter. One of these bore the title that, echoing Buber, Oldham made famous during the war, *Real Life Is Meeting*.[51] Then in 1942, Oldham founded the Christian Frontier, an organization run for and by laypeople, to examine "from the other end"—that is, the secular world in which laypeople spend most of their lives—issues of common concern to Christians and "those who are not Christians and in contexts other than those of organised religion."[52] This too proved of lasting value, with groups working on topics including the management movement, industrial relations, the local community, and education. The Christian Frontier and its journal, *Frontier*, continued for many years after the war.

Oldham had retired from the secretaryship of the IMC in 1938, Paton now taking full charge and serving as an associate secretary of the WCC in London. From that point on, Oldham had no executive position within the ecumenical structures, though he remained on the Provisional Committee until the WCC assembly in Amsterdam in 1948. The projects on which he was most engaged from 1938 were his own—the Moot, the *Christian News-Letter*, and the Christian Frontier—which he could claim represented the WCC agenda in Britain. Any influence he could bring to bear on shaping the WCC and its policies prior to the inaugural assembly depended on his personal wisdom and prestige born out of the thirty years since Edinburgh 1910, which of course were considerable. The most direct channel for such influence was his friendship with Visser't Hooft, as

---

[51] Oldham, Hodges, and Mairet, *Real Life Is Meeting*.

[52] See Clements, *Faith on the Frontier*, 411–12, for Oldham's statement of the principles of the Christian frontier.

testified by the voluminous correspondence and their actual meetings during the war years (Visser't Hooft was able to visit London five times during the war). Oldham worried about the likely woeful underrepresentation of women and youth in the WCC. He and Visser't Hooft disagreed sharply over the role of national councils of churches—Oldham wishing the councils to have a central role in its governance and programs, Visser't Hooft responding forcibly (and successfully) that this would fatally marginalize the individual member churches. Oldham feared the WCC becoming a centralizing body and taking on too many tasks (especially at the expense of focusing on study and utilizing "the best minds" available) and stated that if he had his way, he would have a notice erected above the entrance to the WCC office bearing the Pauline declaration, "This *one* thing I do" (Phil 3:13; emphasis mine). In the midst of all this wartime stress and activity, two great losses by death were suffered, that of Paton in 1943 and, after his tragically short tenure of the See of Canterbury, Temple in 1944. It was now a lonelier furrow that Oldham had to plow in Britain, and this made the connection with Visser't Hooft in Geneva all the more important. But he was also sustained by younger collaborators coming into their own—notably, the Anglican theologian (and SCM product) Kathleen Bliss and the Congregationalist Daniel Jenkins. Oldham's concerns about the WCC remained. He was distinctly cool, for instance, toward the idea of a department of international affairs being created, at least before the first assembly had met.[53] Repeatedly, he argued for the programmatic work to be done in the national and regional constituencies, with the central Geneva staff focusing on the essential tasks of coordinating study and action.

At the same time, Oldham's mind was not occupied primarily with organizational questions. He was still engaging with the social and world issues that the ecumenical fellowship would need to address—as foreseen in the *Christian News-Letter* and its associated publications—and, as he devoutly hoped, would be faced at the

---

[53] The Commission of the Churches on International Affairs was set up at a conference in Cambridge, England, in August 1946, attended by Oldham. According to J. Nurser, "Even Oldham, who earlier had drizzled cold water on the project, came to the party and gave it his blessing." Nurser, *For All Peoples and All Nations: Christian Churches and Human Rights* (Geneva: WCC, 2005), 134.

The Christian News-Letter

Edited by
J. H. OLDHAM

No. 8   DECEMBER 20, 1939

DEAR MEMBER,

I wish you a good Christmas. One hesitates to say a happy Christmas in the midst of such suffering and the seeming ascendancy of the powers of evil. But all the more in such a situation is it possible for us to draw reassurance and strength from the event which we celebrate at Christmas. It is a plain fact of history that in the birth of Christ there entered into the process of human life a spiritual energy of unparalleled power. Into a corrupt society there came silently a new regenerating force greater than any other which history can show.

> " The crazy stable, close at hand,
> With shaking timber and shifting sand,
> Grew a stronger thing to abide and stand
> Than the square stones of Rome."

It is an indisputable fact that in the spiritual life of mankind, as in nature, the death of winter can give place to the life of spring. The power which infused fresh vitality into the decaying ancient world is not yet exhausted. What has been may be again. Why should we preclude the possibility that our age should witness a repetition of the miracle ?

A MESSAGE FROM CHINA

A message has come from the heads of two of the leading Christian colleges in China. One of them is Francis C. Wei, the President of Hua Chung College, formerly at Wuchang in central China and now moved to Yunnan, whom many of you probably know. This message, coming to us across half the world from a country which has been exposed not for three months, but for nearly three years, to the horrors of war, is an encouraging reminder of the reality and strength of the fellowship which had its origin in the birth which we are celebrating at this time. The message is as follows:

" With the approach of the Christmas season our thoughts go round the world to our friends in other lands, many of whom may be going through the same trying experience as we in China. We all share the feeling that this sin-sick and war-torn world is drifting in a direction quite contrary to the Christmas message of peace and good will. But we are confident that these experiences will serve ultimately to bind us closer together in Christian fellowship and in our common determination to find a more effective expression of the spirit of Christ in the life of nations as well as of individuals. We pray that the work in our Colleges, in which you all share, may have its part in the world effort to make this Christmas the beginning of a new realisation of the meaning of Immanuel, ' God with us.'

OPPORTUNITIES OF WAR-TIME

I had a letter a few days ago from one of our collaborators, who writes: "War brings a period when immense social changes can be brought about almost unnoticed. . . . No one can doubt that the real possibilities of the present situation are these possibilities of social reconstruction. If we take thought now we can, I believe, remove mountains, and this ought to be not simply something that is planned for the end of the war, but something that we begin on, here and now." The new agreement between Britain and France in the field of finance, which was announced last week, is an illustration of the rapidity with which, under the pressure of war, things can come about that would be almost unthinkable in times of peace.

You will remember, perhaps, that the same note was struck by Dr. Helen Simpson in a recent broadcast talk, in which she began with a reference to a plan of Sir Christopher Wren for building a new London after the Great Fire of 1666. That fire had ruined London, but Wren saw a chance beyond the disaster. "The narrow old streets, the verminous houses, the filthy accumulations of five hundred years had been brought to ashes. What a chance to start fresh! He set to work to design the city London might have been—ought now to be."

That chance was lost. Shall we take ours?

Yours sincerely,

[signature]

P.S.—I would like to draw your attention to a letter to Christians in belligerent countries from the Primates of the Scandinavian Churches and a representative of the Finnish Church which you will find in the religious press this week.

Christmas Gift Subscriptions. There is still time to order a gift of the CHRISTIAN NEWS-LETTER to be sent to your friends with a signed greeting. But please send us your orders by return of post if you wish your friends to start their subscription with this Christmas number.

Folders. Black rexine folders with adjustable clip and stamped with the C.N.L. monogram in gold for holding copies of the CHRISTIAN NEWS-LETTER are now available at the price of 2s. each, post free.

All communications and subscriptions should be sent to—
THE CHRISTIAN NEWS-LETTER, 20, BALCOMBE STREET, DORSET SQUARE, LONDON, N.W.1.

Published by Dr. J. H. Oldham for the Council on the Christian Faith and the Common Life and printed by St. Clements Press, Ltd., Portugal Street, London, W.C.2.

Two sample pages from the *Christian News-Letter*, December 1939.
Photo credit: Keith Clements.

inaugural WCC, which in 1948 would meet in Amsterdam under the theme appropriate to a war-devastated world, "Man's Disorder and God's Design." Oldham was assigned to "The Church and the Disorder of Society," which was in effect a continuation of the Oxford Life and Work agenda. At this level, even more than on organizational matters, Visser't Hooft valued Oldham's insights. Visser't Hooft recalls a visit to London in 1948 for a preparatory meeting:

> As I walked with J. H. Oldham from the Athenaeum to the place of meeting, he asked me whether we could not find an expression to indicate briefly and clearly what a right ordering of society would mean from a Christian point of view. Could we use "The Humane Society"? Or rather "Responsible Society"? I said that the second was just what we needed. At the meeting Oldham proposed both phrases, but I argued that "humane" could not be adequately translated and so it became "The Responsible Society." Not for a moment did we think that for the next twenty years this phrase would continue to serve as a key-concept in ecumenical thinking about social problems.[54]

Oldham's concern for an understanding of truly human society as relational and communal, in which freedom resided in accountability to the God of grace and in responsibility to others, was as strong as ever, as shown by his two essays in the preparatory volumes for Amsterdam, "Technics and Civilisation" and "A Responsible Society." Now, however, a new challenge is brought on the scene in the form of the immense growth in scientific knowledge and technical expertise. Science and technics, argues Oldham, determine the whole ethos of modern life. They create the atmosphere in which we live. They dictate the prevailing ideas and attitudes in which we live. And above all, they undergird the sense that humans are unique creatures who can break the bounds and transcend the limits of nature and take their future into their own hands. Yet society assumes, at its peril, that the only wisdom is that of science and technology, whereby people conceive of themselves only as objects rather than persons, "and the whole realm of mystery in which the self is engaged, and for this reason cannot be grasped by the investigating mind, becomes

---

[54] Visser't Hooft, *Memoirs*, 205.

J. H. Oldham and his *Christian News-Letter* team, circa 1945. *Seated left to right*: Brenda Snook, Oldham, Kenneth Matthews, Daniel Jenkins. *Standing*: Kathleen Bliss. Photo credit: Deborah Cassidi.

obliterated. Man is thereby deprived progressively of his humanity."[55] Likewise, in "A Responsible Society," Oldham looks at the political dimensions of this situation—particularly in the context of the communist-capitalist, or East-West divide—and affirms yet again that human freedom is rooted in interhuman relationships.[56]

But as well as drawing together his concerns that had developed over the years, during the war and the immediate postwar years, Oldham was voicing some new emphases. One prophetic insight in particular is notable: in the face of the devastation wrought by human exploitation of natural resources, there is a need for a new attitude to nature: "Our schemes for establishing peace on secure foundations and creating a World-State or a Federal Union will achieve nothing, if they only result in greater efficiency of the civilised peoples in exhausting the resources of the earth on which the life of mankind depends. The lack of a humble, understanding, reverent attitude to nature is a religious failing, and it is plain that this *religious* error may have the most far-reaching consequences in the *economic* sphere."[57]

Oldham attended the Amsterdam assembly as a delegate of the Church of England and served as vice chairman of the commission on "The Church and the Disorder of Society." His anxieties notwithstanding, he seems to have been well satisfied at the assembly's outcomes (and not only because he was made an honorary president of the WCC). It was more gratifying that his paper on "The Responsible Society" produced the key idea for the assembly's report on social questions. Moreover, in the final message of the assembly, the phrase that stood the test of time in ecumenical memory, "We intend to stay together," was penned by Bliss.

No End to Adventure

Oldham had passed his three-score years and ten before the end of the war in 1945. Physically aging and with his deafness only partly

---

[55] J. H. Oldham, "Technics and Civilisation," in *The Church and the Disorder of Society: An Ecumenical Study Prepared under the Auspices of the World Council of Churches,* ed. World Council of Churches (London: SCM Press, 1948), 47.

[56] J. H. Oldham, "A Responsible Society," in World Council of Churches, *Church and the Disorder,* 120–54. See chapter 2 in this volume for extracts from this paper.

[57] J. H. Oldham, "The Root of Our Troubles," in J. H. Oldham et al., eds., *The Church Looks Ahead* (London: Faber & Faber, 1941), 15.

J. H. Oldham and Kathleen Bliss meeting friends at the WCC inaugural assembly, Amsterdam 1948. Photo credit: WCC Photo Archive.

mitigated by hearing devices, he was no longer quite the person who could focus intently on issues and command other people's attention toward them either in meetings or in print. Nor could he now assume that others, least of all among the younger generation, shared his predilection for gathering the "best minds" to lead studies and formulate options for action. But he made his best endeavors to be involved, not least in some commissions and working groups of the British Council of Churches, and above all in initiating and chairing the commission on the "Era of Atomic Power" in immediate response to the dropping of the atomic bombs on Japan.[58] For a time, he continued some study groups of his own on the lines of the former Moot, but they were not quite as high powered in membership or as productive in results. He continued to write and, for a time, to give lectures. He wrote the biography of the Anglican missionary Florence Allshorn and published a series of his lectures, giving a lively

---

[58] See British Council of Churches, *The Era of Atomic Power* (London: SCM Press for British Council of Churches, 1946).

contemporary account of Christianity in *Life Is Commitment*.[59] He kept his finger on the pulse of current theology—and on what was happening in Africa through the Capricorn Africa Society. From 1952, he and Mary lived in a residential study center in Sussex, and in 1959, they moved to an elderly residents' home in St Leonards-on-Sea. Mary died there in 1965; Joe in 1969.

Bliss's verdict is that "from the end of the nineteenth century up to the formation of the WCC in 1938 and its foundation in 1948, Oldham was founder and organizer of more significant ecumenical initiatives than any other Christian of his generation, with the possible exception of John R. Mott."[60] That being so, the word to sum up his contribution might be expected to be *organization*. That, however, would entirely miss the spirit with which he acted, which was, to use one of his favorite terms, *adventure*. From his time as a young missionary in Punjab to his later work on the Christian engagement with secular society, he was always wishing to be on the frontier, where the next challenge of mission lay, and calling the churches to find their unity not in shrinking from but crossing together that frontier into the world. Oldham, indeed, habitually spoke of unity in mission as an adventure: "I know that the task to which I have been pointing is utterly beyond our human resources. But the missionary enterprise has always been a perfectly mad adventure."[61] As mentioned previously (see page 31), he had addressed the CMS in similar terms nearly twenty years earlier. Oldham's adventurous attitude outlives whatever he actually established.

---

[59] J. H. Oldham, *Florence Allshorn and the Story of St Julian's* (London: SCM Press, 1951); Oldham, *Life Is Commitment* (London: SCM Press, 1953).

[60] Kathleen Bliss, "Oldham, Joseph Houldsworth," in *Dictionary of the Ecumenical Movement*, ed. N. Lossky et al. (Geneva: WCC, 2002), 846.

[61] J. H. Oldham, *The Missionary and the National State* (London: CMS, 1949), 6.

2

SELECTED WRITINGS OF J. H. OLDHAM

J. H. Oldham was a most prolific writer, with some 36 books and booklets to his name, plus 120 published articles, together with his editorials and short articles in the *Christian News-Letter*, not to mention numerous reviews. Extracts from just five of his writings are presented in this chapter. Arranged in chronological order, they offer in each case a picture of how he was relating imaginatively and critically to the changing contexts and challenges of his world, from the midst of the First World War to the aftermath of the Second.

The World and the Gospel

Oldham's The World and the Gospel *was published in 1916 in the midst of the First World War. It surveys the whole world missionary scene as affected by the conflict and the prospects for further advance. In part, this is a reassertion of the vision of the 1910 World Missionary Conference, but it is also a critique of the assumptions of that conference regarding the commitment and capacity of Western Christianity (not least the British churches) to evangelize the world, given their doubtful record on social justice in their home countries. Positively, it looks forward to a missionary church crossing the barriers of race and culture and transforming society through the work of lay Christians in their secular responsibilities—emphases in Oldham's understanding of mission for the rest of his life.*

J. H. Oldham, *The World and the Gospel* (London: United Council for Missionary Education, 1916), 18–22

It is only a Church that has a passionate belief in its own principles and is thoroughly in earnest about their application that can hope to evangelize the world. The success or failure of foreign missions depends in the last resort not on the number of missionaries or the amount of financial expenditure but on the character of the Christianity that is preached. In the preceding pages we have been concerned with questions that lie at the heart of the whole missionary movement.

What do we mean by preaching the Gospel? The evangelization of the world is sometimes regarded as primarily a matter of preaching, and it has been assumed that if a sufficient number of preachers could be provided to cover the entire geographical area of the mission-field the world would be evangelized. But this view is too simple. It misconceives the nature and ignores the chief difficulties of the missionary task. It takes for granted that words have a meaning apart from the context of life. Missionary experience has proved how unwarranted this assumption is. Here and there a devout seeker after truth may recognize in the Gospel as soon as it is presented to him the prize which he has long sought. But for the most part long years have had to be spent in preparation of the soil. It has been necessary for the Gospel to commend itself in deeds and in the revelation of a new type of life before attention could be gained for its spoken message. The hospital and the school, the exhibition of Christian family life and a Christian home, have played an indispensable part in the presentation of the content of the Gospel.

That a statement is couched in clear and intelligible terms is not enough to ensure that it will reach and influence the mind. An impenetrable wall of prejudice may completely bar the way. Words, however plain and unambiguous, may fail to pierce beneath the surface until the hard covering crust has been broken up by some fresh living experience. A striking illustration of this is furnished by the reception given to the missionary commission of our Lord than its terms as recorded in St Mark's Gospel—"Go ye into all the world, and preach the gospel to every creature." Yet while century followed century this explicit command was almost wholly ignored. Learned and orthodox divines occupied themselves with proving that the words did not mean what they said. It was only as the opening of the seas brought the non-Christian peoples into closer relations with Christendom that the words found an entrance into the general mind of the Church.

Is the Gospel preached to the dwellers in our slums, even though in every street there is a church or mission hall where Sunday by Sunday it is faithfully proclaimed? The conditions of their lives may so completely obscure the love of God that this essential core of the Christian message has for them no conceivable meaning. So in the mission-field the preacher may deliver his message in vain if from the start his hearers regard it as something exclusively foreign, or if national pride and racial antipathy interpose a barrier of steel. In such conditions something more penetrating, convincing and irresistible than speech is necessary, if the Gospel is to reach men's hearts. It must come to them not in word but in power.

The attitude of the non-Christian peoples toward Christianity will be determined in the end by what Christianity actually is in practice and not by what missionaries declare it to be. Some of the earlier successes of Christian missions were gained in fields where the missionary was the only, or at any rate the chief, representative of western civilization. But such a state of things no longer exists. The influence of western civilization is penetrating into every corner of Asia and Africa. The peoples of these continents are feeling its pressure at every turn. Their knowledge of it is increasing from day to day; and unhappily it is easier for them to become familiar with its vices than to recognize its nobler elements. Their representatives are coming in increasing numbers to study in our universities and are able at first hand to form their own opinion of the influence of Christianity in the national life. All these impressions speak so loud that they drown what the missionaries are saying. To evangelize the world, it is not enough to send out preachers; our message must be expressed in clear ringing deeds whose sound none can fail to hear and whose meaning none can misunderstand. The Christian protest against the unchristian forces in social and national life must be clearer, sharper and more patent than it has been in the past. It may be that the Church as it was before the war could never have evangelized the world; that its witness had not the penetrating force necessary for so gigantic an undertaking; that before God could answer the prayers of His people some deep-seated evil had to be removed, however terrible the cost. It may be doubted, for example, whether a Church that was willing to tolerate a state of things that denied to a large section of our population the elementary conditions of health and happiness possessed the moral passion which would enable it to evangelize the world.[1] If a new spirit of repose, joy

---

[1] Editorial note: Here Oldham inserts an extended footnote detailing the appalling statistics of child poverty and deprivation in several English towns.

and creative power is to enter into it, men must learn again to bow in worship and adoration before the Almighty and Living God.

It would be a complete misunderstanding of what has been said, if it were supposed that the energies of the Church should be diverted from its proper religious mission to projects of social and political reform, or that its primary concern is the amelioration of the conditions of our earthly existence. The precise opposite is the truth. It is only in the measure that the Church has a sure hold of eternal things, a clear vision of a spiritual world of truth and beauty, and an unwavering trust in a God of Love and Power, with whom nothing is impossible, that it can hope to regenerate human society and lead mankind into a richer and fuller life. The greatest need of our age is a deepened sense of the living reality and transcendent majesty of God. Western civilization has become materialistic, vulgar, feverish and unsatisfying. If a new spirit of repose, joy and creative power is to enter into it, men must learn again to bow in worship and adoration before the Almighty and Living God, that through fellowship with Him their hearts may be made pure and their hands strong.

Oldham, *World and the Gospel*, 208–214

The life to which we are called in a joyous receiving and perfect obedience is the service of love. Our task is to manifest the spirit of love in all relationships; alike in our personal dealings with individuals of all sorts and kinds, and in our attitude to social and political questions. As we yield ourselves to this divine principle of life, we shall find a human being in every person we meet, and long to break down the barriers of class or education or habit which separate us from those we know to be our brethren. The inventive genius of love will discover new means of bringing the healing influence of sympathy and good-will to bear on the life of the community. Seeing that life has become complex and highly organized, why should not Christian men belonging to the same profession meet together to learn how the Christian spirit can find adequate expression in the work of that profession? Why should there not be federations of Christian employers of labour to consider how industry can be conducted so as to promote the health and happiness of all engaged in it, and unions of Christian workmen for the purpose of finding out how labour can best promote the interests of the community? More important still, why should not employers and leaders of labour meet in frank conference in order that through prayer and the guidance of their common Master they may come to understand one another's point of view and to realize their fellowship in a common service? Whatever our so-called "business" may be, the real business of all of us as Christian men and women must be to protect the weak, to free the oppressed, to lift up the fallen, to secure for every child the best opportunity of healthy growth for body, mind and soul. Knowing, moreover, that man does not live by bread alone and that what matters most to him is the health of his soul, it will be our concern above all else to let our light shine before men and to make known to others that Gospel in which we ourselves have found forgiveness, peace, joy, and power. All this we shall do in the glad and triumphant conviction that the world was made for this kind of thing; that this way, and this alone, can lead to the health, happiness and perfecting of mankind.

For the expression of this life we shall need a transformed Church. The expression of the Christian spirit of brotherhood in social life and relations will need to occupy a much larger place in religion than it has done in the past. In both public and private prayer there is room for more definite and explicit confession of social wrongs; we ought surely in the house of God publicly to acknowledge, as sins for which we have personal responsibility, that millions of our countrymen are living in circumstances which do not permit them to obtain the food and clothing necessary for a healthy life, and that wealth and property are more highly esteemed among us than the succouring of human need and the building up of human life. We need to take a much firmer grasp of the truth that no calling is secular; that Christian teachers, authors, doctors, manufacturers, tradesmen, workmen are first and foremost ministers of Jesus Christ and must be upheld in their ministry by the prayers and fellowship of the Church. In a far greater degree than has yet been attempted, the Church must learn to hallow the secular life by shedding on its struggles and difficulties the light and healing of God's love. It must call those engaged in a common task to go apart to consider together in God's presence the particular and distinctive problems of their calling; and those who are in political or industrial conflict with one another to meet together in order that in prayer and fellowship they may discover the unity which is deeper than their differences, and together learn what God would have them do. It lies with individual Christians to take means to promote and increase such fellowship, and with the governing bodies and officers of the Church to recognize and encourage such efforts as a vitally important expression of the Christian spirit. In no way can the Church more surely take its position in the national life and strengthen its hold upon the loyalty and affection of the people than by becoming in a deeper sense the sanctification and inspiration of the secular life.

But if the Church is in these ways to promote fellowship within the nation it must learn for itself more truly what fellowship means. We must expect that Christian men who differ from one another will spend less of their time in controversy and more of their time in trying to understand one another and to reach through prayer together the higher truth in which their difficulties will be reconciled. Strong conviction and loyalty to truth can co-exist with a recognition that the truth of God is very wide, and that no individual or body has apprehended more than a fragment of it. It is those with whom we most disagree that have often most to teach us. Frankly to acknowledge our differences and yet to meet together as those who are brethren in Christ and have much to give to one another will prove a pathway for all into the apprehension of a fuller and larger truth.[2]

The fellowship which we have been considering in relation to the Church and the nation cannot rest within these limits. It must reach out to embrace humanity. It is the one thing that can surmount the barriers which separate different peoples and races. The chief hope of finding a solution of the difficult racial problems of our time is that little groups of men and women belonging to different races should come together in intimate fellowship, determined to understand one another and to discover the common humanity which underlies their differences.

Seeing that fellowship in its perfection and fulness can be had only in Christ, it will be our deep concern to proclaim His name where it is not known and to plant among non-Christian peoples the seeds which will bear this rich and healing fruit. Never was it clearer than to-day that Christ is the hope of the nations. For those who realize

---

[2] Editorial note: The following paragraph, an extended quotation from an unnamed author on "The Ordeal of the Church" is omitted here.

this truth there can be no higher ambition than to be allowed like St Paul, to preach the Gospel where Christ is not already named.

"Nationality and Missions"

*The First World War had exposed the potent reality of national-
ism among the belligerent nations of Europe. It had also stimulated fresh national consciousness among non-Western peoples
of the "mission field," and in India particularly, movements for
independence from Western rule were stirring. Oldham, in the
immediate aftermath of the war (1920), here recognizes not only
the reality of national identity and loyalty but the need to see
these in the light of the supreme claim of God and the universality
of the Christian fellowship, which transcend nationalities. This
fundamental theological issue soon came to the fore not just for
missions but for all churches and the ecumenical movement as
a whole in facing the challenge of extreme nationalism in Nazi
Germany and elsewhere.*

J. H. Oldham, "Nationality and Missions," *International
Review of Missions* 9, no. 35 (July 1920): 372–383

The consciousness of nationality is at the present time one of the most powerful and active forces of which Christian missions have to take account. It is desirable therefore that those responsible for the conduct of missionary work should try to understand the nature and meaning of this force and the attitude which Christian missions should take towards it.

The first step is to define as clearly as we can what we mean by nationality. It is something distinct on the one hand from the state. The state is a political conception, while nationality has a meaning apart from political organization. It is true that the word nation as generally used conveys the idea of a people organized for political purposes. But the existence of the two words nation and nationality from the same root suggests a difference which needs to be expressed. Whether nationality and the state should always coincide may be a matter for debate. But in many instances they do not coincide. A state may include several nationalities, as the Austrian Empire did while it existed and the British Commonwealth does to-day. On the other hand, people of the same nationality may owe allegiance to different governments as did the Poles, Roumanians and other peoples before the war.

Nationality must be distinguished, on the other hand, from race. While common racial origin may play a large part in the formation of a nation, most existing nations are the product of different racial stocks. The English nation is the product of British, Saxon, Norman and many other elements. American nationality is the result of the blending of many separate races and the assimilation of new racial elements is still going on. Common physical origin is manifestly a comparatively small element in nationality.

Nationality is thus different from the state, which is political, and from race, which is physical. While these rest on the external facts of government and physical origin, nationality is largely the expression of a mental attitude. The bond of nationality is a feeling of national kinship and solidarity. Common racial origin, the possession of a common language and culture, union under the same form of government, enjoyment of the same national institutions may all contribute powerfully to the formation of this sentiment, but it is the consciousness of being bound together by common experiences, community of interest and devotion to common ideals, rather than any of the things which have helped to produce this consciousness that constitutes nationality.

Nationality in this sense of the consciousness of a common spiritual inheritance and of devotion to common ideals is one of the most valuable things in human life. It is a rich soil of corporate life in which the individual life can grow and expand. National achievements in action, art and literature, national institutions slowly built up by the labour, struggles and experience of successive generations are an inexhaustible storehouse from which the individual can draw nourishment and inspiration.

The truth of this can be seen most readily when we observe the effects of denationalization where individuals cut off from their roots in an inherited tradition ape the forms and repeat the catch-words of an alien culture without having absorbed its soul and spirit. A definite and vigorous social tradition gives a strength and stability to character which is lacking in those who are without this mainstay. Cosmopolitanism is a poor and shallow soil for the growth of character. This needs the richer and more nourishing environment of nationality to attain its full maturity.

The nation, it is true, is not the only form of corporate life in which the individual can find support and nourishment. Within it there are smaller social groups such as the public school and trades unions and all the various associations for particular purposes which sustain and mould and enrich the individual life. Some of these unite men in a fellowship that transcends natural boundaries. The future may create forms of human association which may in large part take the place which nationality at present fills in the life of mankind. But in the world as it is today the nation with its common memories, with its institutions and habits slowly formed by the labours of successive generations, with its common store-house of past achievements in action, thought and artistic creation provides by far the richest soil in which the individual life can strike its roots.

Though nationality is thus in itself one of the best and richest of human possessions, it may like other good things be perverted to wrong ends. A nation no less than an individual may surrender itself to self-seeking aims. It may organize itself in opposition to other nations. It may regard the acquisition of new territory or of economic advantages as necessary for the realization of its national aspirations. The tendency in recent times has been for the national life to become more and more highly organized, and in the modern nation economic aims depending on military force for their realization are apt to dominate national policy. It is this materialistic and mechanical aspect of the western nations that Rabindranath Tagore so vehemently denounces in his lectures on *Nationalism*.

When a people is menaced by political or economic domination by another nation or its cultural tradition is imperilled by the invasion of a foreign civilization the feeling of nationality is stimulated to a high pitch. A policy of Anglicization or Russification or Germanization provokes in the subject peoples a strong natural reaction and forces nationality into political channels, since political liberty appears to be the only means through which the national spirit can find its true expression. The feeling of nationality when it is thus roused and stimulated by attempts to suppress it is apt to manifest itself in exaggerated forms and sometimes reaches a morbid self-consciousness.

Nationality is thus both for good and for evil one of the most powerful forces in human life. In its natural and legitimate sphere it is one of the most potent instruments in the hand of the teacher and educator. When perverted it may become the cause of the most bitter antagonisms and the most terrible conflicts. Its tremendous hold over the minds of men has been shown in the recent war. Millions have been ready to sacrifice their lives in defence of their national heritage, institutions and associations. In the course of the war the first spontaneous response to claims of the larger national life developed among all belligerent peoples into a reasoned conviction of the value of the special type of character and culture which had become distinctive of the nation. Rather than allow their ideals and the institutions developed under the influence of these ideals to perish or to suffer they were prepared to spend blood and treasure without stint. Nationality in the war proved itself stronger than the power of international finance; stronger than the solidarity of class, for labour on both sides in the main supported the national cause; stronger even than the bonds of religion, for Roman Catholics, Protestants and Mohammedans fought on opposite sides.

A force so powerful is one which Christian missions cannot ignore. Among the peoples of Asia and Africa the sense of nationality has been stimulated by the experience and fear of political domination and economic exploitation by western nations. In the reaction against these political and economic dangers which threaten them these peoples have become more conscious that they possess a racial, social, intellectual and spiritual tradition different from that of western peoples and they desire to defend this against the disintegrating influence of foreign ideas and customs. The danger in such a situation is lest in their revolt against western domination and reaction against western ideas they may reject the faith which comes to them through the medium of western civilization. If the weight of national feeling is thrown into the scales against Christian missions their task will be made immeasurably harder and they may find themselves confronted with almost invincible opposition.

The first necessity is that Christian missions should learn to distinguish clearly between the eternal truth and life which they seek to communicate and the particular forms which these have assumed at different periods and among different peoples. We are too apt to assume that the form in which we ourselves experienced the blessings of Christianity represents the complete revelation of God to man. The Gospel as we have received it is inextricably bound up by innumerable strands with the whole intellectual and moral heritage of Europe and with the spiritual experience of western peoples. Among peoples with different mental and emotional characteristics, with a different history and different social institutions, the Gospel in proportion as it is really apprehended by them must inevitably express itself in forms of thought and worship different from ours. It is not our part as foreigners to attempt to orientalise Christianity. We can only be what we are and preach the Gospel as we ourselves apprehend it. It would be as easy for us to change the colour of our skin as to divest ourselves of the modes of apprehending truth which are in us the product of an immemorial past. But while it is not our task to try to express Christianity in eastern dress we must be clearly aware that the transformation of its outward form must inevitably take place and that our task is fully accomplished only when the people to whom we bring our message have so completely made it their own that the transformation does actually come to pass.

Though the missionary cannot as a foreigner assist directly in the process by which the Christian message interweaves itself with the social and cultural heritage and so becomes a genuinely indigenous and national possession, he may make it his aim to understand the national inheritance of the people among whom he works and to help them to appreciate justly the elements of moral and spiritual worth in that tradition. He will desire to do this, first, because he realizes that only as Christianity becomes truly national and united by vital links with the inherited modes of thought and feeling of the people is there any hope of its finding widespread acceptance; and, secondly, because as an educator he is aware that, as has already been pointed out, individual character can attain to maturity and strength only when deeply rooted in a corporate life. The task is indeed a supremely difficult one. For many of the accepted ideas and standards and of the prevailing social customs have their roots in a non-Christian view of life, and there is a danger that Christianity in an environment of this nature may lose all or many of its distinctive features. It is noteworthy that converts are often more vehement than the missionary in their denunciation of the non-Christian systems from which they have separated themselves. In the light of the full day into which they have entered the twilight of their past appears to them the darkness of night. It is perhaps inevitable that the breach, if it is to take place at all, should be more or less complete. The somewhat iconoclastic methods of the earlier days of missionary effort may have been the only thing possible. But we can see now in many parts of the mission field that they brought loss as well as gain. On the one hand we are confronted with the undesirable fruits of denominationalisation; we recognise the fatal weakness of character in Christians who have been cut off from their roots in a corporate life and social tradition. On the other hand we find a growing desire on the part of the Christian community to claim its share and part in the national cultural inheritance. A recent issue of this Review contained an article by Mr K. T. Paul on "How Missions Denationalize Indians." Some of the statements in the article have been challenged, but its main contention that Indian Christianity should find expression in ways consonant with the national genius and tradition is indisputable. Christian missions must more and more study the customs, folk lore, literature and art of non-Christian peoples with a view to making them vehicles of an education which will be at once Christian and national.

Secondly, Christian missions must take a definite attitude towards the political and economic aspects of western nationalism. The opposition of the peoples of Asia to the political and commercial domination of the West is one of the greatest and most far-reaching issues of the modern world. The occupation of the continent of Africa by European powers is an historical fact of immense significance which has occurred during the lifetime of the present generation. In these contacts of the West with Asia and Africa there are ideal elements with which Christian missions can heartily co-operate. But there are also at work vast forces of selfishness, oppression and injustice which can only provoke among the peoples of Asia and Africa feelings of bitter antagonism. From these elements in the impact of western civilization it is essential that Christian missions should definitely dissociate themselves. It is not sufficient that they should ignore them as lying outside the religious sphere. The facts are there, and if the hearts of Asiatic and African peoples are embittered against western nations on account of their selfishness and injustice they will be steeled against the teaching of missionaries who are the representatives of these nations. The only means by which this danger can be averted is that it should become known and patent to all that those who bear the name of Christ are actively opposed to policies and practices of selfishness and injustice.

The distinction between the more ideal and the baser elements in western civilization can easily be recognized. Rabindranath Tagore, in the volume in which he so severely denounces the political nationalism of the western nations, acknowledges that this self-seeking nationalism does not represent the whole truth about the West. "In the heart of Europe," he says, "runs the purest stream of human love, of love of justice, of spirit of self-sacrifice for higher ideals. The Christian culture of centuries has sunk deep in her life's love. In Europe we have seen noble minds who have ever stood for the rights of man irrespective of colour and creed; who have braved calumny and insult from their own people in fighting for humanity's cause and raising their voices against the mad orgies of militarism, against the rage for brutal retaliation or rapacity that sometimes takes possession of a whole people; who are always ready to make reparation for wrongs done in the past by their own nation and vainly try to stem the tide of cowardly injustice that flows unchecked because the resistance is weak and innocuous on the part of the injured. These are the knight errants of modern Europe who have not lost their faith in the disinterested love of freedom, in the ideals which own no geographical boundaries or national self-seeking. These are there to prove that the fountain head of the water of everlasting life has not run dry in Europe, and from thence she will have her rebirth time after time."[3] If Christianity is to win the peoples of Asia and Africa it must be made clear to them that in the moral struggle to which this refers the weight of Christian influence is on the side of right and that Christians are the fearless champions of justice, fair-dealing and human brotherhood.

The task is far from easy. The line which separates faithful witness to Christian principle from advocacy of a particular political programme is often difficult to find. To reach a sound judgment in complex and intricate questions of political and economic relations demands wide knowledge and trained intelligence. It would be easy for missionary bodies to commit themselves to courses of action which would merit Burke's censure on those who turn aside from their proper business of religion to interfere in politics—"Wholly unacquainted with the world in which they are so fond of meddling, and inexperienced in all its affairs, on which they pronounce with so much confidence, they have nothing of politics but the passions they

---

[3] *Nationalism*, 66.

excite." But the recognition of these difficulties does not mean that the task should be avoided but that it must be approached with the necessary caution, knowledge and wisdom. If missionary bodies fail to enter their protest where it is needed against the unchristian elements in western nationalism their Christian witness is to that extent impaired. We cannot preach convincingly in word what we deny in national act and policy. In the ultimate mutual relations of different peoples in our complex modern world the range of missionary duty has expanded until it includes not only the winning of individual souls but the endeavour to Christianize the national policies of the professedly Christian nations, and the former part of the task will be handicapped if the latter is ignored. The appointment by the Federal Council of the Churches of Christ in America of a Commission on Oriental Relations and the work undertaken by that Commission are steps in the right direction.

Our consideration of the subject has shown two great and important tasks to which Christian missions must address themselves in face of the awakened national consciousness which is so strong a force in the life of the peoples whom they seek to influence. The first is the necessity of understanding, appreciating and turning to the best educational use the national heritage of each race and people. The second is the duty of bearing Christian witness in respect of the materialistic and selfish expressions of western nationalism. But bound up with these tasks is the need for clear and careful thinking about the place of nationality in the Christian scheme of things. We need a Christian doctrine of nationality to enable us both to determine our own attitudes and to give the necessary guidance to those who are under the influence of strong currents of national feeling. It is possible here to offer the merest suggestion of lines of thought which need to be much more fully worked out.

For the Christian, nationality is not the ultimate loyalty. His highest allegiance is to the Christian fellowship. He cannot be indifferent to the claims of nationality, for the genius and tradition and spirit of the nation have made him what he is. He cannot divest himself of the duties of citizenship. The nation is a fact in the life of the world and we cannot set the fact aside as if it did not exist. There are many points at which the claims of national loyalty and of loyalty to humanity as a whole are difficult to reconcile and create perplexity for the Christian conscience. But there can be no doubt that our great need today in a world fevered and torn by national antagonisms is to be recalled to the simple and universal things, and to realise how much more fundamental are the things that unite men than those that divide them. We need a new vision of eternal things in order that the things of time may be seen in their true proportions and fall into their proper place. We need a new conviction that the real and ultimate conflict is not between peoples but between right and wrong, truth and falsehood, love and hate. The true fellowship is between those who pray and labour for the coming of God's kingdom. One of the most urgent tasks before us is to revive and recreate the Church of Christ as a living fellowship uniting in the bonds of Christian love men of all nations. Nothing would do more to heal the wounds of the world than the clear and unequivocal witness of the Church to this great truth of its own being.

Within this witness and ultimate loyalty there is free room for the expression of national loyalties. These are to be encouraged and not repressed. For love of one's country is the most powerful motive which can bring about its regeneration.[4]

The reconciliation of the narrower and the wider loyalty is found in the truth that nationality can attain its highest and fullest expression only in the service of an ideal greater than itself. The desire of a people to express in its thought, art and the forms of its social and political life its own genius and real self is entirely right. In so far as this desire is a protest against the slavish imitation of a foreign culture it is fully justified. But there is a danger that in reacting against foreign influences a people may concentrate attention exclusively on its own past. To dwell solely on the past is to stereotype the defects and limitations as well as the achievements of bygone times. National genius is not expressed by imitation of any kind but by aiming at the absolute ideal. Self-consciousness, both in the nation and in the individual is a hindrance and not a help to self-expression. A man most truly expresses himself by the gestures of which he is unconscious and by his instinctive actions. He is most intensely himself when he has forgotten himself in enthusiasm for a cause. When a nation has produced great original work it has not been by trying to be characteristically national but by seeking to find the absolute

---

[4] Editorial note: An extended quotation from G. K. Chesterton's *The Problem of Christianity* is omitted here.

truth. The striving after the absolute does not exclude the adoption of things from outside when they are seen to be good or true or beautiful. But they will be adopted because they are really judged to be good or true or beautiful and not merely because they have worldly prestige. It is by keeping steadily in view the ideal and in obedience to the universal claims of truth and love that nationality will reach its highest expression. Thus Christianity as the highest revelation of truth given to man and the noblest interpretation of the meaning of human life is not a menace to nationality and the integrity of the national life but the gateway to its fuller and richer expression.

The solution of the problem of nationality is to be sought in the great Christian law that "he that findeth his life shall lose it; and he that loseth his life for My sake shall find it." Like the individual, the nation can find its highest and noblest expression and self-realization in devotion to an ideal and the unselfish service of mankind. In the measure that we submit ourselves to this law, national loyalty, and loyalty to the universal kingdom of God become one.

Christianity and the Race Problem

Christianity and the Race Problem (1924), Oldham's most substantial single work, was a pioneering study of race from a Christian perspective. It quickly became recognized as a classic instance of how theology and the scientific study of humanity—historical, biological, sociological, and psychological—could combine to illuminate what was at that time just beginning to be recognized by the churches as the most far-reaching ethical challenge of the twentieth century. The extracts given here focus mainly on race according to the basic Christian belief in the love of God for persons equally—regardless of race, class, or nationality—and the critical questions posed to the Christian churches. The first extract contains Oldham's famous description of Christianity as "not primarily a philosophy but a crusade"; the second one his warning that in comparison with Roman Catholicism and Islam, Protestantism in its actual practice of community does not fare too well.

J. H. Oldham, *Christianity and the Race Problem* (London: SCM Press, 1924), 17–27

THE CHRISTIAN VIEW AND ITS RELATION TO FACTS

Before we attempt to lay down the principles by which as guiding stars the judgments and conduct of Christians must be determined, we must remind ourselves that Christianity is not first and foremost a code of morality but a religion. While in ethics and politics we are concerned with what we ought to do and how we are to organize human society, religion affirms the existence of a reality, independent of and greater than man. It "has ever to do," it has been well said, "not with human thoughts, but with Realities other and higher than man; not with the production of what ought to be, but with fear, propitiation, love, adoration of what already is."[5] Its concern is with the unseen, the infinite, the eternal—with God. To Jesus God was everything and the world but dust in the balance.

Christianity, further, is not primarily a command but a Gospel. It reveals what God is like. It tells us that He is love. It bids us recognize His character in One who came not to be ministered unto but to minister and to give His life a ransom for many.[6]

Whether the Christian view is true or not cannot be argued here, nor can it, I think, be established by argument. Each man must live by what he has himself seen. There are plenty of facts which seem to contradict the Christian assertion. Yet notwithstanding these facts, multitudes of men and women through the centuries coming face to face with Jesus Christ as He is presented in the New Testament or manifested in the Christian Society have recognized God, and the experience of life has confirmed and justified the trust they have placed in Him.

From the Christian view of God certain consequences in regard to the relation of man with man inevitably follow. For our present purpose it will be sufficient to refer to three.

First, the Christian's business is to seek first the Kingdom of God and His righteousness. He is dedicated to the service of a God who is overflowingly alive and who has a definite moral purpose for

---

[5] Baron Friedrich von Hügel, *Essays and Addresses on the Philosophy of Religion*, 23.

[6] Editorial note: The remainder of this paragraph has been omitted.

the world. In the light of that commanding, universal purpose of righteousness and love, natural differences which exist among men become insignificant. Moral values are supreme. "Whosoever shall do the will of God," Jesus said, "the same is My brother and sister and mother," thereby making the basis of the society which He founded independent of man's physical origin and natural affinities. God has no favourites. In every nation, as the early Church quickly realized, a man who worships God and orders his life aright is accepted by Him; and what God approves, man dare not reject. [Acts 10:35, 15] The partition wall which separated Jew and Gentile was broken down. On this issue St Paul fought a lifelong battle and would accept no compromise, for in it, as he saw, the whole Christian faith was at stake.

Secondly, God's love for men gives to each human personality an inestimable worth. It is true that it is to the spiritual nature of man that Christianity assigns this transcendent value, and that in anticipation of a speedy end of the world the early Christians looked on temporal conditions, including even the institution of slavery, as matters of comparative indifference. But Jesus Christ drew no sharp distinction between men's bodies and souls. In the brief period in which His mission was accomplished, He thought it worth while to devote His energies and His time as earnestly to healing men's bodies as to saving their souls. It was the man as a whole who was the object of His love and interest. As the lilies of the field excited his admiration and the birds of the air awakened His compassion, so the particular men and women whom He met, with their individual appeal and attraction, evoked His interest and called forth His sympathy and help. This revelation of the value of the individual in God's sight evoked that enthusiasm for humanity which characterized early Christianity.

Apart from the Christian belief in a personal God and His love for men, it is not easy to attach a high value to each individual life. From the naturalist standpoint life is plentiful and cheap. Nature is prolific and seems to care little for the individual. Modern industrialism and militarism lump men in the mass as "hands" and "cannon-fodder." It is worth while on this point to quote the late Professor Ernst Troeltsch. In his monumental study of the social teachings of the Christian Churches, he asks in the concluding section whether exhaustive historical survey yields any results of enduring value and furnishes any insights that may guide us in the present and future.

The first conclusion to which he is lead is that "the Christian ethos alone, in virtue of its belief in a personal God, possesses an idea of personality and individuality which has a metaphysical basis and is a proof against every attack of naturalism or pessimism. Only the personality which, transcending the purely natural, comes into existence through the union of the will and of the whole being with God is raised above the finite and can defy it."[7]

Thirdly, since God loves men and seeks their good, Christians are dedicated to the service of their fellow-men. The love of Christ becomes a constraining motive. Life becomes a mission, a call to uncalculating service. This love, since it is divine, surmounts all barriers.

These principles of conduct by which the attitude of Christians must be governed—the supremacy of moral values, reverence for human personality and the dedication of life to the service of mankind—are, we may thankfully recognize, accepted to-day by many who do not profess and call themselves Christians. Large numbers outside the Christian Church share the conviction that in the more determined application of these conceptions to the life of the world lies the only hope of saving human society from complete collapse. But it makes an immense difference whether we look on these conceptions as expressing merely our own aspirations and desires, or whether we believe that there is something in the universe which corresponds with them and lends them support. But "is it possible," Lord Balfour [in his Gifford Lectures] pertinently asks, "for the ordinary man to maintain undimmed his altruistic ideals if he thinks Nature is against them—unless, indeed, he also believes God is on their side?"[8,9]

What Christianity gives us, then, for our help and guidance in dealing with the problems that come before us is certain fundamental beliefs regarding the meaning and purpose of life. It does not furnish any explicit direction in regard to the problems of race and nationality. For the first Christians, who lived in expectation of the immediate second coming of Christ, these problems did not exist. This expectation was itself only one expression of the overwhelming

---

[7] Ernst Troeltsch, *The Social Teaching of the Christian Churches*.

[8] A. J. Balfour, *Theism and Humanism*, 120–21.

[9] Editorial note: The next paragraph is omitted.

predominance in the New Testament of the purely religious motive, in the presence of which all earthly and temporal distinctions faded into insignificance. The New Testament contains no social programme. No programme adapted to the simpler conditions of New Testament times could have had any application to the conditions of the world today resulting from the growth of capitalism and an industrial proletariat, the formation of modern bureaucratic and militarized states, and the endless complexity and ramifications of international commerce.

But while we do not find in the New Testament any explicit direction for dealing with the ethical problems of the modern world, this does not mean that Christianity has no important contribution to make to the solution of the problems. On the contrary its contribution is one of incalculable value. It sets before our eyes in all our social living and striving—to borrow once more the language of Professor Troeltsch—"a goal which lies beyond all the relativities of our earthly existence and in comparison, with which everything else represents only approximate values." The thought of the future Kingdom of God "does not, as some short-sighted critics suppose, deprive the world and life in the world of their significance, but stretches man's powers, and through all its stages of progression strengthens the soul in the certainty of a final, future, absolute meaning and goal of human life. It lifts man above the world without denying the world. This deepest thought and meaning of all Christian asceticism is the only means of keeping alive vigour and heroism in the midst of a spiritual situation which tends so immeasurably to deepen and refine the life of feeling and to destroy irretrievably the natural motives of heroism."[10] And in addition to this the Christian view supplies here and now an outlook, a temper, a spirit which more than anything else is capable of bringing harmony into the relations of men with one another. Every problem which we shall consider would be immediately transformed if there were general agreement that the only way to settle it was to settle it on the basis of right, and if all concerned in it were animated by the spirit of reverence for man and by the desire to serve.

These convictions regarding the ultimate values of life do not stand in the way of our taking a cool, detached and impartial view of the facts involved in these relations. Indeed, no one should be so

---

[10] Troeltsch, *The Social Teaching*.

eager as the Christian, who believes the world to be God's world, to know that world as it actually is.

Account must be taken of the facts of human nature. Whatever light biological and anthropological science can shed on them is to be welcomed. If physical and mental differences exist between the various races the more we can know about them the better. If it is assumed that a particular quality or capacity is there when it is not there, or that it is absent when in reality it is present, arrangements made on this mistaken assumption will inevitably suffer shipwreck. It might help to cool the passions aroused in controversies regarding the capacities of different races, if the disputants would remember that vehement assertions on the one side or the other make not the slightest difference; the last word lies with the facts.

Just as little can we afford to shut our eyes to the facts of history. Into the making of races as they are found in the world today have gone the slow and silent influences of soil and climate, the toil, struggles and adventures, heroisms, sufferings, discoveries, insights and creative efforts of successive generations. What centuries have built cannot be treated as if it did not exist.

Viewed from the purely religious standpoint, and in the light of eternity, race and nationality are of negligible importance; but from the temporal standpoint and in relation to the course of this world they are of immense significance. In the political sphere they are factors that cannot be neglected. A cosmopolitanism or internationalism which takes no account of them must come to grief on the rock of reality. Humanity exists only in the endless diversities of its component parts, each with its separate history, traditions, customs, institutions and civilization. The individual life must everywhere strike its roots into some particular soil and derive from some particular environment the nurture that it needs.

Again, in particular controversies that may arise, ascertainment of the facts is a first step towards a solution. In many instances half, or even nine-tenths, of the trouble is due to ignorance of the facts. No amount of goodwill can set matters right if the attempted solution fails to take account of essential factors in the situation.

Mr Graham Wallas[11] has shown how in politics, as in economics, quantitative methods are being increasingly substituted for

---

[11] Graham Wallas, *Human Nature in Politics*, 138–66, 245.

abstract conceptions and untried generalizations. . . . Anyone who has followed racial controversies in recent years must have observed how much unnecessary heat has been expended and ink and paper wasted on questions which were simply questions of fact that could be determined beyond dispute by proper enquiry; for example the extent of Indian immigration into Kenya or of Japanese immigration into California. But the quantitative method has wider application than in such matters as these. When sweeping assertions are made, for example, regarding the capacities or qualities or intentions of another people, we ought to insist on knowing to what proportion of the people and in what circumstances the statements apply. As is being increasingly recognized in industrial affairs, so in international and inter-racial relations a vast amount of misunderstanding and friction would be removed by the simple expedient of establishing the facts. And if the facts are to be accepted by both parties as a basis for discussion, it is obviously necessary that they should be collected and set forth by a body in which both have confidence and, as a rule, on which both are represented.

Yet it must all the time be borne in mind that knowledge of the facts is sought for the purpose of action. The scientific attitude of mind has its limitations and dangers.

Modern habits of thought have been profoundly influenced by the historical method. It has become usual to view ideas and institutions in the light of their origin and growth. To this method we owe a much deeper understanding of the world in which we live. But, as Professor A. V. Dicey has pointed out, the historical spirit, and still more the turn of mind to which it gives rise, may prove the enemy of progress and reform. "As research becomes more important than reform," he reminds us, "the faith that legislation is the noblest of human pursuits falls naturally into the background, and suffers diminution. By this science may gain, but zeal for enhancing the happiness of mankind grows cool." It may be a fault of liberalism to emphasize too exclusively the characteristics which are common to all men, but "historical research, especially if it is carried back to, or even beyond, the earliest states of civilization, brings into prominence and exaggerates the dissimilarities between different classes and especially between different races of mankind," and thereby is in danger of quenching the confident enthusiasm for carrying out even the most beneficial reforms. And he adds in a footnote a significant illustration. "The abolition of Negro slavery was not only justified but absolutely required by the principle of utility and by the conscience of mankind; for Negro slavery was a disgrace to civilization and an obstacle to progress. But could the Abolitionists either in England or in the United States have fought with success their desperate battle against oppression had they not been strengthened by an unswerving faith in the essential similarity and equality of all human beings whether blacks or whites?"[12]

A similar danger lies in the application of psychological methods to the study of social problems. The language of psychological science has been made familiar by its use in the press and in popular literature, and its results, real or supposed, are apt to create a feeling of helplessness. An undesirable state of affairs is explained as the result of "mass psychology," and it is assumed therefore to be unalterable. There is enough laziness and cowardice in most of us to make us secretly welcome any plausible excuse for leaving things as they are.

But the scientific way of looking at things, immense as are the services which it has rendered, does not express the whole or the deepest truth about man. We are here not merely to know but to act. Modern psychology has made it plain that the cognitive elements in man's nature are subordinate to the impulsive and conative, that the whole intellectual apparatus from its first beginnings to its highest achievements exists for the purpose of action. "Certain it is," writes William James, "that the acutest theories, the greatest intellectual power, the most elaborate education, are a sheer mockery when, as too often happens, they feed mean motives and a nerveless will. And it is equally certain that a resolute moral energy, no matter how inarticulate or unequipped with learning its owner may be, extorts from us a respect we should never pay were we not satisfied that the essential root of human personality lay there."[13]

Christianity is not primarily a philosophy but a crusade. As Christ was sent by the Father, so He sends His disciples to set up in the world the Kingdom of God. His coming was a declaration of war—a war to the death against the powers of darkness. He was manifested to destroy the works of the devil. Hence when Christians find in the

---

[12] A. V. Dicey, *Law and Public Opinion in England*, 459, 461.

[13] William James, *The Will to Believe*, 141–42.

world a state of things which is not in accord with the truth which they have learned from Christ, their concern is not that it should be explained but that it should be ended. In that temper we must approach everything in the relations between races that cannot be reconciled with the Christian ideal.

In the endeavour to apply Christian principles to public affairs we find ourselves involved in the conflict between two views which are frequently described by the terms idealism and realism. To discuss these conceptions of policy in the abstract is futile. To the question whether the idealist or the realist in politics is right the only possible answer is both. We cannot afford to lose sight either of our ideals or of the facts.

There are those who in their haste and impatience to establish a better order imagine the world to be what they would like it to be. They refuse to look at unpleasant and inconvenient facts. They shut their eyes to the stubbornness of human nature in the mass. They do not recognize the powerlessness of a formula to effect a change in vast multitudes whose ways of thinking and feeling have been formed by influences operating through countless genera-tions, creatures of habit, bound by custom, steeped in prejudices, influenced in their actions far less by rational considerations than by deep-seated, inherited instincts, impulses and desires. They fail to distinguish between the goal and the long, slow and painful steps by which it must be reached, and grasp at great ends without con-sideration of the means which are indispensable for achieving them. They wish immediately to make their ideas prevail, forgetting that nothing that is imposed on men can last, but only what they freely accept, and that it is only by the gradual, divine and costly process of education that truth wins its way in the world and transforms human life into something higher and better.

On the other hand, there are those who claim to be realists and insist on taking account of the facts. But very often the facts of which they wish account to be taken are only some of the facts, and not the most important facts. Those who call themselves realists are apt to make the mistake of unduly simplifying human motive. They assume, for example, that all men are actuated by fear, and forget that forces driven underground by repression may smoul-der there to burst forth later in uncontrollable violence; or they base their calculations on the belief that men always seek their own advantage, which is a demonstrably incomplete account of human nature.

Oldham, *Christianity and the Race Problem*, 261–264

THE UNIVERSAL COMMUNITY OF THE LOYAL

The Christian who believes that God is at work in the world which He has made will joyously welcome and recognize as contributing to the building up of God's kingdom all the fresh knowledge of nature and man which the patient labours of scientists and scholars are pouring at our feet and all new insights, experiments and adventures that are taking place in education, politics, social organization and art. These various stages and ranges of human life, he will believe, "each and all, come from God, possess their own immanent laws and conditions of existence and growth, and deserve our love and service in this their nature and development. . . ."[14] In the same way the Christian will experience a kinship and fellowship with all lovers of truth and goodness in the non-Christian religions, knowing that whatever of truth and goodness is in them has come to them from God to be anywhere.

The Church that is here meant is one, further, that will not be content to be anywhere but in the main stream of the world's life. Only there can its mission be fulfilled. Christians will not be afraid to face any of the facts in God's world. However formidable the menace of modern scientific knowledge or of historical criticism faith must meet it boldly in the open. The Church can meet the need of the world today only if it loves God with all its mind as well as with all its heart, and with all its heart as well as all its mind. It is comparatively easy to do the one or the other; but the Christian witness will be borne to the world only when Christians do both. The Church must be so sure of God that it is afraid of nothing and shrinks from nothing.

Again in a Church which is conscious of its mission to the world there can be no exclusion or separation on the ground of race. This does not mean that as a matter of convenience members of different races living side by side may not worship in separate congregations. If there are differences of disposition and aptitude between races the

---

14 Von Hügel, *Essays*, 239.

genius of each will doubtless find its best expression if the religious life of each is allowed to develop on its own lines. There is nothing in this contrary to the catholicity of the Church of Christ.

But wherever the separation is not a natural segregation but is imposed, a vital and essential truth of Christianity is compromised. It is not for those who are at a distance to pass judgment on what should be done where racial problems are acute. The difficulties in such situations must be acknowledged. Where masses are concerned progress must often be slow. But the discussions in the preceding chapters have shown that the race problem is a world problem. The attitude to be adopted towards it is not merely a question for that part of the Church where the problem is most acute. It is a matter on which the whole Church of Christ is concerned. The essential nature of the witness of the Church to the world is involved. The Church must stand for something in the world's eyes, or it will be swept aside as meaningless. It is committed to the principle that in Christ Jesus there is neither Jew nor Greek, bond nor free. On the Christian view the moral issues of sin, redemption, grace, service, brotherhood are so tremendous that natural differences lose their significance. The body of Christ is one. All partake of the one bread. Take away this unity in Christ and the heart falls out of Christianity.

The Roman Catholic Church has in this matter been truer to the genius of Christianity than the Protestant bodies. Whereas in the latter in the Southern States of America segregation is complete, in New Orleans, where the Roman Catholic Church predominates, Negroes[15] and whites, I am told, may be seen kneeling side by side. Islam too may boast that it can show a brotherhood more real than that of modern Protestantism. A visitor to a Mohammedan mosque enquired what place was reserved for the Nawab during divine service. "What?" exclaimed his guide, "A place for the Nawab in the House of God? The Nawab and the beggar stand side by side." He spoke the simple truth. In the house of God distinctions of class or race count for nothing. Unless the Christian Church can exhibit a brotherhood as real as that of Islam, we cannot be surprised if he latter is more successful in winning the allegiance of pagan peoples.

---

[15] Editorial note: On Oldham's own use of such terms, see the introduction to this volume, page 5.

How this particular problem can best be solved only those who have to deal with it at first hand can decide. But the Church must from its nature be continually striving to break down the barriers which separate men, and to unite them in a fellowship of understanding and love.

Finally the line of thought we have been pursuing illuminates the missionary endeavours of the Church. The aim of missions is to bring men into the membership of the universal community of those who have been redeemed by God from bondage to the world and are dedicated to the fulfilment of His purpose. As the parts of the world are seen now to be inter-related and inter-dependent, so only a Church whose members are drawn from all peoples can truly serve the world. It must be a society which does not merely gather into itself individuals who leave their national and racial distinctions and traditions behind them but one that takes up these differences into its life in order that life may become richer, more varied and more complete. In this fellowship there can be nothing of patronage, nothing of superiority, though differences of function, of experience, of capacity may have full recognition. The fundamental equality of those who all alike depend on God for everything they have and all alike strive their utmost for the coming of His kingdom is of the essence of fellowship.

The Church and Its Function in Society

The leading role Oldham took in the 1937 Life and Work conference at Oxford on "Church, Community, and State" included the preparatory volume 1, The Church and Its Function in Society, *written jointly with Willem A. Visser't Hooft. Part 3 of the volume, from which the following three extracts are reproduced, was Oldham's work.*

The first extract, "The Necessity of the Expression of Christian Faith in the Corporate Life," expresses Oldham's long-held emphasis on the crucial role of laymen and laywomen in their individual secular responsibilities in society—the "corporate" or "common" life, as he calls it. The emphasis on the laity was to become one of the most important features of ecumenical life and thought from now on. At the same time, Oldham makes clear the importance of the church, the divine society, as itself

a corporate body, and affirms that Christian people act in the
world as members of that body and are sustained by it.

The second extract, "The Church as an Organized Society and
as a Community Living in the World," expounds on the calling
of the church to point people to the true aim and end of human
existence, which is community. It includes Oldham's seminal
notion of "middle axioms" as means whereby ethical direction can
be given to life in society, avoiding either moral generalizations
unrelated to specific tasks and contexts or too-detailed attempts to
prescribe actions for every situation.

The third extract, "The Spring of Christian Action," suggests
that in the growth, often spontaneous, of groups and "cells"
of Christians to engage in the multifarious tasks of Christian
responsibility in the world lies the future of Christian life and
witness. At the same time, as a most fruitful form of unity, the
ecumenical movement should enable churches and Christians,
as members of the one universal church of which Christ is Lord,
to help each other in developing common thinking and lines of
action in the world.

**J. H. Oldham, "The Necessity of the Expression of Christian
Faith in the Corporate Life," in *The Church and Its Function
in Society*, by Willem A. Visser't Hooft and J. H. Oldham
(London: George Allen & Unwin, 1937), 189–195**

THE NECESSITY OF THE EXPRESSION OF CHRISTIAN FAITH IN THE CORPORATE LIFE

Christian faith must express itself in the corporate life. There is no
other sphere in which it can express itself. Christians, like other
men, are members of society. They participate in the activities of the
common life. The ways of serving God in the world are infinite in
variety, but none are unrelated to the common life. To live is to act,
and action is invariably conditioned in greater or less degree by the
prevailing practice, customs, and institutions of society.

It is not surprising that in face of the complexities of the corporate life Christians should be tempted to make a separation between
the sphere of public action and the inner life of the soul. The corporate
life appears to be dominated by forces that are irreconcilable with

the Christian spirit of love. But to turn aside from the activities and struggles of common men is an evasion of Christian responsibility. The Christian is called to fulfil God's will, not in some remote and future world, but here and now in relation to the reality which encompasses, challenges, and resists us. Faith in God is real only as it confronts the particulars of history. Only by acting in accordance with God's will in the concrete situation in which He has placed us can we, in the full reality of our being, enter into fellowship with God. As Professor Brunner has written, retreat from the actual world would mean that "real action would be entirely withdrawn from the influence of the Christian ethic. It is *here*, in this borderland between technical action and ethics—in economics, in politics, in public life-that the great decisions are made. If the Christian ethic fails at this point, it fails all along the line."[16]

This insistence is all the more necessary in face of the modern attack on Christianity. It is a vital matter that the Church should open its mind to the full force of this attack. The essence of religion, it is maintained, is the creation of an ideal and imaginary world, which offers consolation for the inevitable frustrations of life. By so doing it diverts men's minds from the struggle in which the reality of human life consists—the struggle to create freedom and community in the world, not of idea, but of fact. Religion is inimical to man's true welfare since it offers him an unreal consolation for material injustices and provides him with an escape from the struggles of society. It is not a sufficient answer to these charges to say that Christianity is concerned with other and higher goods than those which men are seeking. For the sting of the attack is that the cultivation of the religious life of the individual instead of identifying him more deeply with other men in their struggle and need detaches him from the common lot. If that charge can be driven home Christianity will have been betrayed by its own professors. For it will mean that Christianity has nothing to do with the concrete experiences and open conflicts of life, and consequently is without importance for the life which men actually have to live.

---

[16] Emil Brunner, *The Divine Imperative*, 262.

85

The Church as an Organized Society and as a Community Living in the World

The starting-point of a discussion of the witness and action of the Church in the corporate life must be the far-reaching distinction ... between the Church as a society organized for worship and the preaching of the Word and the Church as a community of men and women living in the world but committed through faith in Christ to a new outlook on life and a new way of living. The witness and action of the Church as an organized society, and as such distinct and separate from other forms of human association, and the witness and action of the Church through its individual members who at the same time in an endless variety of callings participate in the activities of these other associations are two entirely distinct, though intimately related, questions. Much confusion of thought has resulted from failure clearly to distinguish them. Although both forms of witness and action are essential, and although the two are inseparably connected, as a rule, in discussing the witness and action of the Church in the corporate life, we tend to think of what can be done by the Church acting in its corporate capacity, whereas, in fact, what can be accomplished by lay men and women actively engaged in the affairs of the world is incomparably greater in its range, effectiveness and importance. The Church as an organized society stands outside the activities of the social and political life. The Christian laity participate in those activities. Transformation from within is immeasurably more effective than any influence that can be brought to bear from without.

In the present chapter we shall examine this influence from within, exercised through the lives of Christian men and women. . . . But while it is important for the purposes of discussion, and in order that matters of vital importance may not be overlooked, to distinguish these two forms of action, they belong inseparably together and have their springs in a common life. It is the one indivisible Church which expresses its life in its corporate action and in the lives of its individual members.

It may seem to some that if this is what is meant it would be simpler and clearer, in the title and text of this chapter, to speak of the witness and action of Christians rather than of the witness and action of the Church. But this change would cut at the root of the whole argument. The point on which we wish most of all to insist is that Christian action in the corporate life, though it is the action of individuals, does not mean isolated action but action by Christians as members of the Church. It is action springing out of the reality of the Christian fellowship, rooted in obedience to the Word which the Church proclaims, inspired and guided by its ministries, supported by its prayers, and examined and tested in intercourse with other Christians. It is with the Church as a divine society that we are concerned in this chapter as much as in the chapter which follows. But while there we shall be dealing the Church acting through its official representatives our present concern is with the manifestation of the life of the Church in the whole body of its members.

The Witness and Action of the Christian Laity

The distinction which we have emphasized coincides, not entirely but in part, with the distinction between the functions of the clergy or Christian ministry and the responsibilities of the lay members of the Church.

The basis of our argument is that Christian faith can be a transforming force in the corporate life only to the extent in which it takes possession of the minds of multitudes of lay men and women and provides the principles by which their conduct in private and public life are determined. There are, of course, already large numbers of lay men and women, who are loyal members of the Church, and who by the integrity and unselfishness of their lives offer a convincing witness to the faith which they profess. Such lives are the salt of society.

But when we consider how this Christian lay-activity may be greatly multiplied we are confronted by problems which call for the most serious attention. As has already been pointed out, there is a far wider gap than there ought to be between the Church as an organized society and the lay world. There are many lay men and women who are conscious of religious need, who in their secret hearts long for the help that they feel the Church might give them, but who do not find that the Church satisfies that need. It is not a real solution of this problem to say that the fault lies in such people themselves; that they are closing their hearts to the Christian message and that the Church must go on trying to convert them. It is at least possible that the fault is to be found equally in our own presentation of the gospel and in its expression in the present institutional form of the Church. We have neither seen the problem, nor is there any hope of solving it, if we assume, as we are too apt to do, that what is wanted is mainly that we should redouble our energies to persuade people to come to Church and to contribute more liberally to Church funds or to take a hand in Church work. All this is right and necessary, but it is to attack the problem only from one side. It has to be attacked from both sides, if a real solution is to be found. It may be that the Church in its present institutional form is not adapted to the real needs of the lay world.

If the gap is to be bridged, new methods must be devised for getting into touch with lay men and women other than inviting them to participate in the present services and activities of the Church. There must be a coming together of churchmen and those who are distrustful of the Church, not on the basis, expressed or implied, that those outside must repent (though the necessity of repentance on the part of all concerned is not in question) and return to the faith of their fathers, but on the basis of equal and frank discussion and a common readiness to learn. Beginnings have been made in this direction, as, for example (to take only one illustration which happens to be within my own knowledge) in weekend gatherings arranged by some Anglican bishops for laymen in their dioceses. But if the gap is as wide and serious as it appears to be, the task of restoring connections between the preaching, teaching, and institutional activities of the Church and the life of the community demands the adoption of new methods on a vastly increased scale. If it is to be undertaken successfully it will certainly require the development of new types of ministry, including probably lay ministries. The vital matter is that, in addition to present forms of ministry (the necessity for which is not in question), approaches to the lay world need to be devised, not on the assumption that the Church is all right and that those who hold aloof from it are wrong, but on the basis that the question is open whether churchmen may not be far wrong and that many things in the Church may need to changed.

That is, however, only one side, though an immensely important side, of the problem. It is essential that in attempting to deal with it we should never forget that our concern from first to last is with the rule of God and not with the laity just because they are lay. In insisting that there is need to discuss with those outside the Church on a basis of complete equality, and with a deep humility and readiness to learn what they feel to be lacking or amiss in its ministries, we do not for a moment mean that the ideas and desires of the natural man have any say in determining the nature of the Church. Christ is the one and only Head of any Church that is entitled to be called Christian. There is no suggestion that those who have never given their loyalty to Christ or been converted to the Christian understanding of life should transform the Church into a cultural association or philanthropic society or something other than the Church of Christ. That would mean not the reformation but the end of the Church. When we speak of action by the laity, we mean always and only specifically Christian action. It is the action of those who acknowledge allegiance to Christ and who are growing in an understanding of the obligations of the Christian life.

J. H. Oldham, "The Witness and Action of the Church as an Organized Society," in Visser't Hooft and Oldham, *Church and Its Function*, 207-213

The Witness of the Church regarding the Purpose of Man's Existence

The primary responsibility of the Church to society is to bear public witness to the truth about the purpose and meaning of life as revealed in Christ. In considering what this means in practice we shall do well to remind ourselves again that what the Church has to proclaim is not a law or a set of ideals but a Gospel. It is this message of divine redemption that sets men free from bondage to the world to serve God in the world as His sons. In the fulfilment of this ministry the Church is calling into existence forces which must have a transforming influence on the social order.

It has to be remembered, further, that the Gospel which the Church has to proclaim is not merely a Gospel for the individual but a Gospel of redemption for the world. The Christian faith is that the coming of Christ has brought about a fundamental change in the relation of man to God and has initiated a new epoch in human history.

It is the principles of this new order into which men may be redeemed that the Church has to proclaim. There is no reason to suppose that the Church can offer any helpful advice as to how the affairs of the world should be conducted on the assumptions of the old, unregenerate order.

It is the task of the Church to remind men of the true end and aim of their existence. It brings to them an assurance of the value and dignity of man as the object of God's love. In face of the widespread devaluation of man to-day the Church has the high mission of recalling men to a sense of the potentialities of their being. In a world where life seems cheap, in which the individual often appears to be nothing more than a cog in a machine, and in which multitudes fritter away a trivial existence in a succession of new sensations and frivolous pleasures, men need to be saved from despair and an aimless existence by the reminder that they have been created for responsible selfhood as the children of God.

Moreover, in Christian faith the Church possesses a true doctrine of community. As against every form of egoism and individualism, it believes and proclaims that those who are redeemed by God and called to His service are bound by an inescapable compulsion to the service of their fellow-men. Delivered from self-centredness, which is death, into a true existence in trust in God and love towards Him, they are impelled to express this love to God in love to men. They are bound in the love of God to an unlimited obligation to their fellows, and these bonds constitute true community. On the other hand, the Christian conception of community as the free and self-giving response of persons to persons is equally opposed to any form of collectivism in which persons are subordinated to organization and the individual is sacrificed to the achievement of impersonal ends. The individual is not merely the instrument of social purposes but as the object of God's love he is an end in himself. There are objective values and purposes which society has to pursue in order to maintain itself, and in so far as these are necessary for the general good the tasks which they impose may be freely taken up by the individual into his will as a means by which his love to his neighbour may find expression and fulfilment. But for the Christian the true meaning and satisfaction of life are found in the dedication of his whole personal being to the service of a loving God and in relations of trust and responsibility, of love and friendship, between himself and his fellow-men.

The Ethical Implications of the Gospel

The Gospel is not a code of morals or a new law. But the new mind which is formed in those who have responded to the revelation of a new reality in Christ must express itself in new forms of behaviour. It belongs to the prophetic and teaching office of the Church to expound the implications of the Christian understanding of life and to make clear the kind of behaviour to which belief in the Gospel prompts.

Such broad assertions as that Christians are bound to obey the law of love or to strive for social justice do not go far towards helping the individual to know what he ought to do in particular cases. On the one hand, there is no way by which he can be relieved of the responsibility of decision in concrete situations. To give him precise instructions to be literally carried out is to rob him of his moral responsibility as a person. It is not the function of the clergy to tell the laity how to act in public affairs, but to confront them with the Christian demand and to encourage them to discover its application for themselves. Hence between purely general statements of the ethical demands of the Gospel and the decisions that have to be made in concrete situations there is need for what may be described as middle axioms. It is these that give relevance and point to the Christian ethic. They are an attempt to define the directions in which, in a particular state of society, Christian faith must express itself. They are not binding for all time, but are provisional definitions of the type of behaviour required of Christians at a given period and in given circumstances. How these middle axioms are arrived at is a question which we shall examine in the next chapter.

In the meantime, it may help to make the issues clearer if we take note of certain questions raised by Professor Tawney in a paper written in preparation for the [Oxford 1937] Conference. He states the opposition between the Christian understanding of life and the standards and values of modern society in the following terms: "Its emphasis on the supreme importance of material riches; its worship of power; its idealization, not merely of particular property rights, but of property in general and as an absolute; its subordination of human beings to the exigencies, or supposed exigencies, of an economic system; its erection of divisions within the human family based, not on differences of personal quality or social function, but on differences of income and economic circumstance—these qualities are closely related to the ends which capitalist societies hold to be all-important. In such societies, as the practice of the latter clearly shows, they are commonly regarded, not as vices, but as virtues.

To the Christian they are vices more ruinous to the soul than most of the conventional forms of immorality."

The conflict between the prevailing practices of society and the Christian attitude to life becomes especially acute in regard to the principle of equality. This principle does not mean either that all men are equal in capacity or that they all ought to fulfil the same functions, or that they all have identical needs. What it does mean is that all men, merely because they are men, are of equal value, and that such differences as will still exist in a juster social order must be made "not on the externals of class, income, sex, colour, or nationality, but on the real needs of the different members of the human family. All social systems and philosophies which discriminate between men on the basis, not of individual differences, but on these externals, are anti-Christian." It is the duty of the Christian Churches to "assert that class privilege, and the gross inequalities of wealth on which it rests, are not only a hideously uncivilised business, but an odious outrage on the image of God. While recognizing that change must necessarily take time, they should state frankly that the only objective which can satisfy the Christian conscience is the removal of *all* adventitious advantages and disabilities which have their source in social institutions. They should throw their whole weight into the support of measures calculated to lead to that end."[17]

To these illustrations from Professor Tawney's paper we may add another. It relates to the meaning and use of power. In one of the most decisive and revolutionary of His recorded sayings Jesus drew the sharpest distinction between the values of His own Kingdom and those prevailing in the world. "Ye know," He said, "that the rulers of the Gentiles lord it over them, and their great ones exercise authority over them. Not so shall it be among you." He illuminated in a flash the problem of power, which is central in the relations of men with one another, and which in spite of its importance has received less attention from Christian thought than it deserves. The word power is highly ambiguous. Power in the sense of validity, adequacy, effectiveness is a quality of being, and the more persons possess it the more they can help their fellows. But power in the sense which concerns us here is power over other men. In that meaning also it may have its legitimate place in the relations of men with one another.

---

[17] Editorial note: The next paragraph is omitted.

It may be an authority derived from God, for the right exercise of which men are responsible to Him. But in the form of power over others it has in it a demonic quality tending always to its perversion. It would seem as though sinful human nature could not be trusted to use this power over other men without abusing it. Jesus asserts in the most emphatic terms that to belong to His kingdom is to renounce such power; or (we may perhaps infer), if in the discharge of their worldly responsibilities, His followers are called to exercise it, they must do so in a continual awareness of its dangers. No issue touches the life of men so closely to-day as that of power and its use. In the economic sphere, science has placed in the hands of those who control the modern state possibilities of power undreamt of by earlier generations. The full extent of what can be done by those who hold the reins of power is only beginning to be disclosed. Men to-day, as Mr Bertrand Russell has put it, are in danger of becoming drunk with power, "The love of power has thrust aside all the other impulses that make the complete human life."[18] This clear insight by one who is not a Christian into the great struggle which is taking place to-day in the souls of men should rouse Christians from their apathy and help them to realize that in it all that the Church means and believes is at stake.

J. H. Oldham, "The Spring of Christian Action," in Visser't Hooft and Oldham, *Church and Its Function*, 250–254

THE SPRING OF CHRISTIAN ACTION

Directions of Advance

If there is to be a release of the creative energies which are brought to birth when men commit themselves in acts of faith and obedience to the will of the living God, what practical forms may the fresh venture be expected to take? The course of our thought suggests two directions in which it may find expression.

The first is in the spontaneous activities of groups of many kinds which recognize and respond to the call to devote themselves to some particular task. No large response from the Church as a whole can

---

[18] *The Scientific Outlook*, 274, 156.

be related to any single centre. The hours of the day are too few and human capacities too limited to permit of the organization from one centre of the infinitely varied responses which are demanded from the Church. It is given, moreover, only to an infinitesimal number of persons possessed of rare capacities and placed in positions of large public responsibility to exert more than a negligible influence on the concerns of society as a whole. What is in some measure in the control of each of us is our immediate environment. It is there that the Christian witness has to be borne and that Christian action can be taken. If the Church is to be a living force in the world its influence will be exerted through an endless multiplicity of "cells," consisting of persons who respond to a call to devote themselves to specific tasks in a limited environment. The separate and independent activities of such groups, drawn together for a great variety of different purposes, is one way in which a rebirth of Christian faith and love and of the creative energies which flow from it would find natural expression.

The other direction in which advance may be looked for has relation to the life of the Church as a whole. We have already been reminded that while Christians differ deeply about the nature of the Church they all believe that there is, and can be, only one universal society acknowledging Jesus Christ as Lord. Yet to-day the Church is divided, not only in organization and government, but in the understanding of the Gospel and of its implications for conduct. The Church cannot hope in such a condition to meet the demands of the present situation. It is a vital question how advance may be made towards a larger unity.

Already the Churches are beginning increasingly to recognize their responsibility for one another. The concern or weakness of one is seen with growing clearness to be the concern of all. This consciousness of the universality and unity of the Church needs to be fostered by all possible means, and on the authorities of the individual Churches rests the responsibility for the systematic education of their members in an understanding of the Church as a universal society. It would seem natural also that increasing appreciation of the oecumenical character of the Church and the deepening fellowship should seek expression in common action. Action, however, is always related to concrete situations, and the situations in different countries differ widely from one another. It is the Churches themselves that possess the necessary authority to act, and it is with them therefore that the responsibility for action lies. The extent to which such action can advantageously be fostered and co-ordinated by an international organization experience alone can show.

The field in which oecumenical co-operation seems to be most urgently needed and likely to be most fruitful is that of common study and thought. But by thought we do not mean thought divorced from action, but thought arising out of and directed towards the living conflicts and tasks of our time. This is not the type of thought which may be criticized as scholastic, academic, and lifeless, since it "does not arise primarily from the concrete problems of life nor from trial and error, nor from experience on mastering nature and society, but rather much more from its own need of systematization."[19] What is required is the kind of thinking which will help the Church to see more plainly, amid the confused struggles of to-day, its proper tasks, to determine more clearly its relation to the forces that are shaping the modern world, and to know more surely the heresies which it must oppose if it would be true to its own faith. Such thinking would be related directly to action, since its aim would be to place at the disposal of those in the various Churches who have to take responsible decisions a growing body of knowledge to the shaping of which the ablest Christian minds in all countries and the insight of the various Christian traditions would have contributed.

The task is one which can with the greatest advantage and greatest economy be undertaken by the Churches in co-operation on an oecumenical basis; with the greatest advantage, because it is the mind of the universal Church with its variety of historical experience and its wealth of different traditions that must be brought to bear on the problem; and with the greatest economy, since the necessary resources will be hard to find, both in money and, still more, in personnel, inasmuch as the persons possessing the combination of qualities and the training necessary for guiding such an undertaking are at present few.

The problem which confronts those who are unable to submit themselves to the rule of a single, central, ecclesiastical authority is how, without surrender of the priceless gift of freedom, they may escape the danger of splitting the truth into fragments and may remain bound together in a common loyalty to a common faith. The only alternative

---

[19] Karl Mannheim, *Ideology and Utopia*, 10.

to truth imposed by authority is truth freely accepted because of its inherent power and persuasiveness. Is it possible for those who, in spite of their real and deep differences, are yet in agreement about what gives to human history its central meaning, and who are united in the common confession, "Christ is Lord," to make provision for thinking out together the implications of this faith and its significance for the social and political tasks of our time? May we hope that, if it were possible to enlist the help of the best Christian minds and the deepest Christian insight on which the universal Church can call, there might progressively come into being a body of Christian thought which, hammered out under the criticism of many minds, and richly fed by the various streams of Christian experience and tradition, might possess a comprehensiveness, balance, and depth that would win for it increasingly wide acceptance freely rendered, and draw together in a deepening mutual understanding those who are now separated? Progress would thus be made towards Christian unity along the surest lines, since it would be by the path of free, inward, spiritual agreement. That would seem to be the great adventure to which the Church in this time may be called.

The Church is not far from the end of the second millennium of its existence. Empires rise and fall and movements take their rise and spend their force. The Church can afford, and ought, to take long views. It has not only to think of the responsibilities of to-day and of to-morrow but to prepare for what the unknown future may bring. In the midst of what seem to be great events weak men, who yet know in whom they have believed, are called to play their part in history. If by a power which is not our own we are enabled to make the ventures to which God may be calling us, it will be in the strength of the assurance given to us in the words, "Ye have not chosen me, but I have chosen you."

"A Responsible Society"

As was indicated in chapter 1 (page 52), Oldham's phrase "responsible society" was seized upon by Visser 't Hooft and others in the preparations for the first World Council of Churches (WCC) assembly at Amsterdam in 1948 to indicate briefly and clearly what a right ordering of society would mean from a Christian point of view. This became (with a minor modification) the title of Oldham's paper prepared for the assembly and its section on "The Church and the Disorder of Society." It was the last major contribution he made to an international ecumenical gathering and summarizes much of his thinking over the previous twenty years, while the "responsible society" itself became the key term for WCC church and society discussion for the next two decades.

The extracts from the paper given here, however, highlight the way in which Oldham's central concept of community involving both interhuman relationships and freedom was now set in the context of two developments coming to the fore in his mind in the period immediately following the end of World War II: (1) the vast developments, with import for both good and harm, in human mastery over nature and humanity's new capacity to determine its own future through advances in technology and (2) the Cold War confrontation between communist East and capitalist West, which was highlighted at the assembly in the public debate between the Hungarian theologian Josef Hromádka and the American diplomat John Foster Dulles. Both technological advance and the Cold War were bringing new challenges to a theology of Christian responsibility, and Oldham's emphasis on the true nature of freedom was part of this major ecumenical discussion.

J. H. Oldham, "A Responsible Society," in *The Church and the Disorder of Society: An Ecumenical Study Prepared under the Auspices of the World Council of Churches*, ed. World Council of Churches (London: SCM Press, 1948), 122–124

If the Church is to fulfil its mission in a world in which such radical changes are taking place, its own thinking must change. There must be an enlargement of the Christian imagination, which perceives that the range of man's freedom is vaster than we had supposed. The great Christian doctrines of creation, sin and redemption have to be thought out afresh in this far wider context. But while we must strive to achieve this larger vision, we cannot as Christians be blind to the greater perils by which the new possibilities are attended. The discovery of new values may so engross men's interest that they may lose sight almost completely of others that are of equal importance, or are even more fundamental.

Through the forgetfulness of these other, deeper truths, men's efforts to obtain mastery over the world have brought them face to face with problems, the range and gravity of which have hardly yet begun to be generally understood. In the first place, in the process of gaining control over physical nature, men have called into existence a vast network of forces and intricate organisation which they are not able effectively to control. This "second nature" which has come into existence by human decision is in many respects far more alien and unfriendly to man than original nature. Of physical nature it was possible to believe that God created it to serve as a home for man, and that man's task was to co-operate with its processes. Men could believe that the process made sense, if they could discern it. But no such belief is possible about the second nature which has been brought into existence by man. No one could suppose that the evils attendant on the industrial revolution, which were the result of human selfishness, stupidity and shortsightedness, called for any reverence, submission and co-operation from those who were their victims. Because the effects of modern large-scale organisation are the product of human will, and bear the manifest traces of human blindness and injustice, they are apt to provoke resentment, bitterness and conflict.

Secondly, the attempt of man to order the world by his own unaided efforts lays on him a terrifying and well-nigh intolerable responsibility of choice. In all directions the range of man's choice is being indefinitely extended. In an unprecedented and increasing degree he holds in his hands the issues of life and death.

It is no accident that the philosophy of atheistic existentialism should be attracting wide attention to-day. It is an attempt to face honestly the predicament of modern man. Men are now beginning to discover in their own experience the implications of the assertion that God is dead. They are coming to see what it means to inhabit a universe which cannot be conceived as in any sense the expression of an intelligent Creator's will. The traditional understanding of truth has been shot through with a sense of an order to which our thought must conform. But suppose that there is no sense of speaking of such an order, no sense in speaking of a universe, what, then, is the status of our thinking?

And what is true of thought is abundantly true also of conduct. Men are only just beginning to see what follows in respect of their judgments of value, if there is no order of values posited and sustained in the universe itself. The old-fashioned hedonist wanted to displace one code of conduct, accepted on the authority of tradition, by another, believed to reflect more adequately the nature of things. To regard pleasure and the absence of pain as the highest good was to make an assertion about what is. But if there is no "nature of things" what then?

If the universe is without intrinsic meaning, the responsibility for man's future must rest wholly on the shoulders of men, since there is nowhere else for it to rest. Without support, without security of any kind and without succour from any source man has to decide at every moment what man is going to be.

This disbelief in any intrinsic meaning in the world makes its appearance at a time when both in thought and practice we have been made aware of the perversions of which human nature is capable. Dostoevsky opened up a new world of understanding in penetrating beneath the world of civilised life and revealing the secrets of the underground man. Freudian psychology has disclosed the dark depths of the unconscious. The bestialities of concentration camps and other horrors perpetrated in Europe have shown the impulses of cruelty and lust that are latent in human nature. If man decides everything by his own unfettered choice, if we live in a world in which everything is permissible, there can be no guarantee that it will not be the underground man who will in the end decide. It is this incalculable creature man with his explosive liberty who is the centre of the human scene and holds human destiny in his hands.

The concentration of interest in recent centuries on the mastery and acquisition of things has brought about an impoverishment of the human spirit. Man develops as a person through his relations with other persons and in striving towards a Perfection beyond and above himself. The subordination of these expressions of his nature to an excessive pre-occupation with things has led to a progressive decay of *human substance*. In their absorption in the task of exploiting the material resources of the earth through technics, men have lost sight of the ends of living. In the exciting pursuit of knowledge, wealth and power they have ceased to ask what these things are for. They have in consequence lost in a large measure even the capacity to understand the meaning and importance of ends, which arise only in the sphere of personal living, *i.e.*, through living in responsible relations with other men and in loyal response to the claims of God. They have acquired all knowledge, but have not love and, in so far as this is true, they have, as the apostle tells us, become nothing. This loss of his true being is the crisis of man.

Oldham, "Responsible Society," 141–154

It is the promise of salvation, even though it be an earthly and material one, that gives to totalitarian societies the attraction which to-day they undoubtedly exert. The totalitarian State, as Canon Demant has observed, "is engendering a conviction that men may work for the future." The appeal of the totalitarian movements is especially felt by those peoples who have been deprived hitherto, or feel themselves to have been deprived, of an adequate share of material advancement. If men are confronted with a choice between economic security and political freedom, they will unquestionably choose the former.

There is no reason in principle why material advance should not be achieved on a basis of political freedom, which has, in fact, been the foundation of American prosperity. But when the matter is viewed historically, it is apparent that there may be conditions in which only a strong centralised government wielding despotic power can overcome the obstacles to economic advance and provide a framework of security within which other freedoms may later develop. It is at least arguable, for example, that the present regimes in the Balkans, or some of them, are the only governments that in existing circumstances possess the necessary strength to solve the basic economic problems of the peoples over whom they rule.

There are . . . no Christian grounds for condemning the effort of men to better their earthly lot and to bring to the task the widest exercise of their powers. But the actual results of the endeavour, as they manifest themselves to-day, cannot but raise serious questions. The consequences of an attempt to find the whole meaning of man's life within the temporal are becoming increasingly evident. If man is not made in the image of God, he has to be made in the image of society, he becomes a function of society, the instrument of impersonal ends. In the end he ceases to be man. Life loses its sacredness. Where the interests of the state seem to require it, the individual may be ruthlessly sacrificed. While in important respects they are completely opposed to one another, communism, national-socialism and fascism are alike in making the impersonal might of the collective an end in itself and in sacrificing individuals without mercy to this god.

This is not, of course, the whole truth about existing totalitarian states. No government could survive that failed to satisfy in some measure the aspirations of the majority of its subjects. In every human society men's natural impulses towards community and co-operation seek some expression. It would be quite misleading to leave out of the picture of Russia is achievements in education, the promotion of health and the care of children and in giving to the ordinary man the sense that the country belongs to him and that he shares fully in a common life.

We are speaking here only of the *logic* of totalitarianism, when no higher authority is acknowledged to which the rulers of the state must have regard, and the state becomes a "mortal God." But the actual facts are terrible enough. Even when full allowance has been made for revolutionary fury, the Bolshevist determination to eliminate ruthlessly an entire class is the expression of a complete disregard of the claims of human beings as such. A recent carefully documented account of forced labour in Russia,[20] on which the Soviet economy seems to be irrevocably based, estimates the number of those employed in slave labour camps at fifteen million persons, condemned to a brutish life of unmitigated toil in intolerable conditions. The expulsion of eighteen million people from eastern Europe, depriving them at a stroke of their homes, tearing up the roots of their historical existence, and leaving their lives at the mercy of an unknown fate, is a similar manifestation of callousness to every human right.

Callous indifference to the individual is common to all forms of totalitarianism. National-Socialism, which deified not a chosen class but a superior race, deliberately put to death ten million persons and carried out experiments on the bodies of its victims with every refinement of cruelty. The infection of this inhumanity has penetrated into the western democracies. The facts which have been cited in the text show that slavery, which the nineteenth century did its utmost to eradicate from the world, has been re-introduced on a vast scale into Europe. By the retention of prisoners of war for labour purposes long after the cessation of hostilities Great Britain and France have

---

[20] Dallin and Nicolaevsky, *Forced Labour in Russia*.

shown how far they have succumbed to the contagion. It would also be difficult to point to a more signal instance of callousness to human life and suffering than the dropping of the bombs on Hiroshima and Nagasaki.

The question which concerns us here, however, is not to pass judgment on communism in the light of an ideal standard but to consider it in relation to the practical political alternatives to-day. These may be described, briefly and inadequately, as the liberal, capitalist society of free enterprise, of which the United States is the outstanding example, and the attempt which is being made by the British government, and by governments or parties in various countries in Europe, to work out a new synthesis of the claims of freedom and equality in the form of a democratic socialism. How are these alternative political systems to be viewed in the light of the fundamental Christian understanding of the meaning of life?

It cannot be too strongly emphasised or too often recalled that the marxist movement, whatever sinister forms its later developments may have assumed, was in its origins a moral revolt against the injustices of a system in which man was exploited by man. Christians must often be put to shame by the readiness of young communists to sacrifice themselves recklessly for the attainment of what they believe to be a higher justice and fuller humanity. We cannot oppose to the totalitarian systems the conception of a "free society" without a constant realisation of the ambiguity of the term "freedom." It may mean the freedom of the Christian man to obey God and to serve his fellow-men according to his conscience. It may mean, on the other hand, freedom to indulge greed and lust, freedom of the strong to exploit the weak, the freedom of property rather than of men.

The question needs to be asked to what extent "free societies" have actually succeeded in realising freedom. We may take the United States as the outstanding present example of a capitalist economy, though the same things could be said in varying degrees of other capitalist countries before the war.[21]

The conflict between the democratic and totalitarian states has its roots in the tearing apart, and the espousal by one side or the other, of two things that belong inseparably together—liberty and equal

---

[21] Editorial note: The next two paragraphs, on economic and governmental policies in the United States, are omitted.

justice. A philosopher of the younger generation in Great Britain writes: "The conflict between marxism and liberalism is a conflict between the need for economic equality and the need for political equality in the ideal state. Marxism will be the ideology of those who feel the one need acutely, liberalism of those who feel the other. The economic need is felt first. In plain terms poverty is more unpleasant to the poor than being regimented, at least when the regimentation is held to be in the interest of a higher standard of living and more equitable distribution of wealth. . . . You will never convince the bulk of the population of the importance of liberty (I am speaking here from five years' experience as a wage-earner), until you convince them, by espousing their claim for equity, that you are not using 'liberty' as a catchword for reaction."[22]

When we take a world view of the situation, moreover, the defenders of western democracy cannot pay too close heed to the fact . . . of the impression made on Asiatic and African peoples by the racial attitudes and economic and political imperialisms of the western democracies. Many of these peoples feel that their aspirations for independence and freedom meet with greater understanding and sympathy in Russia than in the West. The existence of this feeling, whether justified or not, may be of enormous importance in shaping world history. For the Church it is a matter of supreme concern, since Christians in Asia and Africa are torn between the ties which unite them with the western churches from which they have received their Christianity and the attraction of the greater social and racial equality which appears to be offered them by an atheistic communism.

It might seem appropriate at this point to consider what has been called the third force—the attempt in Great Britain to establish a form of democratic socialism. But an adequate discussion of the movements in Great Britain and other countries to find a middle way between American free enterprise and Russian totalitarianism would require far more space than is available. Moreover, the attempts to strike out a new course are still in their beginnings and the shape they will take is not yet clearly visible. The ideas and convictions which will carry them to success have still to be defined.

It is not for the Church to prescribe to its individual members the political decisions they should make, and it is obvious that in

---

[22] Ian Crombie in the *Christian News-Letter*, No. 280, March 5th, 1947.

an ecumenical assembly the political decisions that are open to its members and are demanded of them must vary greatly from country to country. All that ecumenical discussion can provide is aid towards an understanding of the general principles by which Christian action must be guided.

In an attempt to define the beliefs and attitudes which ought to govern the judgements and actions of Christians in relation to the political issues we have been considering, we must beware of lapsing into a moral idealism which supposes that the mere enunciation of moral aims can arrest or deflect the strong tides which are shaping our present social existence. The powerful biological, economic and political forces that hold men in their grip can be mastered not by ideals and aspirations but only by a higher and stronger reality.

The social order which Christians in virtue if their faith must seek to realise will include the following elements:

There can be no question, in the first place, that Christians must stand firmly for the freedom of men to obey God and to act in accordance with their conscience. This is the foundation of a responsible society. What is at stake is not merely the rights of the individual, but the moral progress of society as a whole. Only a society which respects the consciences of its members is open to the creative impulses by which it can attain to a fuller moral and spiritual life.

The question of conscience, which is crucial to spiritual growth, presents itself to-day, in a new form, since, as we have seen, humanity has entered on a new kind of existence. If the way in which men live and the things that they do are determined to a large and increasing extent by corporate decisions, the life of the individual, as expressed in his daily actions, can possess a moral quality only if moral purpose permeates the whole life of society and governs its collective decisions. It is only if men are able freely to participate in the making of those decisions that their life as a whole can have a moral character.

Secondly, to obey God men must be free to seek the truth, to speak the truth and to educate one another through a common search for the truth. Only through the freedom of its members to expose error, to criticise existing institutions and to express fresh creative ideas can society advance to fresh levels of life. In order that this may be possible, there must be free access to sources of information, freedom of expression in speech and writing and freedom to criticise authority.

Sir Norman Angell has written an arresting book[23] in which he directs attention to the widespread disregard of, and even contempt for, facts in public controversy, and the alarming extent to which men refuse to allow their actions to be guided by them.[24] "The present generation," he concludes, "is a generation more perilously threatened by the results of unreason than any which has preceded it."

Thirdly, the Christian is committed by his faith to respect for man as man. Every other individual is equally with himself the object of God's love. He can never allow the individual person to be absorbed in a hated class or disliked race. Every man has the right to an opportunity of expressing his point of view and of having it listened to in affairs that concern him. The principle was given classic expression in a conference between Oliver Cromwell and the officers of his army . . . in the remark of Colonel Rainboro: "I think the poorest he that is in England has a life to live as the richest he."

This religious respect of man for man is the basis if true toleration. Toleration, like all qualities most worth striving after, may easily degenerate into something scarcely deserving of the name. It may mean a supine indifference to intellectual, aesthetic and moral values and a refusal to distinguish between good and bad. True toleration has its ultimate root in the religious belief in man's finitude. Truth is too large and rich to be apprehended in its fulness by any single individual group, school or party. It can be found only by the collaboration of many minds and the clash of opposed opinions. Those who are animated by this conviction will be ready to acknowledge the elements of truth in their opponent's case. They will be prepared to listen to his exposition of it with a view to discovering points which they themselves have missed and to understanding the reasons for what seem to them to be errors. Where no reconciliation between conflicting views can be reached, they will still believe that out of the clash of opinions a larger synthesis will in the end emerge.

This belief in a truth beyond the grasp of any individual or party, in a universal moral law by which all alike are bound, is the indispensable basis of the free society. Those who refuse to acknowledge

---

[23] *The Steep Places.* Hamish Hamilton 1947.

[24] Editorial note: Oldham proceeds in two paragraphs to quote Harold Laski and Norman Angell to detail how the Leninist code encourages Communist parties to act and speak without scruples for truth in the struggle to gain and maintain power.

a spiritual reality of truth and justice to which all owe an obligation can have no valid objection to being totally directed by the state.

What has been called the free society might also (and for some purposes more advantageously because of the ambiguity in the meaning of freedom) be called the non-violent society—that is, a society which has recourse to violence only in the last resort. A fundamental difference between the believers in democracy and communists is that the former believe, as a result of experience, in a way that communists do not, that violence defeats its own object and perverts a good cause. No one who has a sense of realities will deny the necessity of putting restraints on those who seek to overthrow a regime that has the support of a majority of the people. But democrats believe that no unnecessary violence should be employed: that in broad historical issues what you think you are going to attain is never what you do in fact attain, and that you can be much more sure of the injury to social health from intolerance and ruthless violence than of the consequences that will in the end result from this or that particular action.

Fourthly, the Christian will always attach a greater importance to the direct relations between persons than to the collective relationships which threaten to dominate our life. The latter are instrumental to the former and must be judged to the extent to which they foster a genuinely personal life in which true community is achieved. Institutions have an essential place in human life and may become the vehicles of personal living. But this can come about only if there is a revolutionary reversal of values.

We owe a debt to Martin Buber[25] for his persistence in recalling our minds to the immeasurable significance of the living relations between persons, which is the common stuff of every-day existence, and which powerful forces operating in society to-day may filch from us before men are fully awake to the incomparable value of what is in danger of being lost. Neither the individual as such, he insists, nor the aggregate as such, is the fundamental fact of human existence. The fundamental reality is *man with man*. It is in the communication that man is man. To this profound truth the present age is largely blind.

It is evidence of the prevailing confusion of thought that there can be prolonged discussions on the relation of the individual to

---

[25] More particularly in his latest book *Between Man and Man*. Kegan Paul 1947.

the community without any sign of an awareness that there are not two possibilities to be considered but *three*. The first step, as Buber rightly says, "must be to smash the false alternative with which the thought of our epoch is shot through—that of individualism or collectivism." What we are speaking of here is not to be confused with the "third force" which was referred to earlier. That was a possible alternative to communist and capitalist systems in the political field. The third possibility referred to here is a different dimension of life from the political. To recognise this other dimension which is a "primal category of human reality" would make a radical difference to all political thinking and action.

Acknowledgment of this higher dimension is not a way of escape from the realities of man's historical and collective existence. History is always "political" history—the struggle of competing groups to maintain themselves. Christians can refuse to take their part in these struggles only at the price of renouncing all influence on historical life. To occupy themselves only with relations with persons, the very condition for which is dependent on the forces they ignore, would be disloyalty to Christ, who is the Lord of history. The relation between the two worlds of personal relations and of historical reality is one of the most urgent questions which needs to engage Christian thought. What we are urging here is that the extent to which men are inevitably subject to the operation of impersonal forces makes it all the more necessary that these should be balanced by the experience of real community. In a society in which men retain the power to enter into relations with other persons, the working of institutions undergoes a subtle change, because those who work them know something of the true life of the spirit. New possibilities of action present themselves to those who govern. The health of society depends on the permeation of all its activities with the leaven of a rich and full personal life.

Fifthly, belief in the responsibility of men to God and knowledge of human sinfulness will impel Christians to set restraints on irresponsible power and, as has already been urged, to work for the widest distribution of power, responsibility and initiative throughout the whole community.

Sixthly, there are theological grounds for believing that all the varied activities of man, religious, cultural, political and economic, should be given the maximum independence of one another. A tradition in which the independence of each of these is respected is the most powerful of all bulwarks against the all-embracing claims of the omni-competent state.

Seventhly, it must be the aim of a just society, exercising responsibility for all its members, to ensure that the material rewards of the common national enterprise are equitably distributed. This has already been emphasized so strongly that it is unnecessary to say more about it here.

We come finally to the question of political freedom, by which we mean here the freedom of a people to control, criticise and change its government. If that freedom is lost, there is no longer any check to prevent those in power from yielding to the temptation, to which all who bear rule are exposed, to gather more and more power into their hands, and to destroy progressively all social, cultural and religious freedom.

Political freedom is the foundation and guarantee of all other freedoms. It is not the *source* of all freedoms. The ultimate source of all freedoms is Christian freedom rooted in Christian faith. But, so far as freedom in an earthly society is involved, no freedoms are in the long run secure without political freedom.

It may be said that for long periods and over large areas men have had to live without political freedom and that for many peoples to-day it is not a practicable alternative to authoritarian rule. That is certainly true. Men have had in the past, and many have to-day, to be content with such freedom as they can get. But those who appeal to the experience of the past are in danger of leaving out of account the changes brought about by technics. If it is true that the advances in science and technics have effected a radical change in human existence, the consequences must be fully faced.

In earlier societies, when tyranny became excessive, there always remained the possibility of rebellion. The knowledge that, if things were pressed too far, the subjects might rebel had a tempering effect on despotic rule. In the days when weapons were staves and pikes, or even muskets, numbers were a fact to be reckoned with. Modern inventions have placed in the hands of the ruling group not only weapons of mass destruction but means of technical control through the Press, radio and postal system which make successful rebellion virtually impossible.

Of still greater significance is the fact modern inventions have enabled rulers not merely to control the actions, but to give direction to the minds and to play upon the emotions of their subjects. In former days despots could do what they liked with men's bodies, but men's souls remained free. The new powers in the hands of rulers, the potentialities of which are only beginning to be realised, enable them to invade the citadel of the soul. By education and propaganda, through school, Press, radio and cinema they can mould men's thinking in conformity with their own desires. They can deny them access to sources of information which might lead them to form opinions contrary to those which the wielders of power want them to hold. By these means modern dictators can go a long way towards depriving man, not only of the capacity, but even of the desire to resist. Technical advances have weighted the scale so heavily in favour of despotic rule, that it is a question whether political freedom, if it is once lost, can ever be recovered.

No one supposes that political freedom can be immediately achieved throughout the world. It has to contend with widely accepted ideologies which deny its value. In some places conditions are not yet ripe for its exercise. But in the western world there have been developed through the slow growth of the centuries institutions which, with whatever partial denials and shortcomings, are informed by the conception of political liberty. There is also an accumulated experience of the working of free institutions. It is in the interest of mankind as a whole that these freedoms which have been won by long and sustained effort should be preserved and extended as an example, and for the benefit of all.

It has been our aim to show that the conflict between liberty and totalitarianism is not identical with the international tension between the western democracies and the communist societies grouped under the leadership of Russia. The forces opposed to one another in the international sphere are not a white against black but two differing shades of grey. There are elements of freedom within communist societies which, however restricted in scope, contain possibilities of growth. No picture of Russia is complete which does not include the Christian Church with all its unknown potentialities for the future. In the western societies there are those who, both consciously and unconsciously, are the enemies of freedom. The real struggle for liberty cuts across all existing fronts.

But true and important as this is, it is essential not to fall into the opposite and, as it may prove, more deadly error of supposing that, because we have to do not with a difference between white and black but a difference between two shades of grey, there can be no vital issues involved. The difference between a violent and non-violent society, between tolerance and intolerance, is a matter of life and death for the human spirit. It is a complete abdication of responsibility to suppose that because everything human is relative there are no decisive turning-points in history. Where the highest values are at stake, to refuse to make up one's mind and take a stand, because the issues are confused and there seems to be much to be said on both sides, may be a betrayal of humanity. In spite of the relativities attaching to all political systems and political actions the defence and service of political freedom may assume the form of an imperative religious decision. What is involved may be the whole question of what man is in the sight of God and of what God means him to become.

PART II

GEORGE BELL

3

GEORGE BELL

Watchman of Humanity

George Kennedy Allen Bell, nine years junior to J. H. Oldham, was born in 1883, the firstborn child of James and Sarah Bell. James Bell at that time was vicar of Hayling Island on the south coast of England (the vicarage, incidentally, being within sight of the spire of Chichester Cathedral), and after serving several other parishes, he became a residential canon of Norwich Cathedral. George can therefore be considered a child of the English establishment in its ecclesiastical form. Further, he was educated in London at the historic Westminster School located in the precincts of the abbey, that great shrine of centuries of Englishness. From there in 1901, he went to Christ Church, Oxford University, on a classical scholarship to study (like Oldham) "Greats." Apart from his classical and philosophical studies, his main passion at Oxford was reading and writing poetry, and in 1904, he was awarded the university's prestigious Newdigate Prize for English verse for a poem, "Delphi," which waxed romantically on the classical era. His poetic gifts were to find expression throughout his life. Among his student friends at Oxford was William Temple, future archbishop of Canterbury and, like Bell, destined to play a leading role in the ecumenical movement.

Bell does not seem to have been notably religiously active as a student—certainly not in the supercharged evangelical fashion of Oldham and his peers a decade earlier. Asked by another student about his beliefs, Bell described himself as "born a Christian." He was in fact gravitating toward the priesthood and, after graduating in 1906, studied for a year at Wells Theological College. While there, he did experience a converting encounter—with Tissington Tatlow, secretary of the British Student Christian Movement (SCM). Tatlow persuaded the Wells students to run a tent at the SCM camp in Derbyshire for a week. This ignited an ecumenical enthusiasm in Bell and the other Wells ordinands—so much so that on their return, they organized a regular service of intercession for the unity of Christendom, for which Bell devised the litany. Thus he was brought into the SCM orbit within which Oldham, as missions educator, was working along with Tatlow. For Bell, however, who identified with the more Catholic, incarnational stream of Anglican theology, it was the social rather than the missionary element in the SCM that drew him most strongly. There followed ordination as a deacon and four years as curate at Leeds Parish Church. In this northern, largely industrial setting, he worked unsparingly (and, he was warned, to the detriment of his health) in pastoral visitation and leading a men's class, and he was ordained to the full priesthood in 1907. In 1910, he returned to Christ Church as a clerical student, a post that combined chaplaincy work with some academic tutorial supervision. In later life, he would inveigh against Christianity practiced as a "cloistered religion." Oxford had plenty of cloisters, but already Bell was refusing to be confined within them as he immersed himself in projects encouraging students to get involved in social work in the city and in organizations for the study of wider social and political issues. He also lectured for the Workers' Educational Association.

WAR—AND LAMBETH PALACE

The drama of the outbreak of war in August 1914 was accompanied for Bell by a decisive change at the personal level: his appointment as chaplain to the archbishop of Canterbury, Randall Davidson. For nearly ten years from December 1914, Lambeth Palace was to be Bell's home and place of work. Davidson, archbishop since 1903, was a quiet, unobtrusive Scotsman who seemed to embody reserve and caution in all matters both ecclesiastical and political. Working for him at close quarters might seem unlikely to encourage a prophetic mentality, but there was another side to Davidson. He had given the opening address at the World Missionary Conference in Edinburgh in 1910—the conference in relation to which conservative evangelicals and suspicious Anglo-Catholics alike had demanded assurances that it would deal only with matters of practical cooperation and would eschew questions of doctrine and any notions of church union. The archbishop, however, closed his address by pleading for missions to be made central in all future planning and praying. If that were the case, he declared, the outcome would rest with God alone, and "if that come true, there be some standing here tonight who shall not taste death till they see the Kingdom of God come with power."[1] Sanction had, in effect, been given to hoping for outcomes well beyond the stated limits of the conference. Davidson clearly had ecumenical aspirations, and ten years alongside the archbishop gave Bell not only a unique knowledge of how the Church of England worked (or did not work) but also a wide range of contacts with other churches in Britain and with the Anglican communion and non-Anglican churches abroad. Lambeth Palace was to provide a vital tutorial in ecumenism.

Bell took up his post in December 1914, four months after the outbreak of war. By then, several appeals had descended on the archbishop, including one that he resolutely rejected—namely, that the national church should issue prayers for victory in the war. Later, he led the House of Bishops in condemning the use of poison gas by either belligerent side and reprisals of any kind. The most significant challenge, however, had come in September—several weeks before Bell took up his Lambeth post—with the "Appeal to Evangelical Christians Abroad" signed by a large number of German Protestant leaders, theologians, and missionary representatives protesting against the international condemnation of Germany for allegedly starting the war and the "network of lies" being spun by her enemies abroad. It asserted the right of Germany with the assistance of God to defend her frontiers against "Asiatic barbarism." Davidson convened a correspondingly eminent group of British church and academic figures who drew up and signed a reply, stating in measured but firm tones their belief that Britain was bound by moral duty and treaty obligations to act as she did—"dear to us as peace is, the principles of truth and honour are yet more dear"—and earnestly praying for the time when relationships with Germany and the German churches could be restored. Although Bell was not involved in this exchange, the painful rift with the German churches (the signatories included some who had figured prominently in the Edinburgh missionary conference) and the hope of eventual reconciliation set the context for much of his work throughout and after the war. With Davidson's approval, one of Bell's first actions—indeed, one could say the first ecumenical initiative of his career—was to convene at Lambeth Palace

---

[1] Cited in Gairdner, *"Edinburgh 1910."*

a gathering of some fifty Anglican and Free Church representatives (including Quakers) to consider Christian responsibility in wartime. In 1915, he edited a small symposium of essays, *The War and the Kingdom of God*.[2] His introductory chapter, carrying the title of the volume as a whole, argued that while patriotism was a genuine virtue for Christians, the kingdom of God had prior and higher claims, and war itself was incompatible with that kingdom. But the war also came to inflict an especially personal grief on Bell with the loss of two of his brothers, Donald and Benedict, killed in France within a few days of each other in April 1918. The war became a permanently formative experience for him at every level.

As well as tragedy, however, the war years brought Bell the deepest happiness of his life with his marriage to Henrietta (Hettie) Livingstone in January 1918. Then came the armistice in November and the opportunity to begin rebuilding the fractured relationships in Europe. First in the field to explore ecumenical possibilities of reconciliation was the World Alliance for International Friendship through the Churches (hereafter World Alliance), which had been founded (with tragic irony) just as war was breaking out in 1914. Davidson had taken an active interest in one of its progenitors, the Associated Councils of the Churches of the British and German Empires for Fostering Friendly Relations between the Two Peoples, and was its British president. Now the World Alliance was to hold the first postwar international ecumenical meeting of any kind, at Oud Wassenaar in the Netherlands, at the end of September 1919. Determined to show that the British participation should be significant in his eyes, the archbishop delegated his chaplain to attend. Thereby Bell had his first international ecumenical experience.[3] At Oud Wassenaar, he met leading figures on the German Protestant side, including the ecumenist and peace advocate Friedrich Siegmund-Schultze, who was one of the founding figures of the World Alliance; the New Testament scholar Gustav A. Deissmann, who in August 1914

---

[2] George Bell, ed., *The War and the Kingdom of God* (London: Longmans, Green, 1915).

[3] On Bell's early ecumenical work as a whole, see Charlotte Methuen, "'Fulfilling Christ's Own Wish That We Should Be One': The Early Ecumenical Work of George Bell as Chaplain to the Archbishop of Canterbury and Dean of Canterbury, 1914–29," in *The Church and Humanity: The Life and Work of George Bell, 1883–1958*, ed. Andrew Chandler (Farnham, England: Ashgate, 2012), 25–45.

had been among the kaiser's war propagandists but was now seeing encounter and dialogue as the way forward; and the Swiss theologian and organizer of international relief projects Adolf Keller. There too Bell witnessed the continuing bitterness between France and Germany—only when, on Deissmann's initiative, the Germans presented a statement admitting that the treatment of Belgium had been a moral transgression did the French agree to remain at the conference. But *the* decisive presence at Oud Wassenaar was from Sweden, the archbishop of Uppsala, Nathan Söderblom. A scholar of international repute on the history of religions, a vital and engaging personality, and an extraordinarily energetic activist for peace, during the war Söderblom had issued an appeal "for peace and for Christian fellowship," but this was signed only by churches in neutral countries. Now he had come to Oud Wassenaar not only to support the World Alliance but to propose a much more ambitious project—namely, an international conference, more ecumenically inclusive than ever before, to bring Christian principles to bear on international relations and on social, industrial, and economic problems. This was to lead to the Life and Work conference in Stockholm in 1925. Bell was impressed by Söderblom, but no less was Söderblom intrigued by the still-young-looking English priest:

> [Bell] sat just opposite me. He said hardly anything except when he was asked. Then, after consideration, he gave a thoughtful answer which always proved to be reliable. The face is dominated by two large, round eyes, which shine with the life and soul behind and indicate a rich inner life. In my opinion, no man means more for the ecumenical awakening than this silent Bell. This Bell never rings unnecessarily. But when it sounds, the tone is silvery clear. It is heard. It penetrates more than many boisterous voices. He does not speak without having something to say. The strong spirituality of his personality marks everything that he does.[4]

Bell returned to Lambeth enthused but also soon busy with a number of important assignments. He served as assistant secretary to the Lambeth Conference of 1920. Held every ten years, the Lambeth Conferences bring together the bishops of the worldwide Anglican

---

[4] Cited in R. C. D. Jasper, *George Bell: Bishop of Chichester* (Oxford: Oxford University Press, 1967), 60.

communion for consultation under the presidency of the archbishop of Canterbury. This one, taking place so soon after the Great War and attended by 252 bishops, was of particular significance. Most important was its "Appeal to All Christian People" for reunion, sent to the heads of Christian communities throughout the world. Its drafting owed much to Bell, who labored long into several nights, assisted by a small but diverse group of younger bishops.[5] A fruit of the appeal in England was a series of conferences between the Church of England and the Free Churches, for which Bell acted as secretary and coeditor of the official report.

DEAN OF CANTERBURY: LIFE AND WORK

By early 1924, Bell had been at Lambeth Palace for nearly a decade, and it was obvious that he was destined for higher things. Some spoke of a bishopric, but that year, aged forty-one, he was appointed dean of Canterbury Cathedral. This was, of course, a most prestigious appointment. A cathedral dean, compared with a diocesan bishop, generally has more opportunity to set their own priorities, and for Bell, high on the list was the continuing and deepening of his ecumenical activity. The conference on Life and Work met in Stockholm in August 1925, and Bell was in the Anglican delegation. Söderblom's vision was for an event that would set forth the Christian way of life as the world's greatest need; he also hoped to "formulate programmes and devise means . . . whereby *the fatherhood of God and the brotherhood of all peoples* will become more completely fulfilled through the church of Christ."[6] The conference itself, however, did not exactly fulfill these idealistic aims but rather revealed deep differences in understanding how the kingdom of God related to actual human history. The divergence was especially wide between continental Lutherans, for whom the kingdom was not the result of human effort but would come only by divine intervention at the end of time, and "Anglo-Saxon" (notably American) liberal

---

[5] See Charlotte Methuen, "Lambeth 1920: The Appeal to All Christian People," in *From the Reformation to the Permissive Society: A Miscellany in Celebration of the 400th Anniversary of Lambeth Palace Library*, ed. Melanie Barber, Gabriel Sewell, and Stephen Taylor (Woodbridge, England: Boydell, 2010), 521–64.

[6] Cited in P. Abrecht, "Life and Work," in N. Lossky et al., *Dictionary of the Ecumenical Movement*, 691.

idealists, who saw the kingdom as a progressive betterment of life on earth. Bell sat calmly through such debates. It was not just that he had language limitations (notably, he was unversed in German) but rather, as Söderblom had noted, his approach was primarily that of a careful listener. Significantly, he was put onto a group to prepare the conference message, an almost impossible, time-consuming task given the diversity of opinions being voiced, but his final draft carried the day. Then toward the end, as uncertainties surfaced about the way ahead, Bell made a speech that proved decisive, arguing for a permanent international Christian council that could formulate the considered opinion of the churches on grave issues facing the world. As an interim measure, he proposed, there should be a continuation committee of the conference to consider the feasibility and funding for such a body. The proposal was accepted: a sixty-seven-strong international representative committee would be formed. Not surprisingly, Bell was appointed a member, and he also agreed to edit the English edition of the Stockholm report. This was a most critical juncture in the shaping of the ecumenical movement, and one in which Bell had played a key role.

Bell set about applying the spirit and intentions of Stockholm on his home ground: first, in getting the Church of England General Assembly to set up its own council on foreign relations; second, in initiating with Deissmann a series of conferences between British and German theologians. The first of these Bell hosted at Canterbury in 1927. Subsequently, they met at Eisenach (1928) and Chichester (1931). One of the relationships that still needed repairing after 1914–18 was in fact on the scholarly level. On the British side, many could not forget how so many intellectuals had passionately endorsed the German war policy and how Adolf von Harnack, the supreme exemplar of German theological erudition, had reportedly helped draft the kaiser's war speeches. In Stockholm, as previously mentioned, there had surfaced serious differences between Germans and "Anglo-Saxons" on the relation of the kingdom of God to human history. The Canterbury meeting, therefore, focused on the theme "The Idea of the Kingdom of God." Including Bell, the British group comprised the Anglicans E. G. Selwyn, A. E. J. Rawlinson, and J. K. Mozley; the Congregationalist C. H. Dodd; and Oldham, now secretary of the International Missionary Council (IMC) and enjoying high repute as the author of *Christianity and the Race Problem* and as an authority on Africa. From Germany came Gerhard Kittel, Paul Althaus, W. Stählin, and H. Frick. With some slight change in personnel on both sides, the Eisenach meeting focused on Christology. A substantial volume of essays emerged from these meetings, published in 1930 as *Mysterium Christi*, edited by Bell and Deissmann.[7] The essays certainly were scholarly, and they addressed, as was the intention of the meetings, the academic issues of the sources and interpretation of the Christian biblical and doctrinal tradition rather than their application to the issues of the day. Bell contributed a short concluding essay, "The Church and the Theologian." The exchanges were a worthy endeavor to create a theological and scholarly community across national boundaries. Charlotte Methuen comments, "The Anglo-German theological conferences demonstrate Bell's awareness of the necessity for theological discussion as well as shared action."[8]

Three further labors of love were embarked on by Bell while at Canterbury. First, he published the first of his three series of anthologized *Documents on Christian Unity*,[9] itself a major contribution to ecumenical studies. Second, he made a start on his monumental, two-volume biography of Randall Davidson, who died in 1930, which occupied him for almost a decade and was first published in 1935.[10] More than just a biography of an individual, it amounted to a comprehensive church history, including ecumenical developments, of the time. Third, he was able to fulfill—controversially, in some eyes—his passion for the arts by initiating the cathedral's Festival of Music and Drama, commissioning plays by John Masefield (*The Coming of Christ*) and T. S. Eliot (*Murder in the Cathedral*); works by Charles Williams, Dorothy Sayers, and Christopher Fry; and musical performances conducted by Gustav Holst and Adrian Boult.[11]

---

[7] George Bell and Gustav A. Deissmann, eds., *Mysterium Christi: Christological Studies by British and German Theologians* (London: Longmans, Green, 1930).

[8] Methuen, "'Fulfilling Christ's Own Wish,'" 44. See also Charlotte Methuen, "The Anglo-German Theological Conferences 1927–1931: Some Preliminary Findings," *Kirchliche Zeitgeshichte* 20 (2007): 418–49.

[9] Published by Oxford University Press in three series: 1928, 1930, and 1948.

[10] Randall Davidson, *Archbishop of Canterbury* (Oxford: Oxford University Press, 1935). Subsequent editions appeared in 1938 and 1952.

[11] See P. Webster, "George Bell, John Masefield and the Coming of Christ," in Chandler, *Church and Humanity*, 47–57.

But his days at Canterbury were coming to an end; long-expected preferment was beckoning.

To Chichester

Bell was consecrated and instituted as the bishop of Chichester in 1928. It first has to be said that despite all the ecumenical and international commitments that grew even more demanding while at Chichester, he applied himself unflinchingly to his prime pastoral and administrative tasks as a diocesan bishop. Among the ecumenical concerns, it was the follow-up to the Stockholm conference that engaged him most immediately. At the meeting of the Continuation Committee in Eisenach in September 1929—his first appearance at such a meeting as a bishop—he tabled a resolution asking churches of all communions to support the submission of all international disputes to arbitration. It was at Eisenach also that Bell's call made at Stockholm, for a permanent body to be established, was accepted. So there came into existence the Universal Christian Council for Life and Work (hereafter Council for Life and Work). Within a short time, however, the ecumenical bodies were in a critical situation, not least because of the financial crash of 1929. The Faith and Order movement, emanating from the Lausanne Conference of 1927, was particularly affected and was no longer able to sustain a full-time secretariat. For Life and Work and its close partner, the World Alliance, the situation was partly eased by generous funding from philanthropic sources in the United States, and a joint secretariat for both organizations was set up in Geneva, together with a research desk. Bell, however, perceived that funding difficulties were symptomatic of a deeper problem, that of identity and purpose. Life and Work needed to have a distinctive role and profile in the constituency of its member churches, and particularly, it had to avoid overlapping with the World Alliance. In a letter to H. L. Henriod, the Swiss Reformed theologian who was taking up the joint secretaryship of Life and Work and the World Alliance in Geneva, Bell stated the need for "a very considerable reduction indeed of Life and Work activities with a view to making the greatest possible concentration of international Christian interest."[12] Life and Work was very strong

---

[12] Jasper, *George Bell*, 97.

on declaring the ideals of brotherhood and peace, but there was a crying need for direction and focus on what could be done given the few resources available.

Söderblom died in 1931, marking the passing of the apostolic age of Life and Work. Another significant death early the following year, that of Theodore Woods, bishop of Winchester, who had served two years as chairman of the council and as president of the British section, created an immediate vacancy in the leadership. Not surprisingly, eyes were turning toward Chichester. Henry Smith Leiper, ecumenical secretary of the Federal Council of Churches in the United States, wrote to Bell, "We need very much indeed the wisdom and inspiration of your leadership. From my own study of the movement, I can say with the utmost frankness and sincerity that it seems obvious to me that the hand of God points to yourself as the one who can do the most to prolong and increase the influence of the movement, There is not the clear thinking and decisive action which is needed and which it is clear you can bring to the work."[13]

Bell was duly appointed chairman of the Life and Work council and first served in that role at its meeting in Geneva in August 1932. He was now at the helm of the largest and most inclusively representative ecumenical organization yet in being—and thus the person who could come nearest to being the individualized voice of the ecumenical movement. This was a critical moment not just in the story of Bell but in the ecumenical journey as a whole: after a time of drift, the vessel now had a captain able to supply direction and new purpose, and waiting at the dockside, in the person of Oldham, was an engineer looking for a vessel that could put to good use the theological navigational equipment he was developing for facing the challenges now emerging on the world scene. The new leadership and the new crises about to break on the world, particularly in Europe, were to shape the ecumenical movement decisively.

THE GERMAN CHURCH STRUGGLE

The executive committees of Life and Work and the World Alliance convened for their routine meetings in Berlin at the end of January 1933. By uncanny coincidence, as they were gathering, on January 30,

---

[13] Jasper, 98.

George Bell, circa 1930.

Adolf Hitler came to power as the chancellor of Germany. Bell and the other participants from abroad thus saw firsthand the overall enthusiasm that spilled onto the streets for the Nazi revolution. At first, their German hosts, including Hermann Kapler, president of the Evangelical Church Federation and a president of Life and Work, took pains to assure the visitors that there was no need for alarm at this development, which was taking place peacefully and with a good deal of church support. Bell, Henriod from Geneva, and William Adams Brown from the United States made it clear that they needed much more convincing, and so began the ecumenical engagement with the confused and confusing German scene throughout 1933 and beyond. During the following months, events like the boycott of Jewish shops and businesses; the violent manifestations of anti-Semitism; the rise of the so-called German Christian movement, with its strident demand for the "Aryanization" of the church; and the evident designs of the state to unite Protestants in a single "Reich church" conforming to the Nazi ethos, together with all the signs emerging of a police state, were more than enough to alarm church opinion outside Germany. Above all, the bullying actions of Hitler's plenipotentiary for church affairs, Ludwig Müller (a theologically illiterate former naval chaplain and ardent Nazi, in due course accorded the title "Reich bishop"), made it clear that an unprecedented crisis was breaking on German Protestantism. The scenario was perceived by Bell and the Life and Work executive as raising serious concerns for Christians everywhere. Within Germany, opposition to these developments was growing, first in the Young Reformation movement, which morphed into the Pastors' Emergency League led by the outspoken Berlin pastor Martin Niemöller. But most alarmingly of all, in early September 1933, the German Christians had unprecedented success in gaining control of the synod of one of the most important regional churches in Germany, the Old Prussian Union, and resolved to introduce the state Aryan paragraph into the church, which would ban people of Jewish descent from holding pastoral office. Other regional synods followed suit. Almost immediately afterward, on September 9–12, the executive committee of Life and Work, chaired by Bell, met in Novi Sad, Yugoslavia. The German delegation included Theodor Heckel, an official (later, a bishop) of the Reich church with responsibility for the church's foreign relations. He painted a positive, optimistic picture of the developments in Germany and in society, the state, and the church. This was too much for delegates such as Wilfred Monod of France, who challenged the Germans' silence on the synodical anti-Jewish measures. A heated debate ensued, with Heckel declaring that what was happening in Germany was no legitimate concern to those outside—a direct repudiation of ecumenical accountability. From the chair, Bell proposed a resolution recording the great anxieties of churches in Europe and North America, "in particular with regard to the severe action taken against persons of Jewish origin" and the "serious restrictions placed upon freedom of thought and expression in Germany."[14] This was passed—but with Heckel recording his dissent.

---

[14] Life and Work Executive Committee meeting minutes, Novi Sad, Serbia, September 9–12, 1933; see Eberhard Bethge, *Dietrich Bonhoeffer: A Biography* (Minneapolis: Fortress Press, 2000), 312. For an overall account of Bell at the meeting, see Jasper, *George Bell*, 100–104.

Soon after Bell's return home from Novi Sad, a new and vital presence entered his life: Dietrich Bonhoeffer arrived in London to pastor two of the expatriate German congregations there. Aged twenty-seven, Bonhoeffer had already gained high repute as a university lecturer in Berlin, and he came with warm recommendations from the likes of Deissmann and Max Diestel, his Berlin church superintendent and secretary of the German section of the World Alliance. Having shown his mettle in the debates of the German Church Struggle so far, Bonhoeffer was looking for a respite and a chance to discern his own and his church's future direction. His stay in London lasted eighteen months. A warm, almost father-son bond quickly sprang up between the fifty-year-old Bell and the twenty-seven-year-old Bonhoeffer (the Bells were childless) and also between Bell and Bonhoeffer's close friend Franz Hildebrandt, who had come to London for temporary refuge on account of his part-Jewish parentage. Bell and Bonhoeffer shared the same birthday (February 4) and the personal grief of war, Bonhoeffer having lost one brother and Bell two in France in 1918. They had similarly refined cultural tastes. Bonhoeffer reveled in the hospitality of the bishop's palace at Chichester, and Bell, like Oldham, also entertained for confidential conversations at the Athenaeum club in London. In Bell, Bonhoeffer found one of the very few people to whom he could unburden his heart without reserve. But above all, they had a common concern for the German church scene. In Bonhoeffer, Bell had an unrivaled source of reliable information about what was happening in Germany. Furthermore, with Bell Bonhoeffer now had the ear of the highest circle in the ecumenical movement, and ecumenical support would be crucial for those in Germany battling to save the soul of their church. Bonhoeffer, in his meetings and correspondence with Bell, made clear what he understood the church struggle to be about. In his view, it was not so much about who controlled the church but rather about what the church *was* and what it understood itself to be—the church of Jesus Christ or a paganized church of blood, race, and soil? In view of that, it was a struggle for the church everywhere.

1934: THE CRITICAL YEAR

The German scene grew ever more fraught during the early months of 1934. Bell had written, politely but firmly, to Reich Bishop Müller after the Novi Sad meeting and followed events closely through the winter and early spring, expressing concern at the increasing harassment of pastors in opposition to the official policy, the attempt to muzzle protests, and the heavy-handed methods (including imprisonment or expulsion from office) of August Jäger, state commissar for Prussian Protestantism. From London, Bonhoeffer was in constant touch by letter, telephone, and telegram with the church opposition in Berlin and elsewhere, and he relayed to Bell the growing desperation of the beleaguered pastors (one of whom had told him that "absolutely everything" depended on the attitude of the bishop of Chichester) who wanted a sign that the ecumenical community was awake to the situation. "The question at stake in the German Church," Bonhoeffer wrote to Bell on March 14, 1934, "is no longer an internal issue but is the question of the existence of Christianity in Europe; therefore a definite attitude of the ecumenic [sic] movement has nothing to do with 'intervention'—but is just a demonstration to the whole world that Church and Christianity as such are at stake. . . . Please do not be silent now!"[15] Bonhoeffer was also hoping for an ecumenical delegation to be sent to Berlin and even an ultimatum threatening a form of ecumenical excommunication to be delivered to the church leadership. Bell wanted to help to the utmost, but the statutes of Life and Work would not allow him, as chairman, to speak on behalf of the movement without authorization by the council. There was nothing, however, to prevent him from speaking *to* all the member churches of Life and Work and expressing his deepest concern for the German churches as a sign of solidarity with them. What therefore transpired—after further consultation with Bonhoeffer, Oldham, the Swiss Alphons Koechlin, and Hans Schönfeld of the ecumenical office in Geneva—was a pastoral letter over his name to all the members of Life and Work, issued on Ascension Day, May 10, 1934.[16] It appeared in the London *Times* two days later. It did not deliver the ultimatum Bonhoeffer had hoped for, but he was more than grateful to Bell and said about the letter, "In its consciousness it strikes at the chief points and leaves no escape for misinterpretation."[17] Bell

---

[15] Dietrich Bonhoeffer, *London, 1933–1945*, Dietrich Bonhoeffer Works 13, ed. Keith Clements, trans. Isabel Best (Minneapolis: Fortress Press, 2007), 118–19.

[16] For the full text of the message, see chapter 4 in this volume, pages 165–67.

[17] Bonhoeffer, *London*, 147–48.

could not actually say "This is what Life and Work says," but he had cogently personified the ecumenical commitment and solidarity that were required. Later in this chapter, we will look more closely at the Bonhoeffer-Bell exchanges, which reveal how Bell was willing to learn from Bonhoeffer about the actual issues at stake.

On April 22, three weeks before Bell's Ascensiontide message, a first "Confessing synod" had met in Ulm. Three weeks after the message, over May 29–31, the Evangelical Free Synod of Protestants, opposed to what was happening to their churches, met at Barmen in the Ruhr. Inspired chiefly by Karl Barth, it issued the now famous theological declaration recalling the church of the Reformation to belief in the word of God in Jesus Christ as the sole foundation of the church, in contrast to the false and heretical beliefs of the German Christians and others. The Confessing Church was born.

THE FANØ CONFERENCE

Three months after Barmen, in late August, the full Council for Life and Work, together with the Ecumenical Youth Commission of the World Alliance and Life and Work, met on the Danish island of Fanø. As noted earlier (page 1 in this volume), a main agenda item was the decision to hold the next Life and Work conference in 1937 at Oxford, its study program to be coordinated by Oldham. Thus Fanø, with Bell in the chair and Oldham now accepting such a high responsibility, saw Bell and Oldham coming into the closest and mutually supportive collaboration. Bell wrote the introduction to Oldham's preparatory booklet for the Oxford conference, and Oldham was not only taking responsibility for the Oxford program but, as already noted, deeply concerned with the German issues and was co-opted onto the group, which drafted the resolution that Bell put before the conference for decision. For many, this was the key issue at Fanø: Would the most significant ecumenical gathering since the Barmen synod side with the Confessing Church?[18] It belongs to ecumenical

---

[18] The conference (and especially the ecumenical youth section, which met concurrently at Fanø) was also addressing the question of peace, on which Dietrich Bonhoeffer made two radically challenging presentations.

history, of which full accounts are to be found elsewhere,[19] that after three days of plenary debates, closed sessions, and meetings of a working group (which included Oldham), the main conference did effectively take sides—despite vigorous protests from Heckel.

The momentous resolution passed on August 30 covered a lot of ground. It stated the concern for church-state relations as a fundamental worldwide issue of Christian faith. It expressed the "grave anxiety" of many representatives, "lest vital principles of Christian liberty should be endangered or compromised at the present time in the life of the German Evangelical Church." It stated the belief of the council in "the special task of the ecumenical movement to express and deepen the essence of mutual responsibility in all parts of the Christian Church."[20] It recognized "the peculiar difficulties of a situation of revolution" but went on to declare autocratic church rule, use of force, and the suppression of free discussion as "incompatible with the true nature of the Christian Church" and asked "in the name of the Gospel" for proper freedom of teaching and life in the German Evangelical Church.[21] It endorsed the Ascension Day action taken by the bishop of Chichester. And most decisively, the resolution declared, "The Council desires to assure its brethren in the Confessional Synod of the German Evangelical Church of its prayers and heartfelt sympathy in their witness to the principles of the Gospel, and of its resolve to maintain close fellowship with them."[22]

This represented a major triumph for the ecumenical support of the Confessing Church—as may be measured by Heckel's lengthy and vigorous protest (alleging that the council had exceeded its competence and denying many of the alleged infringements of liberties in Germany)—and had a considerable impact among the churches at large. It was not quite, however, a flawless success. At the request of

---

[19] See in Rouse and Neill, *History of the Ecumenical Movement*, 583. For more detail and interpretation, see Klaus Scholder, *The Churches and the Third Reich*, vol. 2, *The Year of Disillusionment: 1934 Barmen and Rome* (London: SCM Press, 1988), 234–43; and Keith Clements, *Dietrich Bonhoeffer's Ecumenical Quest* (Geneva: WCC, 2015), 127–48.

[20] "Resolutions on the German Church," Universal Christian Council for Life and Work, minutes of the meeting of the Council Fanø, August 24–30, 1934 (Geneva archive), 50.

[21] "Resolutions on the German Church," 51.

[22] "Resolutions on the German Church," 51–52.

Heckel, a short additional clause was inserted into the resolution, conveying the sympathy of the council "to all its fellow Christians in Germany" in their present difficulties and its wish "to remain in friendly contact with all groups in the Evangelical Church." Seen at the time as an innocent gesture of goodwill, it was in due course to generate difficulties in relations between the Confessing Church and the ecumenical movement. For the moment, for those such as Bonhoeffer, there was sheer relief and gratitude that the Confessing Church was recognized and supported in its claim to be the true expression of witness to the gospel in Germany. Soon afterward, Bonhoeffer wrote to Bell on September 7, 1934, thanking him for his great help. The resolution, Bonhoeffer said, "has become a true expression of a brotherly spirit, of justice and truthfulness."[23] Indeed, thanks greatly to Bell's firm but patient leadership, the ecumenical fellowship had not just sensed a direction in which to go but dared to take a step in that direction—beyond uncommitted dialogue to solidarity with those witnessing through suffering to the truth of the gospel. If *ecumenism* means "readiness to take sides when loyalty to the gospel requires it," that is a central element in the Bell legacy.

Fanø was the last occasion on which Bell chaired the full Council for Life and Work, and as Andrew Chandler says, "Perhaps it marked his greatest achievement in ecumenical statecraft."[24] But Bell remained an effective presence on the council and its executive, chairing the meetings of the latter at Chamby, Switzerland, in 1935 and 1936; strongly supportive of Oldham's preparations for the Oxford conference; and ever mindful of the plight of the Confessing Church. The greatest unresolved issue in the 1934–37 period was that of German representation at ecumenical meetings. The Confessing Church leadership was adamant that as the church that from Barmen onward had rejected heresy (or its toleration within the Reich church) and held steadfastly to Christian truth, it alone should be recognized by the ecumenical movement as having a right to a German place at the table. Bell and Oldham and the likeminded did their utmost to support this claim. But there was a difficulty in implementing it. First, that seemingly innocent clause added to the resolution at Fanø,

---

[23] Bonhoeffer, *London*, 213–14.

[24] Andrew Chandler, *George Bell, Bishop of Chichester: Church, State, and Resistance in the Age of Dictatorship* (Grand Rapids, MI: William B. Eerdmans, 2016), 56.

offering "friendly contact" with all Christian groups in Germany, gave Heckel a pretext to demand Reich church participation at Life and Work meetings despite the suspicions of the majority who would be present. This issue became especially fraught with the approach of the conference at Oxford in 1937. Who from Germany should be there? The Confessing Church Council of Brethren insisted they would not attend if Reich church representatives were there too. Second, while Bell and Oldham shared the same suspicions about Heckel and his machinations, as the official responsible for foreign relations in the Reich church, Heckel could claim that all German delegates to international events had to be sanctioned by his desk. An awkward reality had to be recognized. If only Confessing Church people were invited, Heckel would see that travel permits for them would be refused. This meant that if a Confessing Church presence was wanted, then Reich church people would have to be invited too. This was the invidious choice as 1937 approached. At the 1936 Chamby meeting, under Bell's guidance, a formula was proposed whereby there would be three German delegations to Oxford, nominated by, respectively, the Confessing Church, the Lutheran Council, and the Reich church. But a further complication arose over the German youth delegation to Oxford. Bonhoeffer had insisted that in accordance with previous meetings of Life and Work and the World Alliance, it should be the Ecumenical Youth Commission, and not the churches, that should issue the invitations. In this, he had Bell's full support, but late in the day—February 1937—he discovered that Henriod, the secretary in Geneva, had overruled him. Bonhoeffer felt this to be a capitulation to the Reich church. There followed an angry exchange of letters with Henriod, and Bonhoeffer resigned from the youth commission.[25] The Confessing Church in fact eventually decided not to participate in Oxford when it was revealed that one delegation under Reich church leadership would be required by the German authorities. The matter became academic when the German authorities banned *all* Germans from attending Oxford—apart from a tiny and embarrassingly pro-Nazi group from the Free Churches.

The German absence from the conference at Oxford, however, illustrated the costly witness being made in the Reich. Bell was on the conference business committee and served on the section on church

---

[25] See Clements, *Dietrich Bonhoeffer's Ecumenical Quest*, 177–78.

The Life and Work council meeting at Chamby, Switzerland, August 1936. George Bell and German delegates discuss the vexed question of German representation at the 1937 Oxford conference. *Left to right*: Präses Karl Koch, General Superintendent Zoellner, Bell, General Superintendent Otto Dibelius.
Photo credit: Gütersloher Verlagshaus.

and state. He urged—in face of demurrals from the archbishop of Canterbury, Cosmo Gordon Lang, who was nervous about the possible dangers to which this would expose their German friends—that a letter to be sent from the conference to the German churches, expressing (as did the Fanø conference in 1934) definite solidarity with the Confessing Church: "We are greatly moved by the afflictions of many pastors and laymen who have stood firm from the first in the Confessional Church for the sovereignty of Christ, and for the freedom of the Church of Christ to preach His Gospel."[26] By contrast, the Faith and Order conference in Edinburgh, which followed shortly afterward, could only issue a vaguely worded statement about all Christians suffering in Germany, with no specific mention of the Confessing Church.

Following the Oxford and Edinburgh conferences, Bell participated in the process of setting up the World Council of Churches

---

[26] Oldham, *Churches Survey Their Task*, 275.

(WCC),[27] and at the Utrecht meeting in May 1938, he was appointed to its provisional committee. That year proved tumultuous thanks to Hitler's expansionist successes with the Austrian Anschluss in March and the Munich agreement on Czechoslovakia in September. Bell, like many other church and political leaders in Britain, supported the policy of "appeasement" not out of any sympathy with Nazism but in the hope that war might still be averted (indeed, he proposed that the Austrian churches, which acceded to the Anschluss, be thanked for their selfless role in upholding the peace of Europe).

The year 1938 also marked a notable step for Bell personally, since having advanced to senior status among the Church of England bishops, he now had a seat in the upper chamber of the British parliament, the House of Lords. From now on, his voice on public affairs became very public indeed. His first speech in the chamber was on a subject that had been close to his heart and increasingly consuming his energy since 1933: the refugees from Nazi Germany. During the slide to war in 1939, he continued to share in ecumenical peace efforts. In 1939, he suggested a meeting of theologians in Rome to "discuss fundamental principles in a true international order and in social justice."[28] But Pope Pius XII could not see the utility of this when he had already, so it was argued, made the church's position on these matters totally clear. Bell strongly encouraged British support for the pope's "Five Peace Points" issued at Christmas 1939. But any ecumenical consensus was disintegrating fast. Willem A. Visser't Hooft at the WCC was concerned—the more so after the actual outbreak of war in September 1939—by the evident denial by some church leaders (Scandinavians in particular) of the specific menace from Nazi Germany as distinct from the danger of war in general. As late as January 1940 in Apeldoorn, Netherlands, the WCC's administration committee was discussing a plan for peace negotiations devised by the Norwegian bishop Eivind Berggrav, while Visser't Hooft wanted a clear protest against the violations of humanity and freedom that were already taking place. Temple suggested a statement on basic moral principles, while others felt that such generalities would be worse than silence. Virtually nothing was agreed. Later,

---

[27] See pages 45–46 in this volume.

[28] On this and other ecumenical peace initiatives during 1939–40, see Visser't Hooft, *Memoirs*, 106–12.

in May, Temple commented resignedly on the "plethora of counsels" among the churches. By now, Hitler's forces, already occupying Denmark and Norway, were storming across Holland and Belgium into France. Temple advised Visser't Hooft that the only realistic possibility now was for everyone "to prophesy individually" via the WCC office in Geneva.[29] Until this fateful month of May 1940, Bell himself maintained hopes, woefully unrealistic in the view of most of his contemporaries, for a negotiated settlement with Germany. Thereafter, he recognized and publicly affirmed the need for the military defeat of the Nazi state.

Bell felt deeply the separation from his German friends brought by the war, and on the eve of the conflict or just after, he had written personally to as many as possible. His note to Bonhoeffer on September 6, 1939, was as warm as it was brief:

My dear Dietrich,

You know how deeply I feel for you and yours in this melancholy time. May God comfort and guide you. I often think of our talk in the summer. May He keep you now. Let us pray together often by reading the Beatitudes. Pax Dei quae superate omnia nos custodias.

> Your affectionate
> George[30]

They had last met in the spring of 1939, when Bonhoeffer, accompanied by his friend Eberhard Bethge, visited London in an effort to strengthen the ecumenical contacts of the Confessing Church and to visit his twin sister, Sabine, and her non-Aryan husband, Gerhard Leibholz.[31] They with their two children had, like so many other escapees from the Reich, been aided by Bell and found refuge in London, in due course settling in Oxford for the duration of the war. During that visit, Bonhoeffer had also gone to Chichester for

---

[29] Visser't Hooft, 123.

[30] Dietrich Bonhoeffer, *Theological Education Underground: 1937–1940*, Dietrich Bonhoeffer Works 15, ed. Victoria J. Barnett, trans. Victoria J. Barnett et al. (Minneapolis: Fortress Press, 2012), 268.

[31] See Bethge, *Dietrich Bonhoeffer*, 638–48.

counsel from Bell on the agonizing dilemma of whether to leave Germany to avoid his pending military call-up or to stay and work there with all the attendant risks.

CHRISTIANITY AND WORLD ORDER

It was in 1940—that year when the starkest peril of war burst upon Britain, the year of conflicting fears, hopes, and perplexities in the world at large and no less confusion among the churches—that one of the relatively few books that Bell wrote was published: the paperback *Christianity and World Order*.[32] A mere 154 pages in contrast to the mighty two-volume biography of Davidson, and shorter even than his other ecumenically themed paperback of 1955, *The Kingship of Christ*, it offers as nowhere else a distillation of his thinking on Christian faith, the church, and the ecumenical movement in relation to the unprecedented challenges of the war. In significant ways, it parallels Oldham's *The World and the Gospel*, which appeared in the crisis year of 1916, and provides the summa of his thinking on the church in relation to the community and the state (drawing much on the 1937 Oxford conference), Christianity and war, peace aims, the universal ecumenical church, the church and the future, and the personal Christian life of responsibility.

It opens soberly but with an implicit hope: "A great search is proceeding side by side with the War. It is a search for world order, and for such a world order as shall satisfy the real needs, alike of the individual and of the community. It has been going on for years before the War which is now ravaging Europe." In dialogue with a remarkably wide range of writers, both Christian and secular, Bell offers no easy diagnosis or prescriptions but deals in fundamental questions about human society, modern secularism, and the nature of Christianity. The real conflict, Bell asserts, is not national or geographical, for both godlessness and Christianity are found in all countries now at war. His vision is profoundly Christian in its basis and hopes. It is generously humane while arguing that secularism by itself offers no real basis for humanity: "No amount of secular Declarations, no number of claims for human rights, without spiritual sanctions, will save us from destruction. What is wanted now more than anything else in

---

[32] George Bell, *Christianity and World Order* (London: Penguin, 1940).

the world, is an awakening of faith and unflinching belief in God, and an unlimited love of my neighbour. They must go together."[33] But the church at present, according to Bell, was not yet awakening people to that unflinching and unlimited commitment in their lives and responsibilities in the world and was thereby betraying its own calling: "Christianity is not a fugitive and cloistered religion. It does not slink out of the race. It endures the dust and the heat. It sallies out and sees its adversaries. It is exercised and fully breathed."[34] Within three years, the book had sold eighty thousand copies. Some found their way to neutral countries and to the WCC in Geneva, where Bonhoeffer read it gratefully during his visit there in 1941.

Among Bell's many activities with an ecumenical bearing that challenged nationalistic assumptions during the war years, three areas must be highlighted for their bearing on his ecumenical commitment: help for refugees from Germany and Nazi-occupied countries; contact with the German resistance, bringing its significance to public and political attention in Britain; and opposition to the Allied policy of area bombing civilian populations.

The Refugees

While president of Life of Work in 1933, Bell had become chair of the International Christian Commission for Refugees. By the outbreak of war in 1939, an estimated eighty thousand refugees from Nazi Germany and Czechoslovakia were in Britain, mainly Jews but also intellectual and political opponents of the Nazi regime. From the outset, Bell had a passionate and often frustrated concern for all such, campaigning persistently but with limited success in getting the Church of England and other British churches to raise enough funds for their support. His first speech in the House of Lords in 1938 was on the subject. In February 1939, he was invited to address the Jewish Historical Society and chose the topic "Humanity and the Refugees."[35] Of specific concern to him were the non-Aryan Christians, both pastors and laypeople, who had been in no less danger than those categorized simply as Jews but whose status and needs were not always

---

[33] Bell, 105.

[34] Bell, 145.

[35] Published in George Bell, *The Church and Humanity, 1939–1946* (London: Longmans, Green, 1946), 1–13. See pages 167–76 in this volume for an extract.

recognized by the reception organizations in Britain. Bell effectively became their guardian, in many cases at an exhaustively personal as well as organizational level. "He saved my life," said Eberhard Wedel simply, his family's flight and reception in Britain in 1939 having been sponsored by Bell, as had those of so many others.[36] After the outbreak of war, the plight of the German refugees was compounded by their indiscriminate internment as "enemy aliens" regardless of the fact that they were actually victims and, in many cases, known opponents of the regime. Bell visited the internment camp on the Isle of Man to see the conditions for himself and spoke vigorously on the injustice of the policy. This earned him unpopularity in some sections of the press; in one instance, he was dubbed the "self-appointed champion of captive Nazis and Fascists."[37] The policy, which had been justified by the government as a precaution against German "fifth columnists" who might be lurking in the refugee constituency, was largely discarded by late 1941, though many internees had been transported to Canada and Australia.

The German Resistance

Via the WCC office in Geneva, during the war, clandestine communication took place between a number of individuals in Britain and among members of the various opposition groups in Germany, such as the Kreisau Circle led by Helmut von Moltke and Adam von Trott. Bonhoeffer, on his second wartime visit to Geneva in September 1941, was able, with Visser't Hooft, to read William Paton's book *The Church and the New Order* and send comments on it back to London.[38] Paton was now the associate secretary of the WCC in London, and among his various internationalist activities, he serviced the Peace Aims Group, largely comprising academics and church-related officials. Bonhoeffer, as noted, was also able to express appreciation to Bell for his *Christianity and World Order*. It is also known that some copies of Oldham's *Christian News-Letter* were seen by von Trott while visiting Geneva. Such communications, however, were mainly about the aims and basis of a postwar peace. Implicitly, of course, those on the German side were opposed to the regime and

---

[36] Eberhard Wedel, personal communication with the author, May 10, 2014.

[37] Jasper, *George Bell*, 151.

[38] William Paton, *The Church and the New Order* (London: SCM Press, 1941).

thereby considered resisters. But what political resistance was being offered beyond the holding of such views and the making of plans for the future was largely unknown. It is unlikely, for example, that Bell, or anyone else in Britain, was as yet aware of how deeply Bonhoeffer was involved in the plot, located in the Abwehr (German military intelligence), to overthrow the regime, as a go-between between the conspirators and potential sympathizers abroad.

This changed dramatically in May 1942. In that month, Bell made an extended visit to neutral Sweden under the auspices of the British government's Ministry of Information, which was seeking to foster links between different departments of British and Swedish cultural life. While in Uppsala, he met with the Swedish ecumenist Nils Ehrenström, who took him to the Swedish SCM, where, to his surprise, he found Schönfeld, director of the ecumenical research institute in Geneva, waiting to see him. Schönfeld proceeded to supply Bell with much information on conditions in Germany, the situation of the churches, and the nature and aims of the political resistance and its plans to overthrow Hitler. Three days later, Bell went to the ancient lakeside town of Sigtuna for talks at the Nordic Ecumenical Institute. He records, "Then, to my astonishment, after tea, arrived a second German pastor, Bonhoeffer. He had known nothing of Schönfeld's visit (nor Schönfeld of his)."[39] Bonhoeffer had been on his third wartime visit to Geneva, and while there, he heard that Bell was in Sweden. Bonhoeffer rushed back to Berlin and discussed with leading members of the conspiracy in the Abwehr (his brother-in-law Hans von Dohnanyi and General Hans Oster) the possibilities that might be offered for the resistance by a meeting with Bell. They, with the approval of General Ludwig Beck, supplied his travel permits, and soon Bonhoeffer landed in Sweden. While Schönfeld had poured much information into Bell's ear, the bishop had evidently listened with some caution, knowing that Schönfeld was not thought wholly reliable in Geneva owing to his close ties to the Reich church and, officially, his accountability to Heckel. But what Bonhoeffer now told the bishop substantially agreed with Schönfeld's account and not only amplified but confirmed its significance. Bonhoeffer went into

---

[39] George Bell, "The Church and the Resistance Movement," in *I Knew Dietrich Bonhoeffer*, ed. Wolf-Dieter Zimmerman and Ronald Gregory Smith (London: Collins, 1973), 196–211.

much more detail than Schönfeld had done, listing names of crucial leaders on both the military and civilian wings of the movement. All this was with a view to Bell passing on the information to the British government in the hope that, suitably convinced about the reality of the movement, the Allies might signal that in the event of a successful overthrow of the regime, they would negotiate a peace with the non-Nazi government. They also talked about Bonhoeffer's personal situation and the immense dangers he faced. Schönfeld then spoke of the conspiracy in tactical and strategic terms (how the takeover would proceed once Hitler was dealt with; who would hold key positions in government, industry, and law enforcement; and what guarantees were to be given to the Soviet Union). Bell recalls Bonhoeffer's unease at this point. The overthrow, Bonhoeffer said, must be seen as an act of repentance by Germans, not of self-preservation. They had to endure God's judgment as Christians if God willed it. Before leaving Sweden, Bonhoeffer and Bell met again briefly in Stockholm. Three years later Bell said, "Very moving was our talk; very moving our last farewell. And the last letter I had from him, just before he returned to Berlin, knowing what might await him there, I shall treasure for the whole of my life."[40]

Back in London, in a personal meeting, Bell relayed what he had learned to Foreign Secretary Anthony Eden. There was some sympathy, but the Foreign Office was not persuaded. Were the approaches to Bell any more than indirect peace-feelers from the regime? Why had these supposed emissaries of resistance been allowed to travel to Sweden if not at the behest of the regime? What hard evidence was there of any concerted action likely by the conspirators? How would the Soviet Union react if it appeared that the Western Allies were seeking a separate peace with Germany? It had been agreed in Sigtuna that Bell would communicate the London response by a coded message to Geneva. Sadly, it had to be in the negative. This did not mean a complete stop to Bell's efforts. In public, he persistently argued the case for there being "another Germany" than the Nazi version. Could not the government at least give some recognition and encouragement to those Germans working for an overthrow and a just peace? But following the Casablanca

---

[40] From Bell's sermon preached at the memorial service for Dietrich and Klaus Bonhoeffer, July 27, 1945, in London. The full text is in Eberhard Bethge, ed., *Bonhoeffer Gedenkheft* (Berlin: Verlag Haus und Schule GMBH, 1947), 8.

meeting in January 1943 between Churchill, Roosevelt, and Stalin, the Allied line was that only Germany's unconditional surrender and total disarmament could guarantee a non-Nazi Germany and Europe. Nevertheless, Bell did not give up, and on March 10, 1943, he made a powerful speech on the issue in the House of Lords, challenging the government on whether (like Stalin, reportedly) it made a distinction "between the Hitler state and the German people in their prosecution of the war and their view of our war aims?"[41] Dissent in Germany, he declared, had not been totally terrorized into submission, and hope should be given to those Germans striving against the Nazi regime.

The Area Bombing

The issue most famously associated with Bell's name was the area (or obliteration) bombing of German cities. Right at the start of the war, in his *Diocesan Gazette*, Bell had welcomed the stated commitment of the British and French governments that any aerial bombardments would be strictly limited to military targets. By the autumn of 1940, this principle was being rapidly eroded on all sides. In early 1941, the destruction of Belgrade by German bombing prompted Pope Pius XII on Easter to broadcast an appeal to all belligerents to limit the sufferings of noncombatants. Bell followed the pope's lead with a letter to the *Times* (April 17, 1941) appealing for restrictions on aerial warfare: "It is barbarous to make unarmed women and children the deliberate object of attack. . . . If Europe is civilised at all, what can excuse the bombing of towns by night and the terrorising of non-combatants who work by day and cannot sleep when darkness comes?"[42] He appealed for the British government to declare solemnly that they would refrain from night bombing—at least of towns with civilian populations—provided that Germany would give the same declaration. Controversy ensued, both in the public at large and in Church of England circles, through the summer.

In 1943, the British night bombing offensive was being pursued relentlessly, especially in the spring against the industrial areas of the Ruhr, followed by Hamburg in July and, in December, Berlin itself. Overall, vast stretches of cities of all sizes were laid waste, and an estimated 410,000 civilians were killed by the offensive—49,000

---

[41] See Chandler, *George Bell*, 103.
[42] Jasper, *George Bell*, 262.

in Hamburg alone and 35,000 in Berlin. Most British public opinion acquiesced in the policy, not just because London and other cities had suffered from German bombing during 1940–41, but because, according to the official line, the only way to win the war was to destroy the industrial base of the German war effort, and the only way to do that was by bombing.

It was Bell's House of Lord's speech on February 9, 1944, that caused the greatest public stir—mostly in opposition but not wholly without significant support. Bell was not a pacifist, and he prefaced his speech by paying tribute to the personal courage and skill of the air crews involved (upward of twenty thousand British aircrew lost their lives in the offensive). His opposition to the policy was based on a careful application of the "just war" doctrine, which includes the stipulation that the means employed in war must be proportionate to the goal and the requirement to discriminate between combatants and noncombatants—a distinction, he asserted, that the British government had repeatedly claimed to recognize. So Bell questioned the morality of obliterating whole towns simply because certain parts of it contained military or strategic industrial targets, thus operating with no distinction between military personnel and civilians, a policy that smacked of the Nazi philosophy that "might is right" and ran contrary to the British government's own declared commitments. As always, Bell had done his homework on the facts on both the bombing operations thus far—including the stated objectives of the chief of the Royal Air Force (RAF) Bomber Command, Sir Arthur Harris—and government spokespeople. In both actual methods and stated objectives, Bell argued, it was now a policy of total obliteration:

> The point I want to bring home, because I doubt whether it is sufficiently realised, is that it is no longer definite military and industrial objectives which are the aim of the bombers, but the whole town, area by area, is plotted carefully out. This area is singled out and plastered on one night; that area is singled out and plastered on another night; a third, a fourth, a fifth area is similarly singled out and plastered night after night, till, to use the language of the Chief of Bomber Command with regard to Berlin, the heart of Nazi Germany ceases to beat. How can there be discrimination in such matters when civilians, monuments, military objectives and industrial objectives all together form the target? How can

the bombers aim at anything more than a great space when they see nothing and the bombing is blind?[43]

Bell's public protest was almost, but not completely, a lone one. In the church, a few other bishops (Hensley Henson of Durham, A. C. Headlam of Gloucester, and E. W. Barnes of Birmingham, for example) agreed with his views but did not publicly address the matter in the way he did, whereas Archbishop Temple was a confirmed supporter of the bombing policy. Strident accusations of undermining the war effort were vented on Bell in the press and in correspondence arriving at Chichester. It was a moment when Christian morality and the assumed claims of national loyalty had turned on each other as rarely before in twentieth-century Britain, and perhaps only a senior bishop of the established church could have achieved this so dramatically.[44] At the same time, signals were being received at Chichester of disquiet at the morality of the air offensive, even among some serving personnel in the RAF. And few, whatever their views on what Bell had said, were prepared to doubt the thoughtfulness, honesty, and sheer courage of his stand. When eight months later the See of Canterbury fell vacant with the unexpected death of Temple, there were many who felt that Bell was an obvious candidate to succeed him. But it was Geoffrey Fisher, bishop of London, who was translated to Canterbury, and Bell was also passed over for the vacancy thus created at London. There have been rumors ever since that Prime Minister Churchill would not countenance such a troublesome prelate and that it was Bell's stand against the bombing policy in particular that had cost him his preferment.

The Postwar Future of Europe and the Churches

Long before the end of the war, Bell and other British Christians were giving thought and speech to the postwar reconstruction of Europe and its church life, not least in Germany. Bell wrote on this for Oldham's *Christian News-Letter*, and speaking in the House of Lords in

---

[43] George Bell, "Obliteration Bombing," in *Church and Humanity*, 90.

[44] One interesting response on the ecumenical level was that of Bell's friend Eivind Berggrav, bishop of Oslo, who under the Nazi occupation had endured months of solitary house arrest. He confessed to bafflement on reading in a Finnish newspaper an account of Bell's speech, which at the time he thought contradicted all the protocols for sound relations between church and state. See Chandler, *George Bell*, 119.

December 1944, he stated, "Not only has Europe never attained political organization as a real society of peoples, but something deeper than a political impulse is required to secure lasting unity now. . . . We are more likely to achieve the goal of European unity if we build on the culture which all European peoples have in common."[45] Bell recognized that that "culture" comprised the diverse traditions of humanism, science, law, and government as well as the Christian religion, although not surprisingly, he considered this last "to be the most important and potentially unifying of them all." We may note, however, that slight qualification—"most potentially" unifying. In other words, European unity would be an ecumenical challenge for the churches as well as a political one for governments. European unity and Christian unity would require each other.

The end of the war, and of Nazism, in Europe in May 1945 brought relief and thankfulness to Bell. In that month, he visited New York with Visser't Hooft for meetings with American ecumenists and philanthropists on restarting ecumenical life in earnest. While there, Bell received the news of the death in April of Bonhoeffer in Flossenbürg concentration camp. On Bell's return, he helped organize the memorial service for both Dietrich and his brother Klaus, who had also been executed for his part in the resistance. It was held on July 27, 1945, in Holy Trinity Church, Kingsway, in central London. It fell at a significant time, just when people in Britain were coping with the images of bestiality from the liberated death camps and a new demonization of everything and everyone German might be expected. Moreover, the service was broadcast by the BBC and transmitted on its German service, where it was heard in Berlin by the Bonhoeffer parents, the first confirmation they received of their sons' fates. Bell preached in English, followed by Hildebrandt in German. He outlined Dietrich's life and career and movingly told of their last encounter in Sweden in 1942, when Bonhoeffer had not only informed Bell about the conspiracy but shared his own anguish at Germany's shame. The last two paragraphs merit quoting in full, for they say so much not only about Bonhoeffer but about Bell's vision of what such costly witness could mean for the whole ecumenical community:

---

[45] George Bell, "The Unifying Forces of Europe," in *Church and Humanity*, 107.

And now Dietrich has gone. He died, with his brother, as a hostage. Our debt to them, and to all others similarly murdered, is immense. His death is a death for Germany—indeed for Europe too. He made the sacrifice of human prospects, of home, friends, and career because he believed in God's vocation for his country, and refused to follow those false leaders, who were the servants of the devil.

Our Lord said, "Except a grain of wheat fall into the ground and die, it abideth alone; but if it die, it bringeth forth much fruit. He that loveth his life shall lose it, and he that hateth his life in this world shall keep it unto life eternal." To our earthly view Dietrich is dead. Deep and unfathomable as our sorrow seems, let us comfort one another with these words. For him and Klaus, and for the countless multitudes of their fellow victims through these terrible years of war, there is the resurrection from the dead: for Germany redemption and resurrection, if God please to lead the nation through men animated by his spirit: for the Church, not only in that Germany which he loved, but the Church Universal which was greater to him than nations, the hope of a new life. "The blood of the martyrs is the seed of the Church."[46]

Three months later, Bell was the senior figure in the group of ecumenical representatives who in October 1945 met in Stuttgart with leaders of the German Evangelical Church. The other members of the ecumenical delegation included Visser't Hooft, Pierre Maury (France), Hendrik Kraemer (Netherlands), Koechlin (Switzerland), Samuel McCree Cavert and S. C. Michelfelder (United States), and Gordon Rupp (England). The Germans, who had all witnessed in the Confessing Church—in some cases, to the point of imprisonment—included Niemöller, who had endured eight years in a concentration camp; Hans Asmussen; Hans Lilje; Bishop Otto Dibelius; and Bishop Theophilus Wurm. The memory of Bonhoeffer, with his repeated emphasis on the church's calling to confess its own guilt, was an unseen but effectual presence, and indeed, his friend (and in due course, biographer) Bethge was in attendance. On both sides, there were misgivings. How far apart would the hosts and guests find themselves after the years of separation and war? Would it be another story of recriminations as in 1914–18? How forthcoming were the Germans prepared to be about their country's actions? How

---

[46] Bethge, *Bonhoeffer Gedenkheft*, 8–9.

judgmental would the ecumenicals be? By all accounts, it was the knowledge that Bell would be there that greatly helped the spirit of the meeting and engendered a hope that by grace, a first step toward bridge building might be possible. In the event, the Germans, without prompting, volunteered a statement that more than met expectations:

> With great pain do we say: through us has endless suffering been brought to many peoples and countries. What we have often borne witness to before our congregations that we declare kin the name of the whole church. True, we have struggled for many years in the name of Jesus Christ against a spirit which has found its terrible spirit in the national socialist regime of violence, but we accuse ourselves for not witnessing more courageously, for not praying more faithfully, for not believing more joyously and for not loving more ardently. Now a new beginning is to be made in our churches.[47]

The Stuttgart Declaration of Guilt had a mixed reception in Germany itself, where many felt ill-disposed toward contrition, their country lying so devastated in defeat. But it was used to great effect by those who had been at Stuttgart, and those pastors who supported them, to point the way toward reconciliation through confession and prayer for renewal. In Allied countries, it was held up as yet more evidence that there was indeed "another Germany" than that of the swastika. In later years, the declaration has been stringently criticized for saying nothing about the greatest of all Nazi misdeeds, the Jewish Holocaust, and the Christian complicity in it. But in its time, it had an irrefutable significance. Not everything that needs to be said can always be said at once. Sometimes the building of a bridge has to be in stages, beginning with the frailest links of ropes and planks. Stuttgart was one such beginning on which much else came to be built. And though it was a German statement, merely by being who he was, Bell was one of its inspirations. It was at Stuttgart that for Bell, the war with Germany was truly over, and the declaration was a pivotal moment in the process of reconciliation and healing. We shall return later to reconsider some aspects of Bell's role in it.

Over the next few years, Bell kept a close eye on the work of the Allied Control Commission in Germany, making recommendations

---

where he considered it weak; after his 1945 visit, for example, he expressed concern that the needs of the minority Free Churches, the Baptists and Methodists, and the contribution they could make to reconstruction should be recognized.[48] He voiced criticisms where he thought the commission's actions on "de-Nazification" were unjust or unhelpful to the rehabilitation of Germans and Germany in the family of nations. He also sought to ensure that in a number of cases, the trials of Nazi war criminals, however dire the evidence against them, did not violate the canons of justice.[49] He also made a particular point of visiting Bishop Otto Dibelius and the churches in the Soviet-occupied Eastern Zone.

CONTINUING IN PROPHETIC ECUMENICAL MODE

Other issues kept Bell in prophetic mode. He had publicly protested against the dropping of the atomic bombs on Japan and was a member of the British Council of Churches group, led by Oldham, which produced the report *The Era of Atomic Power*, and spoke at its launch in 1946.[50] But central to his concerns was the consolidation of the WCC still "in formation." The first full postwar meeting of the Provisional Committee took place in Geneva in February 1946. A touching record of the spirit of the meeting is a photograph of two former prisoners under Nazism, the Norwegian Berggrav and the German Niemöller, warmly greeting each other in Visser't Hooft's office. Berggrav and Niemöller, together with Chester Miao of China, preached at the celebratory service in St Peter's Cathedral. The Geneva meeting also, however, had to solve a delicate matter. Temple's death in 1944 meant that a new chairman of the Provisional Committee had to be appointed. By the end of 1946, a consensus seemed to be developing in favor of Temple's successor as archbishop, Fisher. But Bell suddenly

---

[48] Edwin Robertson, interview with the author, June 21, 2006. This point reflects Robertson's experience with the Allied Control Commission in the 1940s. On Bell's work as a whole in Germany, see Edwin Robertson, *Unshakeable Friend: George Bell and the German Churches* (London: CCBI, 1995).

[49] For a careful and not uncritical discussion of Bell's role here, see Tom Lawson, "Bishop Bell and the Trial of German War Criminals: A Moral History," in Chandler, *Church and Humanity*, 129–48.

[50] British Council of Churches, *The Era of Atomic Power* (London: SCM Press, 1946).

found himself being sounded out by the Swedish bishop Yngve Brilioth, who considered him to be the ideal candidate in view of his standing with the continental churches and who spoke disparagingly of "a common type of Englishman who has a certain constitutional difficulty in taking a real interest in things outside England."[51] Bell, however, made it clear that he would not stand against his own archbishop's candidature, and indeed, Fisher was well aware of his own lack of experience in the ecumenical field. In the event, Pastor Marc Boegner of France was asked to take the chair.

In August 1948, ten years after its constitution had been laid down, at last came the full inauguration of the WCC at its first assembly in Amsterdam. While relatively inconspicuous in the immediate preparations and at the assembly itself, Bell was truly one of its enablers. Visser't Hooft said that without Bell and Stuttgart, there would have been no Amsterdam, "for if that meeting had not been held or if it had not succeeded in restoring fraternal relations, it would have been impossible to create the necessary spiritual conditions for the inauguration at Amsterdam."[52] But Bell was not just seen as a symbolic figurehead. He was appointed first chairman of the Central Committee and served until the second assembly in 1954. Chairman (or moderator, as known today) of the Central Committee may not sound like a very glamorous title, but in fact, it is a crucial role in the life of the WCC. The Central Committee comprises over one hundred members, all representatives of member churches and elected by the assembly. It meets every year or so between assemblies. It is where decisions are made on priorities and policies, where the work of staff and particular committees is scrutinized. Here is where real encounters take place. Here East meets West, Protestant meets Orthodox, lay meets clerical, youth meets age, South meets North, male meets female, traditionalist meets liberal, and so it is often the place of impassioned debate. Here is seen ecumenism often at its finest—and sometimes, inevitably, at its less than best. The final message of the Amsterdam assembly includes a notable phrase, penned by the young Anglican leader in the laity movement, Kathleen Bliss: "We intend to stay together." That this commitment was fulfilled in those first years of the WCC, facing as it did the new division in Europe and the world

---

[51] Jasper, *George Bell*, 320.

[52] Visser't Hooft, *Memoirs*, 194.

Bell taking the longer view.
Photo credit: Jimmy James.

between East and West and crises such as the Korean War and the new atomic age yet also, on the positive side, the steady emergence to prominence of the so-called younger churches of the South and East, owed an immense amount to Bell and his steady, mediating, and compassionate discharge of his role. He hosted the first meeting after the Amsterdam assembly, at Chichester in 1949. Particularly crucial were the Central Committee meetings in Toronto, Canada (1950), which laid down a strong policy on religious freedom and clarified the basis of membership and mutual acceptance of churches within the WCC, and Lucknow, India (1953), the first time such a gathering had taken place in Asia. This was a deliberate attempt by the WCC to combat the idea of its being a Western-based and Western-oriented organization and an attempt to call the "older" churches into a new partnership with the "younger" churches. And Bell really did lead. As Visser't Hooft said of him, Bell always came to the meeting "with something in his pocket"—whether a proposal concerning refugees or a persecuted church or some new idea to increase understanding or cooperation among the churches—and described his chairmanship as "that of father of a family rather than a keeper of hard and fast rules of procedure."[53] As his term in office concluded in 1954, he could report on "the steady growth of mutual trust" among the Central Committee members. But Bell was not only a chairman. He was an ecumenical pastor as well, and he made a special point of visiting, in company with Visser't Hooft, the churches of Eastern Europe under the new totalitarianism—not least the Eastern Orthodox Churches, most of which had not yet joined the WCC.

When the second WCC assembly met in Evanston, Illinois, in 1954, it was in a thoroughly confident, forward- and outward-looking spirit. For Evanston, Bell wrote his second Penguin paperback, *The Kingship of Christ*, dedicated to the members of the Central Committee with whom he had served those six years.[54] The book is a further telling of the ecumenical story and the work of the WCC but also a wide-ranging survey of the challenges facing the world and the world church's responses to them at both the global and local levels. The churches had not just stayed together; they were now more conscious of their common mission. It was a growing family that would grow still further with the arrival of more of the Orthodox Churches—most notably, the Russian Orthodox Church—at the next assembly in 1961, a development Bell had longed to see happen but, like Moses on the top of Mount Pisgah, had only been able to envision from afar. The extent of Bell's regard for the Orthodox Church became controversially apparent during 1956–57, when he was severely critical of British policy over Cyprus and supportive of Archbishop Makarios, who was leading the Greek Cypriot cause for independence. Bell had to face accusations in the British Parliament that he was more loyal to the WCC than to British interests. No less was he critical of British policy during the Suez Crisis of 1956.

Loyal to the WCC he certainly was, and the WCC at the Evanston assembly underlined its gratitude by electing him one of its presidents. As such, he died four years later, in 1958, in Canterbury, having just retired there from Chichester.

This, in summary, is a sketch of *what* Bell did to deserve that phrase on his epitaph in Chichester Cathedral, "Tireless worker for Christian unity." Many things of importance worth mentioning

---

[53] Jasper, *George Bell*, 337.

[54] George Bell, *The Kingship of Christ: The Story of the World Council of Churches* (London: Penguin, 1954).

The WCC Central Committee meeting, Lucknow, India, 1953. George Bell chairs the session addressed by Prime Minister Jawaharlal Nehru. Photo credit: WCC Photo Archive

have had to be left out because what needs to be emphasized now are features of the *spirit* that drove him, the why and how of his apostleship for unity. This requires that we step back a little from the chronological, episodic treatment of his life and look at four main marks of his ecumenism and, as appropriate, illustrating them with a closer look at some of his activities.

An Ecumenism of Relationships

"I seek my brethren" (Gen 37:16), the text on which Bell chose to preach at his installation as dean of Canterbury Cathedral on March 21, 1924, signaled a theme that had already marked his entry into ecumenical life and responsibility and was to do so for the rest of his life. It is often remarked that the ecumenical movement is not only a matter of conferences, agreements on interchurch action, cooperation in social and evangelistic programs, common prophetic witness on issues of justice and peace, building and strengthening ecumenical organizations, and (it is hoped) moves toward mutual agreement on basic doctrines of the faith and the nature and governance of

149

the church but also the personal relationships and friendships that grow through and strengthen such common activity. Friendship, it is recognized, is often the oil that enables the ecumenical mechanism to move. For Bell, however, friendship was at the heart of the ecumenical life, not merely the lubricant but one of its main energies. Such friendship is not to be taken for granted but has to be sought if not initiated. Already during the First World War, Bell was developing international friendships. In 1915, for example, he was meeting with the young Serbian priest Nikolaj Velimirović, who had come to London on behalf of the Serbian Relief Fund and for whom a meal in an Indian restaurant with the archbishop's chaplain was a good business opportunity. Andrew Chandler comments, "Yet there was evidently something more to share with this personable, intellectual young Serb. By February 1917 the two were evidently getting along famously." Likewise, during these years, Bell struck up a significant, heart-to-heart relationship with a French monk, Lambert Beauduin, "a persevering ecumenist and a reforming liturgist." Further, says Chandler on the basis of Bell's preserved papers, there were "far, far more" of these friendships.[55]

For his part, Bell knew that friendships, and even family relationships, sometimes have to be dared, across boundaries and in the face of prejudice and unreconciled memories, not least between Christian traditions. During the Second World War, Bell experienced firsthand the continuing difficulties in establishing cooperation with Roman Catholics in Britain. The Catholic-led Sword of the Spirit movement, launched in 1941, at first held great promise for a new ecumenical advance, but difficulties arose on the Catholic side on the issue of joint prayer at public meetings, while non-Catholics had misgivings about becoming a subgroup within an essentially Catholic movement. There was, however, no doubting the sincere hopes on both sides for cooperation. In October 1941, Bell was even an overnight guest of the head of English Catholics, Cardinal Arthur Hinsley, and recorded, "Went to stay with Cardinal Hinsley on October 14–15 at Hare Street House to discuss Christian cooperation and the Sword of the Spirit. Cardinal a fine old man of 76—keen, eager and alive." Hinsley and Bell shared their difficulties with complete openness. Bell remarked, "On prayer at Sword meetings—Lord's Prayer, yes:

---

[55] See Chandler, *George Bell*, 16.

knowing that those present need not take part unless they wished. As to using collects common to both, this would cause trouble. He would get into hot water: so, he thought, would I. He was very appreciative of the value of the whole talk. He had been much criticised: so, he supposed, had I. But it was good to meet and understand one another."[56]

Eight decades on, it takes some effort to appreciate just how impenetrable the official walls between Catholics and other Christians at that time appeared to be. It was Bell's ecumenical style to seek his brethren even among those who might not yet be seen as brethren and to be open to friendship when historical memory and ecclesiastical protocol remained so divisive.

It was, however, in his relations with the German churches and the German opposition to Hitler that Bell's commitment to friendship was most definitive. Historian Klaus Scholder, author of the most complete and authoritative history of the German Church Struggle, has given the definitive accolade to Bell: "Whereas for most English people the theological traditions of the continent were remote, Bell had a sure feel for the basic positions in the German church struggle. From summer 1933 on he followed the Confessing Church indefatigably and without a moment's hesitation or uncertainty, and even during the war, when everything seemed to sink into a flood of hatred, he remained the unshakeable friend of the other Germany, of whose existence and credibility he tried in vain to convince the Foreign Office."[57]

"Unshakeable friend" is indeed the truest description of Bell in that context, and it was aptly used by Edwin Robertson as the title of his book on Bell. But his was a friendship not just in the abstract but realized in particular friendships with real people such as Otto Dibelius, Hermann Sassed, Niemöller, Theophilus Wurm, Hans Asmussen, Hans Lilje, Hildebrandt, and above all, Bonhoeffer. Bell had been moved to the depths by his last meeting with Bonhoeffer at Sigtuna in 1942, when Bonhoeffer had not only confirmed and amplified the details of the conspiracy to overthrow Hitler but emptied his heart in what was a confessional moment of what, as a German, he believed to be his country's guilt and its need to accept the judgment of God in whatever form that judgment might take.

---

[56] See Jasper, *George Bell*, 253.
[57] Scholder, *Churches and the Third Reich*, 75.

In October 1945, as Bell journeyed to Stuttgart for the ecumenical meeting with the German Evangelical Church leaders—like Joseph in the Genesis story, unsure of what to expect from his brethren—the memory of Sigtuna must have been much in his mind as he prepared notes for his address. His speech in response to the Germans' statement came after Visser't Hooft, Maury of France, and Michel Elder of the United States had spoken. Bell began by expressing his joy at meeting face-to-face with these leaders. He came, he said, as a bishop with greetings from the archbishop of Canterbury, "as a brother in Christ, and as an old friend of the Confessional Church." He spoke as one who had followed with great admiration the witness of those who had stood up against the crimes of the Nazi state, and he specifically mentioned "the brave, utterly dedicated, most gifted and ardent soul Dietrich Bonhoeffer."[58] He discussed the terrible scourge of war, the untold cruelties brought to Jews and millions of others. Now, he declared, they must turn to the future, for which the new WCC was a means of manifesting the incarnate love of Christ in the social, national, and international life of humanity. Thus was the hand of ecumenical friendship being offered from the start. In fact, the most time and weight in the discussions at Stuttgart were given to the plight of Germany itself. The future of which Bell had spoken was already being embarked upon. We have noted Visser't Hooft's comment that without Stuttgart, there would have been no Amsterdam in 1948. One could add that without Sigtuna in 1942, there might have been no Stuttgart three years later.

The unshakeable friendship continued in the difficult and complex postwar situation in Germany—as, for example, in the painful matter of August Marahrens, bishop of Hannover, a president of the Lutheran World Federation (LWF) and a member of the WCC Provisional Committee. In the view of many in the Confessing Church, since 1939, Marahrens had fatally compromised himself by making, at best, equivocal (and certainly in Bell's eyes, at worst, shameful) statements in support of Hitler. Neither the LWF nor the WCC could accept his continued participation in their governance, and the younger pastors could not accept his continuance as a bishop. But Marahrens refused to step down, protesting his innocence, and Bell was asked to mediate. He visited Marahrens in 1946, his approach

---

[58] See Chandler, *George Bell*, 133.

as always as diplomatic as possible but also firm, pointing out that if all the churches had been as acquiescent under the regime as Marahrens had been, "there would have been no Church resistance in Germany."[59] In April 1947, Marahrens did resign, succeeded as bishop by Hans Lilje. Friends are also those who, when needed, speak unwelcome truths.

Bell's friendships always extended well beyond the European scene, however. At the 1920 Lambeth Conference, Samuel Azariah, the bishop of Dornakal in South India, was with Bell in the group that drafted the famous appeal,[60] and the two met again in London in 1927. In 1931, in the midst of Gandhi's campaign for Indian independence, Bell welcomed Gandhi to Chichester, had a lengthy discussion with him, and sought to mediate his concerns to the British government.[61] In fact, it was Bell, together with the Anglican missionary C. F. Andrews, who provided an introduction to Gandhi on behalf of Bonhoeffer, who in 1933–45 was hoping to visit Gandhi at his ashram and draw inspiration from his methods of nonviolent resistance and also to visit the poet and philosopher Rabindranath Tagore. Another important Indian relationship was with the philosopher and statesman S. Radhakrishnan.[62] In 1949, Bell visited India out of particular concern for the Church of South India, whose formation and relation to the Church of England he vigorously supported (in face of Anglo-Catholic opposition); he visited again in 1953 for the meeting of the WCC Central Committee in Lucknow. Vital to his interests were the Indian friends themselves. After Bell's death in 1958, Russell Chandran, the first Indian principal of the United Theological College at Bangalore, recalled a meeting with him in New Haven, Connecticut, the year before. Chandran wrote to Henrietta Bell, "Bishop Bell always impressed me as a 'humble man of God.' . . . The way he made inquiries about his friends in India showed the

---

[59] Jasper, *George Bell*, 301.

[60] See Jasper, *George Bell*, 57. Whether Azariah was actually a member of the drafting group has recently been questioned by the historian Charlotte Methuen, who suggests there may be confusion here with the bishop of Bombay (personal communication with the author, February 22, 2021). Jasper does mention that the bishop of Bombay, Edwin James Palmer, was present along with Azariah and others.

[61] See Joseph Muthuraj, "An Indian Scholar Looks at Bishop George Bell," in Chandler, *Church and Humanity*, 59–76.

[62] Muthuraj, 74–75.

amount of personal affection he held for people. He always made me feel that he was a personal friend, not just a great man."[63]

A Holistic Ecumenism

Enthused by his first encounter with Söderblom and other ecumenicals aspiring to peace and social justice, Bell returned from Oude Wassenaar in late 1919 to be plunged into preparations for the conference in Lambeth the following year, at which, we have seen, he made a major contribution to drafting the "Appeal to All Christian People" to work for a reunited church. The times, stated the appeal, called for a new orientation and vision, for "the battle for the kingdom cannot be worthily fought while the body is divided." Thus,

> The vision which rises before us is that of a Church, genuinely Catholic, loyal to all truth, and gathering into its fellowship all "who profess and call themselves Christians," within whose visible unity all the treasures of faith and order, bequeathed as a heritage by the past to the present, shall be possessed in common, and made serviceable to the whole Body of Christ. Within this unity Christian communions now separated from one another would retain much that has long been distinctive in their methods of worship and service. It is through a rich diversity of life and devotion that the unity of the whole fellowship will be fulfilled.[64]

It was this vision of a church "genuinely Catholic" in "battle for the kingdom" that inspired and directed Bell's whole ecumenical commitment. "The context in which all of Bell's diverse works transpired," says Andrew Chandler, "was a rich, vivid vision of the universal church, in which all Christians could find each other and labour for justice, not merely as members of different confessions but together, as brothers and sisters."[65] It was a remarkably holistic ecumenism that he pursued and served. It is a well-worn truism that the modern ecumenical movement arose in three main streams: the world missionary enterprise, highlighted at the 1910 Edinburgh conference;

---

[64] Anglican Consultative Council, *The Lambeth Conference: Resolutions Archive from 1920*, 2005, https://www.anglicancommunion.org/media/127731/1920.pdf, 6.

[65] Chandler, *George Bell*, xi.

Life and Work, launched at the 1924 Stockholm conference; and Faith and Order, beginning with the 1927 Lausanne conference. Each had its own emphases, aims, and methods. Each was also capable of generating its own loyalty, sometimes in anxious competition with the others, and claiming to represent the authentic ecumenical movement from which the others were diversions. "Doctrine divides, service unites" was a slogan popular in some Life and Work circles in the 1920s, an implicit swipe at Faith and Order. But among the ecumenical leaders of the time were those active in all three streams: Temple is an outstanding example. Bell above all exemplifies a commitment to all three strands. Only someone so committed would devote so much time and energy to his series *Documents on Christian Unity*. Bell's summaries of the ecumenical story in *Christianity and World Order* and *The Kingship of Christ* deal equally, fully, and fairly with the IMC, Life and Work, and Faith and Order and also recognize the vital role the youth movements played in the story. His inclusive vision is further seen in *The Kingship of Christ* where he highlights the growing concern for the role of women in the church—in particular, the pioneering efforts of Sarah Chakko of Lucknow, India—to bring this to the attention of the Amsterdam assembly as a "concern of the Church as a whole, and not a problem for women alone."[66]

If it is indeed through "a rich diversity of life and devotion that the unity of the whole fellowship will be fulfilled,"[67] this implies not just mutual regard or cooperation between the different members and churches of the ecumenical fellowship but an actual *symbiosis*, a mutually dependent life at every level from the corporate to the personal. This is well illustrated by the way Bell and Oldham worked closely to their own benefit and to the greater good of the ecumenical movement from the early 1930s onward. Oldham, we have seen, during the later 1920s was increasingly concerned that the IMC, which he had largely parented, seemed locked in the missionary agenda of the past and was unwilling or unable to respond to the wider challenges facing human society at both national and international levels, in particular the growing threat of totalitarianism in Europe. He was looking for an instrument that could analyze the contemporary social scene and identify the relevant tasks for the church. At the same time, Bell had

---

[66] Bell, *Kingship of Christ*, 157.
[67] "Appeal to All Christian People."

taken the lead in insisting that after the Stockholm conference, Life and Work needed a permanent basis and a focused agenda instead of being just a platform for idealistic speeches and resolutions. By 1932, Bell was at the helm of Life and Work, and its research institute was being set up in Geneva. Oldham, who at first had been dismissive of the Stockholm initiative, was now attracted and negotiated his invitation to the Fanø conference; thereafter, he was in charge of the study program for the 1937 Oxford conference. It is probable that without Bell and the prestige that as a bishop of high repute he could bring to Life and Work, Oldham would not have had the effective tool with which to operate in his social theology projects. In turn, without Oldham, Bell and Life and Work would not have had the benefit of a mind that could ground the churches in engagement with the challenges that were making the world a much more complex and less optimistic scene than was apparent at the time of the Stockholm conference ten years earlier. Oldham, the Scottish Presbyterian by upbringing (though now registering as a lay Anglican), still retained a slight reserve about bishops as a species but notably exempted Bell (and Temple) from suspicion. The close Oldham-Bell collaboration continued through the German Church Struggle. During the Second World War, Oldham provided a particularly important service to Bell through the *Christian News-Letter*. Bell's vilification in much of the British press for his stand against the obliteration bombing—and in some circles also for his pleading the cause of German refugees—was countered by the space Oldham gave him for a fair hearing in the *News-Letter*. No less, Bell in *Christianity and World Order* draws extensively on Oldham's work and thinking for the Oxford conference and highlights Oldham's perception of the dangers in the "increasing organization of the life of the community, which is made possible by modern control of economic forces [which] coincides with a growing secularization of the thought and life of mankind."[68]

Bell was greatly inspired by Söderblom's approach to Christian unity, "the method of love and Christian cooperation,"[69] which became the approach of Life and Work as a whole. This did not mean that he ignored the doctrinal issues in which he was well versed and that as the collator of *Documents on Christian Unity* he had followed closely—not to mention the fact that he was a stalwart

---

[68] Bell, *Christianity and World Order*, 67.
[69] Jasper, *George Bell*, 39.

supporter of the Church of South India.[70] Indeed, it has been suggested that "with hindsight he would later declare a preference for the more narrowly doctrinal concerns of . . . the Faith and Order Movement."[71] It would of course be expected that having become the moderator of the WCC Central Committee in 1948, Bell would be motivated to affirm the concerns of Faith and Order no less than of Life and Work. But in the frame, there was also the IMC, which would not be incorporated into the WCC until 1961 and also called for recognition. Pertinent to Bell's state of mind post-Amsterdam is the sermon "The Approach to Christian Unity," which he preached in Cambridge in 1951.[72] Strikingly, he takes as his text Matthew 28:19, the Great Commission: "Go ye therefore, and make disciples of all the nations" (ASV). In that sermon, we see the aims of Stockholm and Lausanne being marshaled for energizing under the banner of Edinburgh 1910: a truly holistic ecumenism oriented toward mission in the world.

AN ECUMENISM IN TRUTH

To say that Bell's ecumenism was inclusive does not mean that it was open to the point of disregarding matters of belief and truth, for it was an inclusivity emanating from *the* truth who is the living Christ in his church. Bell grew up in an age of successive Anglican debates on the interpretation of traditional belief in the light of modern historical and scientific knowledge and on who or what had the authority to decide such questions. In 1913, during Bell's clerical studentship at Christ Church, there appeared the volume of essays *Foundations: A Statement of Belief in Terms of Modern Thought* by a group of Oxford scholars with liberal inclinations, including some who later were to be significantly involved in the ecumenical movement, such as Temple, Walter Moberly, and B. H. Streeter.[73] Lively

---

[70] To be noted also are the lectures Bell gave in Uppsala in 1946. See George Bell, *Christian Unity: The Anglican Position* (London: Hodder & Stoughton, 1948), on which, see Jaako Rusama, "George Bell and the Promotion of Anglican-Lutheran Relations," in Chandler, *Church and Humanity*, 195–208.

[71] Rusama, "George Bell," 200.

[72] See pages 203–8 in this volume for an extensive extract.

[73] B. H. Streeter et al., *Foundations: A Statement of Belief in Terms of Modern Thought* (London: Macmillan, 1912).

controversy was stirred both within and well outside Oxford. Bell was not a member of the *Foundations* group, and his own response to the essays can best be described as one of detached sympathy: "Of course there must be creed and dogma, the intellectual presentation of the Word. But the Word itself is alive, quick and powerful. To me 'faith' in the New Testament suggests something very living, creative, rather than something settled and deposited once for all. . . . Christianity is a life before it is a system and to lay too much stress on the system destroys the life."[74]

This emphasis on the life rather than the system remained with Bell. He was aware that the church as a believing community and the theologian, as a servant of that community, needed to be in constant mutual relationship for the sake of the truth that is the Christ himself and ever to be explored as well as worshipped. His concluding essay, "The Church and the Theologian," to the volume of essays *Mysterium Christi*, produced by the Anglo-German theological conferences of 1927–28 (see pages 119–20 in this volume), expounds well the need for the theologian to be accorded proper respect and freedom in their scholarly work and equally the integrity of the church community and the historic landmarks of the faith to be respected by the theologian who serves that community:

> I would give great liberty, as well as great honour, to the theologian, and encourage him to ever fresh endeavour and ever new research. But he is, after all, the servant of the Church, and it is the faith of the Church speaking through the ages that he studies and expounds. He may be endowed with such insight that he perceives an aspect unperceived before in some Christian doctrine. He may find a new and true way of interpreting *Mysterium Christi* to his own generation. Or he may have the genius which is able to relate fundamental Christian theology to modern categories of science and philosophy. If this be so, sooner or later (and if the Church is truly living in the Spirit sooner rather than later), his contribution will be taken in and absorbed, his new light will become a permanent part of the Church's faith.[75]

---

[74] Jasper, *George Bell*, 16–17.
[75] Bell and Deissmann, *Mysterium Christi*, 281.

This affirmative and hopeful glance at their common theological task was doubtless welcomed by all participants in these dialogues. But within five years, the very possibility of such fellowship would be thrown into question. With the German Church Struggle, the question of the truth to which church and theologians alike owed fidelity was thrust with unprecedented urgency into the center for churches and the ecumenical movement. Certain Germans (notably, Gerhard Kittel, Paul Althaus, and Heinrich Frick) would become identified with the nationalist theology that under Nazism declared ecumenism anathema, while Hermann Sasse, another member of the *Mysterium Christi* group, was strongly opposed to Nazism and identified with the Confessing Church—albeit, as a Lutheran, critical of Barth's strongly Reformed influence upon it.

Bell, we have seen, was foremost in the ecumenical concern for the German church scene during the first year of the struggle, and his Ascension Day message in May 1934 to the member churches of Life and Work was a landmark in that concern (see pages 165–67 in this volume). Behind the final text of the message, however, lies an instance where Bell himself realized that the quest for truthfulness is indeed a learning experience in ecumenical relations no less than in others. Typically, he had first circulated a draft of his proposed statements to a number of trusted advisers, including Bonhoeffer. In referring to the persecuted pastors, his draft spoke of the loyalty of the persecuted pastors "to what they believe to be Christian truth." Bonhoeffer was deeply grateful for the message as a whole but respectfully took issue with Bell over his wording at this point. In a May 3, 1934, letter, Bonhoeffer comments,

> You speak "of the loyalty (of the pastors) to what they believe to be Christian truth." Could you not say perhaps: to what *is* the Christian truth—or "what we believe with them to be the Christian truth"? It sounds as if you want to take distance from their belief. I think even the Reichsbishop would be right in taking disciplinary measures against ministers, if they stand for something else but the truth of the Gospel (even if they believe it to be the truth)—the real issue is that they are under coercion on account of their loyalty to what *is* the true Gospel—namely their opposition against the *racial and political element as constituent for the Church of Christ.*[76]

---

[76] Dietrich Bonhoeffer, letter to George Bell, May 3, 1934, in *London, 1933–1935*, (Minneapolis: Fortress Press, 2007), 140.

Bell duly took note, and his final text spoke of disciplinary measures against pastors "on account of their loyalty to the fundamental principles of Christian truth." This was more than a verbal quibble. Continually in the English-speaking world, the German Church Struggle was seen as a fight about "religious freedom." To the Confessing Christians themselves, especially such as Barth and Bonhoeffer, it was about not the general principle of religious freedom (a very "Anglo-Saxon" notion, they said) but obedience to the gospel. This was the crux of the matter. So Bell, thanks to Bonhoeffer, was acknowledging this three weeks before it was etched indelibly in the Theological Declaration of Barmen, and this proved crucial in securing his enduring understanding of and support for the Confessing Church. His was an ecumenism that for the sake of truth was prepared to travel contextually—not just geographically but mentally and culturally—into the scene of the others and view that scene as those involved saw it and experienced it. Bell, the Catholic-minded Anglican, came from a rather different world from that of the continental Protestant churches, where the issues were seen in terms of loyalty to the Reformation formulations and the concept of a *status confessionis*. But he knew instinctively that what was at stake in Germany was loyalty to the gospel, and Bonhoeffer helped him see and express this more definitively: Bell the Anglican bishop was prepared to be corrected by the young German Lutheran. This, as was shown at Fanø in August that year, secured an ecumenical integrity in the truth. Moreover, Bell's significance to the German Church Struggle was recognized by no less a figure than Barth, who in 1939 with Koechlin, facilitated the award to Bell of an honorary doctorate in theology from Basel University (though the actual conferral was delayed by the war).

WATCHMAN FOR HUMANITY: GOODNESS, TRUTH, AND BEAUTY

Addressing a largely Jewish audience in February 1939, three months after Germany's infamous *Kristallnacht*, Bell stated, "But an end will come: justice, mercy and liberty will re-assert their sway. The oppression will cease, as it has ceased before. Belief in God, and the lessons of history, forbid us to despair."[77] He saw the sympathy

---

[77] George Bell, "Humanity and the Refugees," in *Church and Humanity*, 13.

and generosity unleashed among the British public after the pogrom as a hopeful augury. It may well be asked if Bell would have spoken with such seeming confidence had it been known just what unimaginable horrors still lay ahead for the Jews, but Bell's partnering of belief in God and the resilient values of justice, mercy, and liberty in society at large characterized his fundamental beliefs throughout his adult years. The gospel and humanity were not one and the same, but neither could they be divorced from each other. As Bell put it, "The Church is the divine society; the community of believers; the organ of the will of the divine Lord,"[78] functioning as a fellowship of love in worship, preaching, and witness. But it is also set in the wider world, where it is to exhibit what true community is, call others into that truly social way of living in which people find their true fulfillment as human beings, and declare God's justice and mercy: "The Church has still a special duty to be a watchman for humanity, and to plead the cause of the suffering, whether Jew or Gentile."[79] But should it be claimed that the church or Christians are themselves the sole exemplifiers of these values? Pertinent in this regard are the comments Bell made in his sermon at the memorial service for Bonhoeffer in July 1945:

> [Bonhoeffer] was inspired by his faith in the living God, and by his devotion to truth and honor. And so his death, like his life, marks a fact of the deepest value in the witness of the Confessional Church. As one of a noble company of martyrs of differing traditions, he represents both the resistance of the believing soul, in the name of God, to the assault of evil, *and also the moral and political revolt of the human conscience against injustice and cruelty.* He and his fellows are indeed laid upon the foundation of the Apostles and the Prophets. And it was this passion for justice that brought him, and so many others in the Confessional Church who were in agreement with him, into such close partnership with other resisters who, though outside the Church, shared the same humanitarian and liberal ideals.[80]

---

[78] Bell, *Christianity and World Order*, 43.

[79] Bell, 107.

[80] Bethge, *Bonhoeffer Gedenkheft*, 9 (emphasis mine).

The same point could be made about Bell himself, the priest in the Anglican Christian socialist tradition, who knew that if the church is to be a watchman for humanity, if faith is to take form in the public sphere for the common good, it will at some point have to seek collaboration and alliances with people whose conscience and inspiration may stem from sources quite other than the specifically Christian but whose practical, short- or medium-term goals may be very similar. That is a concomitant of an incarnational theology that seeks to identify in the life of the world immanent resonances with the kingdom of God while being aware of the kind of catastrophic mistakes made by the "German Christians" and their like who regarded Hitler as God's new voice on earth. There needs to be a search for genuinely common moral ground. Bell knew this each time he rose to speak in the House of Lords, whether on refugees, the plight of the Jews, the peace aims of the Allies, the reconstruction of postwar Europe, and not least, obliteration bombing. There is a moving story of how another member of the Upper House, Lord Woolton, went up to Bell shortly before he made his dramatic speech and said, "George, there isn't a soul in this House who doesn't wish you wouldn't make the speech you are going to make. . . . You must know that. But I also want to tell you that there isn't a soul who doesn't know that the only reason why you make it, is because you believe it is your duty to make it as a Christian priest."[81]

Yet what is striking about that speech is that while delivered out of passionate Christian conviction, it is not a sermon, not larded with biblical citations or references to the will of God. Bell is not in the pulpit but alongside his fellow peers (in every sense) and appealing to a common ground of conscience, citing the government's previous statements of the aims of the bombing policy and, most fundamentally, the "just war" doctrine of proportionality and discrimination between combatants and noncombatants that, though historically Christian in origin, had been essentially accommodated in the West into the corpus of natural law. Bell's speech concludes, "The Allies stand for something greater than power. The chief name inscribed on our banner is 'Law.' It is of supreme importance that we who, with our Allies, are the liberators of Europe should so use power that it is always under the control of law. It is because the bombing of enemy

---

[81] Jasper, *George Bell*, 277.

towns—this area bombing—raises this use of power unlimited and exclusive that such importance is bound to attach to the policy and action of His Majesty's Government."[82]

Bell had questioned the bombing policy on the grounds of humanity and the "just war" doctrine. It was Oldham who took up the issue while pointing to what he saw as an unanswered question prompted by Bell's position. In almost the very next issue of the *Christian News-Letter*, Oldham wrote under the heading "War and Civilisation" with full praise for Bell's courage in raising the issue and the humanitarian considerations involved. Is such inhumanity, Oldham asks, the price to be paid for winning the war? He continues,

> The importance of the Bishop of Chichester's action lies in its reminder that we cannot afford to forget that even in war we are not simply combatants but also men, and as such are bound by inescapable obligations to our fellow-men, to the tasks of civilisation and to God. The vital matter is not the decision we reach in regard to a particular act of war, e.g. whether we agree with the Bishop of Chichester about the bombing policy of the Government, but whether we are alive, as he is, to the momentous choice which the nation has to make, and from which there is no escape.[83]

We are powerless, Oldham concludes, to escape the spiritual danger that encompasses us, and only a spiritual renewal from God can lighten our darkness. Oldham's responses to Bell's protests against area bombing might be seen as evasive fence-sitting. That is too superficial a reading. What he is wanting is a fair hearing for Bell and the centrality he places on the moral and spiritual factors involved in warfare. If Oldham appears to be equivocal in his support for what Bell is saying, it is because he is also insisting that in the context of the war, Bell's moral argument cannot be the *only* sort of argument employed. Having accepted, as Bell himself did (certainly from mid-1940 onward), that the military defeat of Nazi Germany was morally necessary, then that becomes the overall framework—moral as well as political—within which decisions on policy have to be made. The question of the *means* to that end cannot be avoided. Oldham had wisdom here, and in fact, at the time, there was

[82] Bell, "Obliteration Bombing," 94–95.
[83] J. H. Oldham, "War and Civilisation," *Christian News-Letter* 202, February 23, 1944.

debate within government military and scientific circles on the strategic value of area bombing and on technically feasible alternatives to it.[84] To have opened this up more fully could have made the moral case still more pertinent. In his speech, Bell referred in passing to official estimates that the bombing had not hitherto affected German industrial output as greatly as had been envisaged. But the technical knowledge involved in strategic decision-making was not fully in the public domain.[85] Those who press governments to stay their hand must make clear their attitudes to these consequences or at any rate be prepared to engage with the technical and strategic issues. Oldham and Bell were here in a critical kind of symbiosis, or a sympathetic disagreement.

A final note on Bell's opposition to the area bombing is pertinent. In his criticism of the policy, he was as distressed at the destruction of the cultural wealth of German art galleries, libraries, and museums as he was passionate in his patronage of the arts in Britain, in Canterbury, and in Chichester in particular. The arts were for him essential to the humanity that came under the blessing of God and the gospel. Indeed, he refers to them as "auxiliaries" to the gospel.[86] They uncover truths, often more cogently than any other medium, about our nature and the meanings of our experience, to which is offered the gospel. Perhaps Bell would say that if the church is to be a watchman for humanity, the arts can be the spies out in the world, giving early signals to those keeping the watch.

---

[84] See, for example, R. V. Jones, *Most Secret War: British Scientific Intelligence 1939–1945* (London: Penguin, 1978).

[85] Oldham's own sense of frustration at the way the debate proceeded was evident in the *Christian News-Letter* 225, January 10, 1945, when he wrote of his impatience "with those in this country, and America, who plead in the name of Christianity or humanity for restrictions on bombing, but restrain from stating clearly whether they intend, or do not intend, that the range of air attack should be restricted, even if this involves the prolongation, or conceivably the loss, of the war."

[86] Bell, *Christianity and World Order*, 146.

4

SELECTED WRITINGS OF GEORGE BELL

Archbishop Nathan Söderblom, the founder of the Life and Work Movement, said of George Bell, "He does not speak without having something to say." Bell was not as prolific a writer as J. H. Oldham, and with the exception of his biography of Randall Davidson, his published works are relatively short. But they are always to the point and address a particular situation or issue. Indeed, in many cases, they were originally given as addresses or sermons. Those selected here are in chronological order, beginning with his clear statement of May 1934 on the grave threat to the Christian church in Nazi Germany and concluding with his ecumenical vision of hope in the newly dangerous world of the 1950s.

"A Message regarding the German Evangelical Church"

On May 10, 1934, Ascension Day, Bell, as president of the Life and Work Movement and chairman of its executive committee, issued this statement in response to the serious situation facing the Evangelical (i.e., Protestant) Church in Germany. Those pastors opposed to the "Reich church" and the Nazi racial policy were under increasing pressure and harassment. The message was addressed to the member churches of the Life and Work Movement and was the first direct public comment on the German Church Struggle from an international ecumenical quarter, making clear that the events in Germany were of immediate concern to Christians everywhere. In drafting his message, Bell consulted with other ecumenical figures including Dietrich Bonhoeffer, who asked Bell to strengthen the wording at a crucial point (see page 159–60 in this volume). Bell agreed.

Three weeks later, in opposition to the pro-Nazi German Christian movement, the Free Synod of Barmen issued its now famous theological declaration, the foundation of the Confessing Church.

George Bell, "A Message regarding the German Evangelical Church," in *London, 1933–1945*, Dietrich Bonhoeffer Works 13, English ed., ed. Keith Clements, trans. Isabel Best (Minneapolis: Fortress Press, 2007), 144–46

A MESSAGE REGARDING THE GERMAN EVANGELICAL CHURCH TO THE REPRESENTATIVES OF THE CHURCHES ON THE UNIVERSAL CHRISTIAN COUNCIL FOR LIFE AND WORK FROM THE BISHOP OF CHICHESTER

I have been urged from many quarters to issue some statement to my fellow members of the Universal Christian Council for Life and Work upon the present position in the German Evangelical Church, especially as it affects other Churches represented on the Universal Christian Council for Life and Work.

The situation is, beyond doubt, full of anxiety. To estimate it aright we have to remember the fact that a revolution has taken place in the German State, and that as a necessary result the German Evangelical Church was bound to be faced with new tasks and many new problems requiring time for their full solution. It is none the less true that the present position is being watched by members of the Christian Churches abroad not only with great interest, but with a deepening concern. The chief cause of anxiety is the assumption by the Reichbishop in the name of the principle of leadership of autocratic powers unqualified by constitutional or traditional restraints which are without precedent in the history of the Church. The exercise of these autocratic powers by the Church government appears incompatible with the Christian principle of seeking in brotherly fellowship to receive the guidance of the Holy Spirit. It has had disastrous results on the internal unity of the Church; and the disciplinary measures which have been taken by the Church government against Ministers of the Gospel on account of their loyalty to the fundamental principles of Christian truth have made a painful impression on Christian opinion abroad, already disturbed by the introduction of racial distinction in the universal fellowship of the Christian Church. No wonder that voices should be raised in Germany itself making a solemn pronouncement before the whole Christian world on the dangers to which the spiritual life of the Evangelical Church is exposed.

There are indeed other problems which the German Evangelical Church is facing which are the common concern of the whole of Christendom. These are such fundamental questions as those respecting the nature of the Church, its witness, is freedom and its relation to the secular power. At the end of August the Universal Council will be meeting in Denmark. The Agenda of the Council will inevitably include a consideration of the religious issues raised by the present situation in the German Evangelical Church. It will also have to consider the wider questions which affect the life of all the Churches in Christendom. A Committee met last month in Paris to prepare for its work, and its report will shortly be published entitled, "The Church, the State, and the World Order." I hope that this meeting will assist the Churches in their friendship with each other, and in their task of reaching a common mind on the implications of their faith in relation to the dominant tendencies in modern thought and society, and in particular to the growing demands of the modern State.

The times are critical. Something beyond conferences and consultations is required. We need as never before to turn our thoughts and spirits to God. More earnest efforts must be made in our theological study. Above all more humble and fervent prayer must be offered to our Father in Heaven. May He, Who alone can lighten our darkness give us grace! May He, Who knows our weakness and our blindness, through a new outpouring of the Spirit enable the whole Church to bear its witness to its Lord with courage and faith!

(Signed) George Cicstr:
Ascensiontide 1934

"Humanity and the Refugees"

Bell was invited by the Jewish Historical Society to give the Lucien Wolf Memorial Lecture to a largely Jewish audience in London on February 1, 1939. Less than three months earlier, in November 1938, the infamous Kristallnacht *(Night of Broken Glass) had taken place in Germany, unleashing mob violence and destruction against Jews and their property. The refugee situation was becoming ever more critical. Bell here speaks out of his long-standing concern for refugees in a way that combines a sense of history and past wrongs with a comprehensive grasp of facts and statistics about the present crisis and, above all, a plea for humanity by governments, individuals, the churches, and all religious groups. He sees the crisis as a spiritual issue: "Our attitude to the refugees is a test of our attitude to God, well as of our attitude to man."*

George Bell, "Humanity and the Refugees," in *The Church and Humanity, 1939–1946* (London: Longmans, Green, 1946), 1–13

There is a striking sentence in the Epistles of St. Ignatius, one of the earliest Christian writers outside the New Testament, which I venture to quote.[1] St. Ignatius, Bishop of Antioch, is warning the members of his flock against certain dangers attending the association of Christian and Jew. And he makes this remark—"The Jew talking Christianity is better than the Christian talking Judaism." Well, ladies and gentlemen, I am here as a gentile Christian speaking to an audience mainly Jewish. But the principles of which I desire to give my witness are principles of humanity. And it is because I believe that the problems of the refugees, of whatever epoch or race, are the problems of humanity, that I am here on this platform. The problem of the refugees to-day, though in a special sense a problem of refugees of Jewish race, concern not Jewry alone, but mankind. And if there were no non-Jewish refugees in the whole world, it would still be the concern of mankind.

Again, the term "refugee," in the sense I have in mind, is not to be applied to those whose flight is due to natural calamities such as flood or pestilence or famine. I wish to use it only of those whose flight is caused by the action of human agents, other than themselves. It is, therefore, not action for which the particular refugee is, so to speak, criminally culpable. The distinction is nicely shown in the preamble of a statute of Edward I for the Government of London:—

---

[1] Editorial note: Some sections have been omitted from this extract: Bell's self-introductory opening paragraph, a poem by an unnamed author, and four paragraphs of general historical background in section 1.

Whereas divers persons do resort unto the city, some from parts
beyond the sea, and others of this land, and do there seek shelter
and refuge, by reason of banishment out of their own country,
or who for great offence or other misdeeds have fled from their
own country, and of these some do become brokers, hostelers and
innkeepers within the said city, for denizens and strangers, as freely
as though they were good and lawful men of the franchise of the
city; . . . It is provided, etc.[2]

II

I turn now to those huge refugee movements of which we ourselves
have personal and contemporary experience. They certainly are on
a scale much greater in their total bulk than any yet on record. And
there are signs that they have not reached their climax. Their causes,
partly political, partly religious, are the old causes, also greatly intensified, for the forces which drive men from their countries now are
Dictatorships and ideologies which, exercised and pursued with
fanatical fervour, are at once political and religious systems totalitarian in their claims. It is right, I think, to use the term 'religion'
of an ideology, even though it denies God, and knows no world
but the material world; because there is something apocalyptic about
the tremendous will to create a new order out of the disasters and
distress of the present, which has in fact placed each dictator, be he
Communist or Fascist, Kemalist or National-Socialist, at the head
of his State.

But these refugee movements also represent a challenge to humanity. Indeed in some ways I believe that our attitude to the refugees
is a test of our attitude to God, well as of our attitude to man. It is a
question of the quality of our faith. To despair of being able to do anything, or to refuse to do anything, is to be guilty of infidelity, just as to
be the cause of men becoming refugees is to sin against the Almighty.
The evil can be cured. Its cure requires an awakening, not only
in the State which creates the refugees, but in the other countries of
the world. It requires the aid of a counter-religion, deeper and stronger than the Fascist or the Communist. It cannot be cured by politics
alone, though political acts, perhaps world-embracing, indispensable

---

[2] W. Cunningham, *Alien Immigrants in England*, 92.

for its final solution; political and economic acts, which break down the walls of nationalism and are directed to the return of freedom, and are inspired by far-reaching spiritual principles.

Since the beginning of the European War wave upon wave of refugees has broken on the Old World and in part on the New. Sir John Hope Simpson in his masterly report on *The Refugee Problem*[3] has given a clear and precise account of the existing situation. There are the Greek, Bulgarian and Turkish national refugee migrations, involving over two million people in all, which are practically completed. There are the Armenian and Assyrian deportations, massacres and flights, leaving refugee problems still, to our dishonour, unsolved. There is the Russian emigration, dispersed in many countries and most variously composed, numbering rather less than a million, stabilised, to a certain extent, after twenty years, but faced with the grave economic problem of supporting aged unemployables from rapidly diminishing resources. Finally, there are those later movements from European countries caused by civil wars, or the rise of Fascist States, the Italian, the German, the Czech and now the Spanish, refugees.

I must ask your indulgence if I speak at greater length of the refugees potential and actual from Germany. But these refugees for various reasons make a special claim on our thoughts; and although their problem is not a solely Jewish problem, it is obvious that Jewish interests are very deeply involved. I shall not burden you with facts and figures, or the details of the various processes and laws which the National-Socialist regime has set in motion against the members of the Jewish race. You know them only too well. It is sufficient to say, regarding numbers, that in addition to the 165,000 refugees who have actually fled from Germany, there are another 500,000 Jews who are potential refugees in Germany and Austria, and a body of 'non-Aryan' Christians of unknown magnitude, in addition to the very many others who are potential refugees on grounds other than race. It is sufficient to say that the Nuremberg laws and their sequel revive in modern dress some of those very practices and persecutions which the fourth Lateran Council initiated, as already described, just 734 years ago; denial of civic rights, exclusion from public office and employment, prohibition of marriage with non-Jews, segregation, confiscation of goods, persecution and expulsion. It is a terrible

---

[3] Oxford University Press, 1939.

catalogue of crimes, of unspeakable damage to both oppressor and victim; for the degradation of the persecutor is no less terrible than the humiliation of the persecuted people.

But what are we to do when confronted with a tragedy so great? Let me put and answer a preliminary question often asked by official spokesmen in the National-Socialist State. "What business is it of other countries like England?" It is our business because we are human beings. If humanity means anything it is impossible to shut our eyes. It is equally impossible to refuse to take action. But let me give a further argument. We all appreciate the soundness of the general rule which forbids intervention in the domestic affairs of other states. But many eminent authorities, from Grotius to those of our own day, have recognised the right of intercession to protect the victims of persecution and oppression. Grotius, writing early in the 16th century, qualified the general rule of non-intervention by pointing out that

> The case is different if the wrong be manifest. If a tyrant ... practises atrocities towards his subjects, which no just man can approve, the right of human social connection is not cut off in such a case.[4]

And other well-known jurists, German as well as British and French, can be quoted in the same sense. There are also precedents for successful humanitarian intercession; amongst them one, I am glad to say, by Great Britain on behalf of the Jews in Bohemia. When in December, 1744, Jews were banished from the Kingdom of Bohemia, the sympathies of Great Britain and Holland were enlisted to make representations to Empress Maria Theresa. Lord Harrington instructed the British Ambassador in Vienna to exert himself 'with all possible Zeal and Diligence' in the endeavour

> to dissuade the Court of Vienna from putting the said Sentence in Execution, hinting to Them in the tenderest and most friendly Manner, the Prejudice that the World might conceive against the Queen's proceedings in that Affair, if such Numbers of innocent People were made to suffer.[5]

---

[4] *De Jure Belli et Pacis*, Whewell trans. Cambridge 1853 II, 308, 440.
[5] Quoted in *International Aspects of German Racial Policies*, Janowsky and Feagan, 52.

The appeal to humanity proved effective and the edict was revoked. But still more interesting as declarations of the right to intercede are two American utterances. The first is from the Note of the Secretary of State, John Hay, in 1902, regarding the flight of the Jews from Rumania. Describing the physical and moral oppression which sent them as refugees to the United States, he says:

> This Government cannot be a tacit party to such an international wrong. . . . It is constrained to protest against the treatment to which the Jews of Rumania are subjected, not alone because it has unimpeachable ground to remonstrate against the resultant injury to itself, but in the name of humanity.[6]

The second utterance is by President Harrison in 1891, and refers to the terrible persecution which caused the exodus of the Jews from Russia. He points, amongst other considerations, that the State which expels is *ipso facto* interfering with the rights of other States—

> The banishment, whether by direct decree or by no less certain indirect methods, of so large a number of men and women is not a local question. A decree to leave one country is, in the nature of things, an order to enter another,—some other. This consideration, as well as the suggestions of humanity, furnishes ample ground for the remonstrances which we have presented to Russia.[7]

No, I do not think that there is any doubt that other nations have the right to intervene on grounds of humanity, where conditions exist which create refugees. They have the right to show the prejudice that the world does conceive against the proceedings of the German State in the present affair. They have also the duty to do everything they can, in proportion to their means, for the succour of the victims.

III

Mr Chairman, I am not a statesman; I speak simply as a fellow minister of religion, who feels the plight of the refugees upon his conscience. But I believe that if only we could get the national conscience,

---

[6] *International Aspects*, 8.

[7] *International Aspects*, 18.

and the consciences of other nations, aroused, the statesmen, who must contrive the proper solution, will attack their task with decision, and, because they are determined, will succeed. I believe myself that it is possible to absorb in this country and other European countries a far greater number of Jewish, Christian and other refugees than have yet been envisaged. In France, apart from the Spaniards now pouring in, they already have 250,000 refugees, including 40,000 Jews. In Switzerland, with a population of five million there are 15,000; in England, till the other day, there were only 11,000 German refugees. It involves planning, of course. But actual experience has already proved that the employment of skilled refugees in England has created work for our own people and reduced unemployment. And apart from entry into the labour market, people in this country should be able and willing to receive a far larger number of refugees than have yet found an entry, whether in transit to other countries, or in homes for the older people, as well as the children now being introduced under a generous scheme for education in English schools. As Sir John Hope Simpson says of Great Britain

> Her initiative and role in International work would be greatly strengthened if she could show a braver record as a country of sanctuary.[8]

—in other words, if England would to-day live up to her reputation for hospitality in the past.

But when all allowance has been made for possible absorption in the old countries, the fact remains that the principal hope for the future of the refugees must lie out of Europe. It may be in Palestine. It may be in Northern Rhodesia, and other parts of Africa. But the hope must especially lie in the New World—the Americas, Australia and New Zealand.

It is also both a notable and an encouraging fact that when the terrible pogroms broke out in Russia in 1881, lasting thirty years, it was, apart from the much smaller influx into England, the United States that proved the sanctuary and the refuge for the Jewish refugees in their hundreds of thousands. Between 1881 and the close of the century over 600,000 Jewish refugees from Eastern Europe

---

[8] *The Refugee Problem*, 345.

landed in the American ports, and another half million had joined them by 1908.

The United States cannot do again on the same scale what it did 50 or 60 years ago, but what the United States achieved then is possible to-day for many parts of South America, and for Australia or other British Dominions, if only the will to help and the determination to succeed are present. Of course, there are all sorts of difficulties in the settling of hundreds of thousands of refugees. Colonisation as such, for refugees as such, is beset with problems, which have been frankly stated by Sir John Hope Simpson. But infiltration may be on so large a scale as to reach the proportions of a mass movement, such as it has reached in the case of Jewish refugees in Palestine. And the difficulties met in colonisation may be overcome, if a nation or body of nations could be found which will sink capital in a colonial experiment, without expecting a financial return for some generations, not because it is the nation or government of the refugee, but just because it sees that the refugee has no government or nation of his own behind him.

If humanity, as a quality, is to prevail, or if the interests of mankind are to be regarded as the dominant interests, such an exhibition of human brotherhood should not be ruled out as a sentimental dream.

I agree that all liberal countries, in the New World as well as in the Old World, should organise the right of asylum and assure the refugees of an undisturbed place in the community which has given them shelter. But the right of asylum, which carries with it the true kind of hope and encouragement, is that which is given in countries and in circumstances which allow new scope for creative living, and afford the refugee the chance to make the fullest contribution of his own gifts to the wealth of the community. The governments of the British Empire would act both wisely and nobly if they took the opportunity which the plight of the refugees provides for linking the problem of their migration with the problem of empire migration, and empire population generally.

I have spoken long enough. Permit me a few remarks only in conclusion. The movement of the refugees is an immense movement, and even in the last week the flood has grown through the coming of many thousands from Spain. There are signs that it may grow larger yet for a while, if the clouds of persecution extend to Hungary, Rumania, Poland and Lithuania.

But an end will come: justice, mercy, liberty will re-assert their sway. The oppression will cease, as it has ceased before. Belief in God, and the lessons of history, forbid us to despair. And it is of very good augury for a more liberal attitude all round, that the sympathy and generosity of the public have increased in a remarkable way since the events of November. In the meantime we must do everything we can to help the victims, of all classes and occupations and creeds. And this 'everything we can' means more than philanthropy or private charity.

I cannot conceal my admiration of the magnificent activities of the Jewish community for their co-religionists, and for some of my co-religionists, too. The Friends have done much. The academic and industrial and other organisations have done much. And the Christian churches, following Lord Baldwin's appeal, are doing far more than they have done before. But the refugee problem, on the scale it has reached to-day, is a problem which the State itself cannot escape. It is a problem which not only cannot begin to be solved without determined government action, but is of such a character that, if governments continue to let it drift, it may poison our whole civilisation. The High Commissioners, Mr. James Macdonald and Sir Neill Malcolm, have done what they could; and Sir Herbert Emerson will apply himself with zeal to the same task as High Commissioner. There is the Evian Intergovernmental Committee. But, as Sir John Hope Simpson says in the closing sentence of his book, while "the machinery for governmental action was created at Evian in July, 1938; the need is no longer for a machinery but for action."[9] The collaboration of the governments in a determined way and using their financial resources is the only possible cure. Political features, as well as economic, are involved in the problem of Eastern Jewry: and nobody can pretend that private charity can deal effectively with this. Everyone must sympathise deeply with the present preoccupations of Prime Ministers and cabinets. Their burden is extraordinarily heavy. But the refugee problem is inextricably bound up with the peace problem. Prime Ministers and their cabinets cannot afford to be passive here; for it is an essential part of the whole business of creating a true international order. The problem of the refugee is a political and economic problem, which cannot be solved unless the governments are determined that it shall be. It is a task which requires

---

[9] *The Refugee Problem*, 550.

generosity and courage and insight in the Heads of the governments and their advisers in the New World and in the Old. It is a task, the proper handling of which will make all the difference not only to men and women living to-day, but to posterity. For the problem of the refugee is the problem also of humanity.

"Christianity and War"

Bell's Christianity and World Order *appeared in 1940, the year in which Adolf Hitler was winning his most dramatic military victories in western Europe. Britain was successfully resisting the threatened invasion, but the longer-term outlook for the world remained dark and uncertain. In the book, Bell faces the crisis fully yet places it within a longer and wider crisis of thought in the light of Christian faith. He sees hope in certain responses of the churches, particularly on the ecumenical front.*

Chapter 7, "Christianity and War," is especially important for an understanding of Bell's mind in relation to war. He is sometimes, wrongly, labeled a pacifist, due largely to his outspoken opposition to the Allied obliteration bombing of German cities. This chapter, however, makes clear that while for several months after the outbreak of war he had hoped for a negotiated settlement with Hitler, the events of April and May 1940 had convinced him that the military defeat of Nazi Germany was essential to the future of Europe. Equally, however, he believed in the application of the "just war" doctrine to the conduct of war and in the nature of the church, even in the midst of world conflict, to hold to its calling as the universal body of Christ and not "to say ditto to the State." The passages extracted here also reflect his conversations with young people who had sought his counsel in relation to their personal decisions on whether to fight or take the noncombatant route.

George Bell, "Christianity and War," in *Christianity and World Order* (London: Penguin, 1940), 73–87

There can hardly be a greater contradiction than that between the teaching and example of Christ and war. Christ declares the fatherhood of God. War blasphemes God. The gospel of Christ is salvation.

War is destruction. The gospel affirms community. War denies it. The gospel stands for the imperishable worth of the individual personality. War shows the individual suddenly as an "isolated, helpless, powerless atom in a world of irrational monsters." Modern war is the demon that not only kills human lives, but by its awful unreason, its organization and invention, its perfection in the technique of mass murder, turns the individual from a *person* into an *unmeaning thing*. Unemployment is one of the demons which causes the despair of the masses. War is the other. Both are the fruits of a society founded on the doctrine of the economic man, both are unnatural because the social order out of which they come is an unnatural order—a radical disorder which requires a radical cure.

I think that it is more constructive to state the situation in these essential terms than to begin by posing the problem simply from the point of view of the justifiability of war, as an expression of force, or by asking whether a Christian may take up arms in this or any war. I shall have something to say about these questions before I have done. But it is impossible to begin even a brief treatment of the relations between Christianity and war, on the basis of the particular crisis of September 3rd, 1939.

We are often reminded that "justice," not "peace," is the supreme Christian aim. I understand what is meant, although in fact not only is real justice the foundation of real peace, but real peace and real justice are fundamentally inseparable. It is better to say that the Christian seeks Order; peace being (as S. Augustine said) "the tranquillity which springs from Order." And by "Order" is meant "a system of right relations."

There is an admirable essay on the "Tragedy of War" by V. S. Demant in the [1937] Oxford Conference volume of essays on *The Universal Church and the World of Nations*.[10] The tragedy of war, he says, is that "men are moved not so much by what they hope to get out of war, as by what they hope war will get them out of." We may put it in another way. Nobody wants war for its own sake; while practically everybody wants peace. Those who make war make it because they want an alteration to existing conditions, and can find no other way of making that alteration. To be an ardent supporter of peace need not, however, prove very much about the attitude adopted towards justice

---

[10] *The Universal Church and the World of Nations*, 175.

by the particular individual or nation. The maintenance of peace, without any provision for securing alterations by peaceable means is perfectly consistent with a hardened injustice. As Professor E. S. Carr reminds us with great point in *The Twenty Years Crisis*, every great power (except perhaps Italy) for many years after the World War repeatedly did lip service to the doctrine of the common interest in peace, by declaring peace to be one of the main objects of its policy, "Peace must prevail, must come before all" (Briand, 1928). "The maintenance of peace is the first objective of British foreign policy" (Eden, 1935). "Peace is our dearest treasure" (Hitler, 1937).[11]

It is profoundly true that peace is the common interest of humanity. But it is a part of the consequence of this truth that peace, as the tranquillity which springs from Order, often demands great sacrifices from those who are the immediate beneficiaries from the *status quo*. It is also true that those who have opposed all non-warlike procedures for the alteration of the *status quo* in the interests of Order, are in effect enemies rather than friends of peace. It is part of the pathos of the immense movement in favour of peace in many European countries, that their Governments have failed to understand "the things that belong to their peace," by failing to recognise the legitimate needs of others. It is part of the tragedy in which we are involved that the British and other great Powers could not bring themselves to see that peace, as dependent on Order, must be costly to them; and that a sincere devotion to peace involves a sharing of goods, and a redistribution of possessions so as to secure right relations between all the Powers.

Nobody wants war for its own sake. But some will go to war, will "put up" with war, for the sake of getting something which they cannot get without it. Hitler's own behaviour affords an excellent illustration of this truth. He said he did not want war. But he "put up" with war because he did want (let us say) the cancellation of the Versailles Treaty, and Czechoslovakia, and Poland, and Danzig, and Germany for all the Germans, and iron-ore and raw materials, and colonies, and a world empire, etc.[12]

---

[11] Editorial note: Bell here inserts a quotation from E. H. Carr, *The Twenty Years' Crisis* (London: Macmillan, 1939), 68.

[12] Editorial note: Bell here inserts a quotation from a letter of Hitler to the French prime minister Deladier, August 27, 1939, in which Hitler insists, "The diktat of

Hitler's astonishment and disappointment that the Allies should in fact go to war because of his proposal to make a bloodless conquest of Poland are similar evidence of the truth of the argument. The proposal was a criminal proposal. The threat was a terrible weapon to use, a criminal threat. Hitler's object was remorselessly clear. It was the reversal of the Treaty of Versailles, without war if possible, but reversal whatever the price.

II

War springs from disorder. Deep among the causes of the present disorder is economic aggressiveness. Commerce is said to be a peaceful occupation. But as carried on to-day it is a grim struggle for existence. It is not a struggle for existence, says Demant, except to a minor extent: "It is the absence of an economic mechanism for reciprocal trade in goods and services that prevents satisfaction of the claims of dissatisfied nations."

Yet the world is so rich. The material resources of the earth, more abundant than ever, are now made immeasurably more available than ever, through human organization and invention. It is a tragedy that, instead of combining in order to distribute those resources in due proportion among all human beings, men keep up the prices, and in order to do so, throw the surplus away.

Why is the world the scene of such struggling? Why do men turn commerce into a grim struggle for existence? The root cause is—they have forgotten God.

To remember God means that men have peace, together with life's good things duly shared and used. S. Augustine says in the *City of God* that he that uses the good things (light, air, water and all the other necessaries of meat, drink and clothing) "in their due manner, and with reference unto human peace, shall be rewarded with gifts of far greater moment, namely with the peace of immortality, and with unshaded glory, and full fruition of God, and his brother, in the same God. *But he that uses them amiss shall neither partake of the former nor the latter.*"

Our world has forgotten God. In Demant's words:

Versailles was intolerable."

> The natural social order minus supernatural truth has become
> unnatural. It is this unnaturalness of present-day secular exis-
> tence that causes the economic, social, and psychic dilemmas
> which drive peoples into militant attitudes. The social problem
> is therefore intimately related to the central religious problem of
> our time.[13]

All is godless, and therefore all is unnatural. In our godlessness we
have become so complicated. We are confused with organization.
We pour out money on buildings and machines! We incur vast expenditure on artificial amusements, and colossal public debt! Indeed, it
may be truly said that we spend so much on *doles* and *cinemas* (the
modern equivalent of *panem et circenses*) that we have quite forgotten
the natural things on which the human being lives, and have failed to
demand the simple social and economic arrangements which would
make these natural things generally available.

We might have used all our strength, nationally and internationally, to secure the easy enjoyment by all of the world's wealth, and so
have done something to save the world from war. Instead we have
promoted an artificial short-lived prosperity by a fantastic development of the armament industry. We have sought to cast out the Satan
of unemployment by the Satan of war! When we might all the while
have been casting out war by making economic order!

So we sink under the terrifying burden of trying to make the
over-complicated human organization work better and harder on
the old lines, instead of believing in God's power to save and to give
men tasks and put them in places where personal effort and spiritual
freedom will have far greater play. God has the power, if we will let
Him use us. He gives us His Grace to work the revolution which will
make life both purer and simpler, distributing His goods for the use
of human beings according as they are needed and can be enjoyed.

Thus we must base all peace work on the assumption implicit in
Christian theology that sin is a fall and redemption a recovery. Just
as sin is a fall and redemption is a recovery, so war is a fall and peace
has to be recovered. Peace has to be re-discovered by re-discovering
order. Peace and true prosperity can be achieved together if man
is faithful to the purpose for which God made him. And we must

---

[13] *The Universal Church*, 194.

begin here and now in the particular national community to which we belong in the effort to that peace. We must not wait for other nations and places before we ourselves make a start, for that means waiting for ever.

God alone has power to save. It is for men to respond to God's leading. It is when men have broken God's law and have pursued their own interests, and have refused to share their goods with their brothers, that war comes. War descends as the judgement of God. It is not some quite foreign corruption superimposed upon a body healthy up to that point. It is not the gathering of thorns from vines, or thistles from fig trees. On the contrary, it is the unescapable consequence of the reign of violence, cruelty, selfishness, hatred among men and nations. "From whence come Wars and fighting among you? Come they not hence, even of your lusts that war in your members?" (James 4:1) They are a judgement brought by men upon their own heads. "When the natural moral law is denied and rejected," says Cardinal Faulhaber in a recent pastoral letter, "darkness descends upon the earth."[14]

We have all sinned and fallen short of the glory of God. Part at least of the origin of the Nazi reign of violence now established in Germany, with its fearful consequences in the brutality to the Jews, in the persecution of political opponents, in the antagonism to the Christian religion, in all that is involved in the system of the secret police and the concentration camps, is to be found in the blindness and unbrotherliness to Germany after the World War of those who defeated Germany. No doubt other causes also existed in Germany itself, such as the cruel strain which is found not seldom in certain expressions of the German character. Yet it is surely also true that historians of the future will connect the uprush of Hitler and the regime of terror which he began in 1933 with failures and faults on the Allies' part since 1919. This is in no sense to excuse Hitler's treachery and falsehoods and violence, for his "offence is rank, it smells to heaven." If the spirit by which he is infected were to prevail, it would be the destruction of that order and liberty which are ours, and the overthrow of those standards of morality on which the civilization of Europe and the world depends. Yet war is a judgement, and it may

---

[14] Editorial note: Cardinal Michael von Faulhaber, archbishop of Munich, a critic of Nazi policy.

well be a part of the judgement exacted from us British people, that we should be compelled, as a matter of stern duty, and at the cost of great suffering, to resist the aggressor with all our power.

III

There are two special questions which have yet to be discussed. Is there such a thing as a just war? And is a Christian justified in fighting against the enemy?

Is there such a thing as a just war? The thirty-seventh Article of religion of the Church of England says: "It is lawful for Christian men, at the commandment of the magistrate, to wear weapons, and serve in the wars." The Roman Catholic Church refuses to condemn war absolutely, but lays down the precise conditions with which a war must comply in order to remain within the limits of justice. These are set out, for example, in *A Code of International Ethics* issued from the Roman Catholic University of Louvain. . . . It is there stated that Catholic theologians and moralists have constantly and unanimously taught that for a war to be just, it must:—

(a) Have been declared by a legitimate authority.
(b) Have a grave and just cause, proportioned to the evils it brings about.
(c) Only be undertaken after all means of peaceful solution to the conflict have been exhausted without success.
(d) Have serious chances of success.
(e) Be carried out with a right intention.

They add further that:—

> "It is also necessary that *moderation* should characterize the conduct of hostilities and should keep the demands of the victor within the limits of justice and charity."

It would seem exceedingly difficult for any modern war to satisfy all these conditions.

If we take the question in a more general way, we are bound to admit that there is no international authority which possesses a recognized power to declare that any particular war is just. On the other hand, it would seem clear that a war genuinely conducted for self-preservation is a justifiable war, and we can enlarge the "self" in this case so as to include a continent like Europe, which appears as a more or less consistent whole. Scrupulous care still has to be taken to be sure that the particular war is a war of self-preservation and is not a preventive war, but a war in which arms are taken up against an undoubted aggressor. It would not, however, apart from any binding obligations solemnly undertaken by treaty or by membership of a league, seem justifiable for Great Britain, for example, to go campaigning into war on behalf of remote places outside Europe with which it had no links whatsoever.

IV

Ought a Christian to fight?—*i.e.*, bear a combatant part in war regarded as actual belligerency.

There is the view of the absolute Pacifist which holds that war is a denial of the nature of God as love, of the redemptive way of the Cross, and of the community of the Holy Spirit, and is therefore always sin. The absolute Pacifist says that it is therefore utterly wrong for a Christian to take part in war. It is a difficult position to justify in the world as it is. For it is not possible to conduct the daily business of the world except by the use and discipline of some kind of force. To refuse to use force absolutely is logically, surely, to be anarchic.

There is the view of the utilitarian pacifist, which, while not regarding war as absolutely wrong in principle, declares that in modern conditions any war is bound to cause more harm, more sin, more suffering than any good it can possibly do. And it is indeed a question whether any war does not involve unspeakable suffering for which, however much may be vindicated by the terrible action of war, compensation, taking a long view, in the moral field, is extremely difficult to discover.

But there is the other view, which is the view of those who are not pacifists. Some would hold that a Christian is bound to fight whenever his country commands. It is to my mind impossible for a citizen to commit his conscience so unreservedly to the rulers of the State. It would seem to me to be that the only justification of combatant service which is ultimately defensible as a Christian view, is that which holds that a Christian is bound to fight for his country because of his duty as a citizen, *unless he is absolutely convinced that the war which his country makes is unjust.* To quote the Report of the Oxford Conference:

> It is therefore a Christian's duty to obey the political authority as far as possible, and to refrain from everything that is apt to weaken it. This means that normally a Christian must take up arms for his country. Only when he is absolutely certain that his country is fighting for a wrong cause (*e.g.*, in case of an unjustifiable war of aggression) has the ordinary citizen a right to refuse military service.[15]

There is clearly, therefore, a division among Christians as to the rightness of Christians undertaking combatant service.

I sympathize deeply with the feelings of those who are tormented with the doubt of it ever being right in any circumstances—not to fight and die for your country—but to kill your brother. "Should a man kill his brother?" that is the question I have heard put by a young man called up for military service by the Military Service Act, and consenting to serve. It is dreadful to kill your brother when you, as a young man, have had nothing to do with the shaping of the process of these last twenty years, which has precipitated the war. It is all the more dreadful when the methods of killing him are as diabolical as those in use to-day. No Christian can fight, as those serving with modern fighting forces are obliged to fight, save (as it seems to me) with extreme reluctance, sustained by a strong sense of duty, and the personal conviction that, in all circumstances, no other course is morally possible for him. And when a Christian says he cannot fight, because his conscience will not allow him to kill his brother, then in my opinion such a man's opinion should be accepted, and he should be able to count on the support and sympathetic understanding of fellow-Christians who take another view.

In any war the decision has to be taken in the face of immediate events.

We are living in a tragic hour. The Christian must use the best means he has, facing a particular crisis, to come to a personal decision.[16]

---

[15] *The Churches Survey Their Task*, 181.

[16] Editorial note: Bell here adds two paragraphs on the terms of the Treaty of Versailles, imposed on Germany in 1919, and the resulting German sense of grievance.

The clash which is now upon us is a clash of moralities. The war is not just the protest of the injured German people against the victors of 1918. It is the war of a barbarian tyrant against civilization, and of violence against freedom. All the persecutions of Jew and Christian, and of political opponents; all the terror which finds expression in concentration camps, and expelled the refugees, is gathered to a head in this cruel war. Woe indeed to the man who unloosed it on Europe! To be whole-heartedly at this crisis on the British side in view of the immediate acts of treachery and pillage, which set the world on fire, seems a very plain duty. This is a moment in human history when it is impossible for the just man to be neutral.

Therefore, for the overwhelming majority of people in Britain, it is as clear as noonday on which side the aggressor is found and on which side the defender; on which side the championship of the just state appears and on which side barbarism. This does not mean that the just State is realized on the side of Britain, or that there are not many good men in Germany silently opposed to Hitler, as there are men in Britain unworthy of their cause. But it does mean that the direction in which the British are striving is towards that end, in contrast with the opposite direction taken by the Nazis. . . . So the overwhelming majority of the young men of the British Empire will back their conviction by fighting with the Forces. I have no doubt in my own mind that the results of a victory by Hitler would be so disastrous, morally and spiritually, that Christians ought to do their utmost to defeat him.[17]

V

But although the war is on, and although there is no doubt in most Englishmen's minds that they are fighting in defence of the Just State, the Christian, whether he be combatant or non-combatant, has a further duty. He will still seek, through the very torment of war, the establishment of order, and with order, peace. He cannot regard any

---

He states, however, that "nothing can excuse the absolute remorselessness of Adolf Hitler."

[17] Editorial note: Here Bell follows with a paragraph quoting from the 1937 Oxford Conference Report, on the calling of the church in wartime, to denounce war as the fruit of sin and for the church to remain united as the one body of Christ. See Oldham, *Churches Survey Their Task*, 59.

war as a "Christian war" or as a "holy war," for no war can be holy, though the object with which a particular nation undertakes it may be just. There is only one holy war—that against sin. The Christian soldier may rightly feel in such a war as the present that he is fighting to secure the *possibility* of the Christian faith's existence. But he cannot see in it a crusade, for a crusade means fighting in the name of the Cross. And because he still seeks order and peace, he will do everything possible to help forward non-violent ways of securing the aims which are sought by war, and be on the watch not to let slip any genuine chance of a negotiated peace which observes the principles of Order and Justice. In particular the Christian will urge that the real guarantee of future security is order, and a freely negotiated treaty. And he will also press for the objective consideration of such a strong guarantee as disarmament all round, as a guarantee which can be actually checked by the limitation of offensive weapons: particularly the abolition of the heaviest arms, especially suited for aggression— *e.g.*, tanks and artillery—and the prohibition of the dropping of bombs on the civil population outside the real battle zone.

It is indeed the duty of Christians—of the Church as Church—to exercise the prophetic function, both humbly and impartially declaring where justice lies, and guiding the moral conscience by the application of principles. The Church will also guard and maintain those moral principles in the war itself. It must not hesitate, if the occasion arises, to condemn the bombing of civilian populations quite outside the military zone by the military forces of its own nation. It should set itself against the propaganda of lies and hatred. It should oppose any war of extermination or enslavement, and enemy measures directly aimed at destroying the morale of a population. It will not be easy, as the war goes on, and the ferocity of attack and defence increases, and new problems, like the effect of a blockade, arise, with their hard consequences for neutrals, and former allies, as well as for the enemy.

One special task must fall to its lot. The Church must do everything it can to prevent the methods of barbarism and tyranny prevailing at home. One of the most tragic features of the war situation is the surrender, in important fields, of the defender of human freedom, good faith, and justice to the very spirit of militarism and oppression, the "evil things" against which we are fighting. For example, I do not hesitate to say that the British nation suffered a real moral defeat when, in violation of the principles of freedom and justice, the Government interned thousands of German and Austrian refugees, lovers of freedom, and suffering for freedom's cause, in Alien Internment Camps, under conditions involving mental cruelty and grave hardship both to those interned and to the relatives from whom they were separated.

And, besides this, Christians will realize that they share with other Christians in the enemy country the universal fellowship of the *Una Sancta*. All Christians acknowledge one Lord, whose claim upon them is such as to transcend all other loyalties. Here is the first obligation of the Church, to be in living fact the Church, a society with a unity so deep as to be indestructible by earthly divisions of race or nation or class. Links should be strengthened between the Churches in warring countries on both sides in any way that is possible, through the help of the Churches in neutral countries. Every effort should be made with the same help to preserve former contacts between Churchmen whose nations are divided by war. The Churches should be eager to minister spiritually and materially to prisoners of war and interned aliens. They should refuse to yield to the unreasoning popular clamour, which brings new suffering to those who fled from Nazi persecution for refuge on British soil. They should counteract and subdue vindictiveness, hatred, and lust for power and the desire for retaliation. Their supreme loyalty will be to Christ. The greatest service which the Church can render is to remain steadfast and loyal to its Lord and to test all claims of national interest rigorously by His Gospel. It is not the Church's function to say *ditto* to the State. And it is healthy to remind ourselves of the epigram composed by Sir John Squire in the world war:—

The Dilemma

God heard the embattled nations sing and shout
"Gott strafe England" and "God save the King!"
God this, God that, and God the other thing—
"Good God," said God, "I've got my work cut out."

Finally, the Church should pray not only for the nation in which God has placed it, but also for the enemies of the nation. To quote the Oxford Conference Report:—

If Christians in warring nations pray according to the pattern of prayer given by their Lord, they will not be "praying against" one another. The Church should witness in word, in sacramental life, and in action to the reality of the kingdom of God which transcends the world of nations. It should proclaim and obey the commandment of the Lord, "Love your enemies."

"The Church and the Future"

"The Church and the Future," the final chapter of Christianity and World Order, was written, Bell says, just as total war was beginning in the first half of 1940. It is a strong assertion of Christianity's distinctive and essential contribution to resist a descent into sheer barbarism and to bring hope for the future. In this, the church—recovering its unity and its strength through the ecumenical movement—is central to the divine purpose. His ecumenical imagination and far-sightedness are apparent here, and he follows up on Oldham's idea of local communities or "cells" as nuclei of Christian fellowship and witness. Further, his proposal for a "joint consultative body" to enable the Roman Catholic Church and other churches to collaborate can be seen as an early foreshadowing of what has only relatively recently come about with the formation of the Conference of Secretaries of Christian World Communions as well as other forms of cooperation between the WCC and the Roman Catholic Church following the Second Vatican Council.

George Bell, "The Church and the Future," in *Christianity and World Order*, 140–154

The answer of Christianity to man's search for order is a Revelation through events in history in which a Man is at the centre and God willed and did immortal things.[18] In that Man, Jesus of Nazareth, His life and death and resurrection, a New Age commenced. Christianity means primarily Jesus Christ with those events and the community of which He is the Head. It stands for God, the God who revealed Himself in Christ; and by that very fact, those who are Christians, also stand for God who is the God of Christ.

---

[18] Editorial note: The extract given here starts partway through the second paragraph of the original.

At the heart of Christianity stands the Church. Christianity without the Church is not Christianity. The Church is the community through which God intended that the life of Christ should find continual expression. The Church needs no justification based upon utilitarian grounds. It was created by the act of God. Its existence cannot be denied or disregarded. It is here. It is a fact. It lives a life. It offers worship to God. It is a rock. It possesses the Gospel, the revelation of the love of God in Christ, who was born and was crucified and rose from the dead. This is a fact of immense significance, which the human mind is compelled to recognize. It is a fact which places the Church among the things which cannot be destroyed.

I know very well that the history of the Church is stained with many instances of weakness, opportunism, inconsistency and wickedness. I know that there are some very poor and some very cowardly Christians. But Christians who obscure or deny or corrupt the witness and life of Christ are just so far bad Christians. . . . The Church, while composed of various kinds of people, some good, some weak, some bad, represents the revelation of God, the First things and the last Things, the supreme law which man is called to obey. It is a living body representing a living force. It owes its being to the act of God and declares God as Sovereign Ruler of Man, as Saviour, and as creative Spirit. Its very existence proclaims that God is, and that He is the truth.

II

These things being so, the Church is something far greater than a private society giving men a private religion and private satisfactions. It is for the world. It declares a law, and offers a Gospel to mankind. And its message is distinctive.

It speaks of the New Age and the new Spiritual Order which Christ has brought to human life. It speaks of the principles which that Spiritual Order embodies being the principles which ought to govern the relationships of men. It does not overvalue material things. On the contrary, it tells men of the citizenship which is in Heaven as being the indestructible possession of those who are united to Christ. And it bids them look not at the things which are seen, but at the things which are not; "for the things which are seen are temporal; but the things which are not seen are eternal."[19] The eternal things are present. The heavenly citizenship is enjoyed now. There is a spiritual world—active, dynamic, living—even here. But Christianity, though not over-valuing material things, draws conclusions in material terms. It insists on translation from the general into the particular; from principles into actions; from the eternal into the temporal. Indeed, the central doctrine of the Christian religion is the Incarnation, which means this very thing: "The Word (God) was made flesh (Man) and dwelt among us. The Eternal was translated into the temporal."

So God is the Lord of all life. Private and public affairs must all come under God's control. The social and the international order must be governed in accordance with God's commands. The relations of human beings to one another ought not to be those of an acquisitive society, but those of the members of a family all having the same care for one another; and all working for the common good and all seeing that there is real equality of opportunity for men and women, food and shelter, leisure and employment being provided in due measure for all, according to their needs and gifts.

Christianity demands such a translation from the spiritual into the temporal. It demands that man should have his due, his elementary rights. But it does not rest here. It does not identify itself with any programme purely social or political. It expects social justice, but is something much more. It still insists that, while the labourer is worthy of his hire, man is not only a worker for money and the things money buys, and that while man ought to have his daily bread, he does not live by bread alone. It teaches that man has a soul and that his nature finds its fulfilment in the spiritual order; that the spiritual is supreme, and that in Christ, and in His Church, the spiritual world is alive and dynamic, and that the enjoyment of its resources is within man's reach, and the experience of its reality open to man to-day, especially to men in community.

Therefore, when I am asked, "What must we do?" or "What shall we do?" there is the authoritative answer. "Change your way of life, be baptized into the Church (or act as baptism requires of every Churchman)." This means conversion and prayer and fellowship, with all its implications for private and public life and worship and

---

[19] II Cor. iv.18.

sharing. It means a vital contact with God in prayer. It means a definite faith. It means also an overhauling of the whole of a man's life
and the application of the Christian standard in all departments, and
it means reaching out to make other men Christians.

That is the general life. But special ways are also open to Christians as members of the Christian community. There is the way of
life lived in community under a rule, meeting the needs of a time
which calls for "new bold and prophetic experiments in Christian
living which might show the pattern for the remedy of community."[20]
It might be an agricultural community settlement. It might be a particular industrial enterprise, all the men and women engaged upon
it, of whatever status, regarding it genuinely not only as a form of
co-operation but also as an endeavour in which every member was
directed by the Church and took his part as a Christian worshipper,
work and worship going hand in hand. It might be a community of
persons following different callings but living under a common rule
of discipline and worship, and sharing their goods, or at least possessing their goods under a common direction. Such a community might
be of the nature of an Order of lay-men and women living in the
world. It was by Orders that civilization was rescued from darkness
or despair in earlier days. Then the religious communities—detached
from the world—kept the flame of religion and the lamp of culture
both burning. Perhaps lay communities of disciplined people living
in the world, yet having a certain detachment from it, might render
a like service to-day. The Third Order of St. Francis might provide a
model; or a new sort of Order, with grades of associates and full
members and novices; all under some kind of obedience, and undertaking a regular practice of worship and meditation.

It might be a parish, or even a portion of a parish, with the Church,
its scriptures and its sacraments as the centre; the church members
(or a company out of the church members) agreeing to live as men
and women who had a common spiritual life and were ready to
consider their material interests together as common.

There is another way also, which may be called the way of "Cells,"
according to which a few men and women—it may be only two or
three to begin with—surrender themselves to God, undertake a

---

[20] G. H. Gibson, "The Call for Christian Community," in *Community in Britain*, 1940.

simple but definite rule of life—public worship, Bible study, daily prayer and personal service—and go out after a while and collect others to join the Cell, each person making himself responsible for drawing in, say, two or three others. So the Cells would grow. And the more Cells there are the more will the work grow in proportion. The agenda for the Cell, in a meeting perhaps once a week for study and worship, need not only be confined to personal service as an outcome, but could include the extension of the rule of Christ in the village, the street, the town or the industry to which different members belonged.

We have to *live* the Christian life. We have been too secure in our attitude and practice, and too little aware of the call to bold witness.[21]

III

Christianity is not a fugitive and cloistered religion. It does not slink out of the race. It endures the dust and the heat. It sallies out and sees its adversaries. It is exercised and fully breathed.

This means, of course (among other things) that, to be really applied and active, Christianity must be in touch with modern needs, and the Church must be alive to modern conditions. . . . And the Church (no less than the State), if it is to meet the needs of modern life in all its pressure and energy, and also if it is to give an answer to the cries of those who despair, must know where it is going, what it has to say, and whither it will lead men and women. When I say the Church, I mean not only the Church of England, nor all the Christian communions in the British Isles, but the Church throughout the world.

In the German Church Conflict . . . men were often seen in the churches where Confessional Church leaders were preaching, who till that time had hardly been inside a church for many years. A prominent leader of the Confessional Church told me in 1934 that, observing the attendance in his own church of a man of independent standing in the town, and well known, but not accustomed to take part in church worship, he had asked him why he came. His reply

---

[21] Editorial note: Bell follows with four paragraphs on the need of Christians to show a deep commitment to Christ—no less than the Communists, Fascists, and Nazis show to their leaders.

was swift and clear. He said at once, "I come because I like to hear a brave word spoken!" The Church everywhere should be the Confessional Church. It should be everywhere the Church of the brave word. And it ought to be a rallying-ground for men who believe in such things. Indeed, I would say that in times like the present all those who stand for the things that cannot be shaken should give support to one another. Believers in justice and truth, in mercy and love, in art and poetry and music, have this as common ground: that the things they believe in are indestructible. Certainly, art, poetry and music are not the same things as the Christian religion. But they can be truly regarded as auxiliaries to it. The Christian religion can stand without them (as it could not stand without justice and truth). It can, and would, survive without them, even in the catacombs. I do not dispute it. But they have noble gifts to bring to Christianity. And without Christianity will *they*, and justice and truth, mercy and love, in the long run be able to survive? How great then is the need that those who stand for the indestructible things should live with, work with, and worship with the Christian Church![22]

All this gives a new urgency to the achievement of unity in Christian effort. This does not mean uniformity of belief, or worship, or government. Such a uniformity would be as undesirable as it would be impossible to secure. But it does mean far greater community in Christian public action. It does mean a very definitely closer collaboration in Christian education, in Christian social and moral witness, in the presentation of the Christian form of community life, and in the conversion of the world, whether that world be London or Paris, England or Germany, Europe or Africa; indeed it should be the whole world. And here again we require not plans for the future, but action *now*, with authority behind it.

We have in many different countries what are known as Christian Social Councils or Christian Councils on an interdenominational basis, and they are all of them representative organizations. . . . But they are as a rule starved financially. They often lack the popular appeal and the immediate contact with the congregations and parishes, partly because of the lack of funds to promote them. And what I am sure they require, to take England as an example, is the challenge

---

[22] Editorial note: Two paragraphs follow on the need for self-sacrificial Christian engagement in public life and, no less, spiritual discipline and prayer.

of a big common task like the conversion of England. They need the great drive which a great, well-planned, unspasmodic campaign towards such a goal would do more than anything else to secure. For by "the conversion of England" I mean nothing less than the turning of the interest and actions, the industries and professions, the sciences, and the arts, the universities and schools, the personal, economic and social life, of England, into the Christian way. Here is a task which is quite beyond the powers of any one denomination by itself. It is a task for which the whole united effort of the Christian Church is demanded, and the putting out of all its strength. There is need of a common plan, a long-range plan certainly, but commencing now. It is a task that brooks no delay.

There are similar Christian Councils in other countries, notably in the United States of America and in the Scandinavian countries. All need the great challenge.

We have also the World Council of the Churches (in process of formation) . . . in which the non-Roman Churches are associated together for common work. And here, too, an immense field opens out, if the constituent Churches, Eastern and Western alike, will co-operate to the full with one another, and with the younger Churches represented on the International Missionary Council, and if all are able to awake to the crucial nature of the task! The World Council might, I know, become merely a useful centre for research and consultation. But given the loyalty, the adequate financial support, the effective self-sacrifice, of the Churches, and their spiritual devotion, it might give invaluable help to the churches in working together in real earnest for the conversion of Western civilization. That civilization has lost its moral bases. Each Church is its own country—or should we not say each organ of the Universal Church in the particular country—revived and rekindled, has its own particular task which it alone can do. But the sense that all Christians are engaged in a common effort in all countries for the "conversion of the West"—and indeed of the world—gives a new *élan* of incalculable value to the action of each. It is profoundly true that "our wrestling is not against flesh and blood, but against the principalities, against the powers, against the world rulers of this darkness,[23] against the spiritual hosts of wickedness in the heavenly places." The conflict in

---

[23] Eph. 6:12.

which we are all engaged—all Christians everywhere, in France and Britain, in England and Germany, in Russia and Poland and Italy, and in all the countries of the world—is a spiritual conflict, for which the whole Church needs the whole armour of God!

VI

What of the possibilities of collaboration between the Roman Catholic Church and the rest of Christendom? Clearly enough every ounce of Christian strength is needed for this spiritual conflict. It will be a sad day indeed, and would add inconceivably to the difficulties of a real extension of the rite of Christ throughout the world, including the reconversion of the West, if the Church of Rome were to stand unalterably apart. She is a great Church. She has great teachers. She possesses a great store of wisdom, and not the least of the treasures in her store consists of the Encyclical Letters issued by successive Popes, especially Leo XIII, Pius XI, and the present Pope, during the last sixty years, dealing with social and political doctrines.

The attitude of Rome in questions concerning Faith and Order has been made abundantly clear. There is no sign of unity in that field. But provided that there are safeguards assuring that the dogmatic field of Faith and Order remains unaffected, the present Pope has used language which has, and was certainly intended to have, a definite encouraging character. In *Summi Pontificatus* he said, speaking of contemporary dangers and anxieties:—

> "Among all those who believe that there is a God and follow Jesus Christ as their Leader and Master they may well give strength to the recollection that a common peril, one and the same everywhere, hangs over us all."

Still more clearly in his Christmas Eve address to the College of Cardinals, December 14th 1939, known as *The Pope's Five Peace Points*, he said, referring to the rulers of the nations:—

> They must cultivate that hunger and thirst after justice which is proclaimed as a beatitude in the Sermon on the Mount and which supposes as its natural foundation the moral virtue of justice; they must be guided by that universal love which is the compendium

and most general expression of the Christian ideal, and which therefore may serve as a common ground also for those who have not the blessing of sharing the same faith with us.

How is the "common ground" to be interpreted? And how are "all those who believe that there is a God and follow Jesus Christ as their leader and Master" to face the "common peril"?

It would be rash for an individual belonging to a different Church to attempt an answer to this question. And yet it may well be that on finding it soon depends more than we can understand at present for the future of Western Civilization and the influence of the Christian faith on the whole world.

There are many difficulties on both the Roman and the non-Roman side. Yet so great is the crisis in the world that ancient difficulties ought not now to be allowed to stand in the way, if there is any possible method of overcoming them, and where the "common ground" is so clearly admitted. The last thing I would wish to give the impression of suggesting in these words is any kind of *dogmatic* unity. I know the Roman, the Protestant and the Orthodox positions too well and I respect them too deeply, for that. But collaboration in a limited field, based on consultation, with safeguards for dogmatic differences, should not be impractical. The Encyclical Letters themselves contain such profound and weighty doctrine, that it ought not to be confined to the enlightenment of Catholic thought. And there are documents, also containing weighty doctrine, issued by other bodies, less authoritative but still of service, which have their real contributions to give. Yet it is not only or chiefly documents that should be considered. It is the contact of minds and experiences, and even of traditions, interpreted by living personalities. We need the meeting face to face of Roman Catholic and other Christian theologians, economists, social and political thinkers, experts in international law, in conciliation, in international action of various kinds; with the releasing of spiritual energies to which such a meeting would surely lead in Christian communions generally.

I should like, in other words, to see some kind of Christian Consultative Body capable of meeting from time to time, over which it would be natural that, probably at Rome itself, the Pope or his representative should preside, while certain of the great Churches of the world would send their own accredited representatives to take their part. Under this Christian Consultative Body I should like to see a Standing Theological and Expert Commission, also representative but quite small in numbers, with a joint secretariat adequately staffed, which should both work out the implications of "that hunger and thirst after justice which is proclaimed as a beatitude in the Sermon on the Mount" and that "universal love which is the compendium and most general expression of the Christian ideal, and which therefore may serve as a common ground"; and be entitled to make definite recommendations to the Consultative Body, or, indeed, to the authorities of the Christian Communions represented, with a view to action. I do not say that the proposal thus sketched would work out exactly as I suggest. It is but a sketch. It might lead to the allocation of some particular position in the total "common ground" to the Roman Catholics. But some such project would lead, I hope, to collaboration and consultation in some specific and evident way which would be known to the world.

VII

And yet, though all these questions of consultation and collaboration are important, the Church is not to be regarded simply on the plane of organization. It is the Spirit-bearing Body of Christ. It brings grace. It offers worship. It is an organ of spiritual life. It is the divine community founded on Love. When Christ came a new allegiance entered into the world. Those who did the will of God He described as His brothers and sisters—his mother and His brethren. It was an allegiance destined to outlive all other totalitarian claims, whether those of Caesar in the early centuries or those of caste and nation and Communism in the twentieth. It is an allegiance also which has nothing individualist about it, but involves the community, and is an integral part of the idea of the Church. The Church is God's own creation. It is a community of life as well as love. As such it stands over against all denials of life. It declares, because it is the Body through which Christ works, that Love is the only possible basis of human unity, and that enmity and estrangement make freedom impossible and are the frustration of life's purpose. It proclaims this truth in all circumstances, and the kindred truth that God's purpose in the world is the creation of Man as a personal community of free and equal persons. Its very existence testifies to the spirit which is the opposite of war. Indeed, it bids men renounce the will to power because the will to power is the negation of the will of God for man. It bids men renounce war not only because war brings bitter suffering, but because it makes men seek power as an end in itself. As the will to power is the negation of the will of God for man, so Love is the fulfilment of His will. The Church is the divine community founded on Love. It is in God's plan the supreme means for the unification of mankind.

"If Thine Enemy Hunger"

Bell addressed this sermon to a British radio audience on March 3, 1946. It was a winter when British people were experiencing increasing postwar hardship with food and fuel shortages and rationing. Here Bell the bishop, theologian, and ecumenical leader speaks simply as an evangelist and pastor, calling his hearers to act compassionately toward people irrespective of their status or nationality, including their former enemies in Germany, who are suffering even more hardship than they. He calls them to act not out of a kind of moral heroism but simply in response to the all-embracing, costly love of God.

George Bell, *The Church and Humanity, 1939-1946* (London: Longmans, Green, 1946), 168-172

> If thine enemy hunger, feed him; if he thirst, give him drink. . . . Be not overcome of evil, but overcome evil with good. —Romans 12. 20, 21.

A good deal of water has flowed under the bridges since the first address was given in this course. Every day brings fresh evidence of the suffering of the world. Every day, therefore, brings home the urgency of the question with which the course deals. It is briefly this: in face of the tragedies which crowd round on all sides, is there any call for me to do something about them because I am a Christian? When a man or a woman is suffering, ought I to help?

Take the latest illustration. Last Wednesday it was announced in Berlin that a drastic cut would be made in the rations for the Germans in the British zone, starting to-morrow. This will have the result that, unless there is a radical change and a great addition is made to present supplies, very large numbers will certainly die of starvation. We in Britain are going through difficult times in the way of food, but nothing comparable to that. Ought we, as Christians, to take any notice of it? Am I my brother's keeper?

That is but a single example of the tragedy of the present situation, and of men's need of help; but it is very apt for our purpose. I am going to talk this morning of justice and love, of the relationship between them. And I hope to show you that while, in this present tormented world the achievement of justice now would be a victory beyond price, justice by itself is not enough. I want to suggest that the Christian has a call, which he may not disobey, to go further than justice demands. If you are a Christian, you must not only be your brother's keeper in the sense of refusing to commit the sin of murder which Cain committed; you must save your brother; you must do everything possible to meet all his needs.

Christianity is a religion of two Testaments, the law and the gospel, justice and love. Justice has indeed been described as a sort of protective fence, within which the life of love can be developed; or as a soil out of which it can grow. It means giving to all their due. The Christian must render full loyalty to justice. He must respect law. He must be very clear about the obligations of the claims of justice, and he must fulfil those claims. It would never do, for example, to behave like that Indian Christian who, being heavily in debt, and having unexpectedly received a large legacy, gave the whole of it away to the poor of the neighbourhood, paying nothing to his creditors and keeping nothing for himself. He forgot that Christian charity begins where legal obligation ends, but not before. But while the Christian must certainly pay his dues, and, for example, must not give away money which is not his, he must not stop there. In the example which I gave of the Germans starving, from the point of view of bare justice one objector might say, 'It serves them right,' on the theory of treating people according to their deserts (though it would be hard to defend the application of his statement to, among others, the children). Or another objector might say, 'Well, there is only a limited amount to go round, and it is surely just that the nations who fought by our side and are still in distress should have the first claim.' But the Christian must go out of his way to help. Whatever may be said about the justice of leaving the Germans to their fate (and I wholly disagree as to its justice), it is quite another thing to defend leaving the Germans to their fate as a Christian action.

This is only an example in a controversial field; and you will want me to justify my statement that, however precious the achievement of justice must be—and it is most precious—the Christian, while doing everything he can to achieve that justice, cannot be content, when it has been achieved, to stop there. So let me offer an illustration from our Lord's parables. The parable of the Prodigal Son describes a father receiving back his sinful but penitent son with open arms. So far as deserving is concerned, the Prodigal had wasted his substance with riotous living, and when everything had failed, and he was completely down and out, he turned his face towards home. If his father had treated him with justice only, he would surely have said, 'My son, I am glad to find that you have thought better of your wild ways. But your conduct has been very bad, and though you tell me you are sorry, I am not yet prepared to receive you back into my house till you have proved by your efforts over a sufficient time that you are cured of your vices. You shall have your due; and if you will go and work in the fields with my hired servants, you shall have the same payment as they have, and later on I will consider the matter afresh.' Nobody could have quarrelled with the justice of such a decision. But the actual picture which Jesus gave of the father to whom the Prodigal Son returned was very different from that. It was of a father who went out and fell on his son's neck and kissed him: who clothed him with the best robe, and killed the fatted calf to feast him, just as he was. There was the difference between justice, giving the Prodigal his due, and love, giving him far more than his due, without desert, and spontaneously.

I need not quote more parables. The whole action of our Lord's life moved on this plane. 'I am not come,' He said, 'to call the righteous, but sinners.' It was a complete reversal of values. 'Joy shall be in heaven over one sinner that repenteth, more than over ninety and nine just persons which need no repentance.' The very substance of legal religion was being transcended in the name of God. It was God who called the sinner to a fellowship with Himself, characterised not by law but by love. It was just the opposite of what the Jew of our Lord's day was expecting. And even now, the more you think of its real meaning, the more completely it takes your breath away. What God offers us in Jesus—through His words and through His Cross—is not justice, not the punishment we deserve, 'Use every man after his desert, and who should 'scape whipping?' said Shakespeare—but love. God is not counting up our good deeds and our bad deeds, with a view to a carefully calculated settlement based on the entries in a ledger: you and I need only look into our own hearts to see how disastrous such a settlement would be, so far as each of us is concerned. But He freely offers us love, and love without ending.

Now, if that is really the case with regard to Jesus, some rather important consequences follow for those who claim to be His disciples. How can a man who has felt the free, generous love of God in the depths of his own soul, fail to be the minister of that love to his fellows? He is bound to love his neighbour, irrespective of whether the neighbour is personally friendly or unfriendly to him, and whether his character is attractive or unattractive. Indeed, the disciple of Jesus is called not only to love his neighbour, but to love his enemy: and he has to love his enemy in exactly the same way as God's love is poured out on sinners. Jesus said, 'Love your enemies . . . and pray for them which despitefully use you, and persecute you; that ye may be the children of your Father which is in heaven: for He maketh His sun to rise on the evil and on the good, and sendeth rain on the just and on the unjust.' And St. Paul said, in exactly the same spirit as his Master, 'If thine enemy hunger, feed him; if he thirst, give him drink: for in so doing thou shalt heap coals of fire on his head. Be not overcome of evil, but overcome evil with good.' The natural thing (he suggests by implication) to do with your enemy is to leave him to his fate—on the ground that, after all, he deserves it. But the Christian thing is to go out of your way to give him the food he so sorely needs. Love is creative. It is not a mere reaction to an outside influence, but a positive, active power. In fact, it is the teaching of the Christian religion that love is not only creative, but the ruling principle of the universe. It is the supreme form of cosmic energy, beside which all other forms, however physically great, in the end must pale. It did once inhabit a man—Jesus of Nazareth. It proved itself in Him to be the strongest force in the world, and its supreme expression was the sacrifice offered on the Cross. It was love revealed there which gave and gives life to millions.

With all the forces of destruction around us, physical and spiritual, it is this cosmic energy which alone can renew the world. It is here, waiting for men to believe in it, and to give themselves to it: or, rather,

God is here, controlling the cosmic energy and appealing to all of us to believe in Him, and to harness our souls to this energy, love. It is impossible to go on unless we heed His appeal. Yet the greatness of the revolution required in men's thinking is equally impossible to exaggerate. Men in the mass, that is, races and nations and classes, all too commonly conceive of life in terms of self-interest, which is the opposite of love; and it is because they do so that we are moving nearer and nearer to destruction. To harness our souls, as human persons, to this energy of love is to join in a re-creation.

But, let us make no mistake, to harness our souls to this energy of love means a spiritual and moral and political revolution. As the evil is so deep-seated, the victory over it, which such a revolution promises, can only come by degrees. Yet it is urgent that we should begin. If more and more people look out on the famine in India, with millions likely to die, on the hunger in Germany, on the misery of the homeless people of many nations, cut off from their families, some hopelessly tramping on the road, some in pitiful conditions in detention camps, with real compassion and a sincere desire to help: if more and more people had their consciences stricken with shame for war and all its cruelties: if more and more people were wounded in their hearts by the spectacle of poverty, of starvation, of unemployment: if more and more people looked with pity on the terror of those who have fled from their own country to find safety in a foreign land, lest the Government of that land should send them back, or compel them to suicide; I say, if more people in every nation took this suffering as a challenge to their humanity, and resolved that such things must not be, in any continent of the world to-day, the net in which all are caught would be broken, and the sense of impotence overcome. The sign that this can be done is the Cross of Christ: the power for doing it is given in the same Cross of Christ. Do not wait for an assessment of the merits of the case. Remember the spontaneousness of Christ. Remember, too, that justice is regulative—while love is creative; that is why justice by itself is inherently defective as a moral ideal. And do not wait till you can see your way clear through all stages. You can begin here and now, by harnessing your soul to the energy of love, for the brother who is with you in your home, the neighbour who lives next door, doing for each what you can, and by the very way you think and speak and pray for your former enemies in Germany and Japan. But let me also give you a warning. You must not think you can be a Christian and escape the Cross. Harnessing your soul to the cosmic energy of love means sacrifice: but it also means that, through the joining of such sacrifice to the sacrifice of Christ on the Cross, the world can be saved.

"The Approach to Christian Unity"

Bell was one of nine theologians of different church traditions who were invited to preach on Christian unity before the University of Cambridge in early 1951. His was the concluding sermon of the series. In the forefront of his mind is the formation of the Church of South India in 1947, which much Anglo-Catholic opinion had opposed over the issue of episcopal succession but that Bell himself had vigorously supported. The 1948 Lambeth Conference had given it qualified approval. Bell here upholds this union as an inspiring example of ecumenical commitment in contrast to the slowness of interchurch dialogue in Britain over the same period—that is, since the 1921 Lambeth Conference—and his sermon manifests his impatience with the British scene. What is striking above all is his highlighting of the missionary and evangelistic calling as the prime motivator of unity.

George Bell, "The Approach to Christian Unity," in *The Approach to Christian Unity: Sermons Preached before the University of Cambridge, 1951,* by University of Cambridge Select Preachers' Syndicate (Cambridge: W. Heffer & Sons, 1951), 57–63

> "Go ye therefore, and make disciples of all the nations, baptizing them in the name of the Father and of the Son and of the Holy Ghost." —St. Matthew 28:19.

The most casual observer of current affairs can hardly miss the steady advance in military force, and the energetic way in which a policy of rearmament is now being pursued on every side.[24] It is all the more melancholy, therefore, that the approaches which the Christian

---

[24] Editorial note: Bell in fact begins his sermon with two references to Charles Peguy and Otto Dibelius.

Churches make to the reunion of Christendom are so halting. It is true that many churchmen of different traditions are more conscious of the scandal of division than their forefathers were. But though there have been pioneers in the cause of unity, with few exceptions the churches have remained untouched. There has been little result in the achievement of unity between East and West since the Great Schism, or, since the Reformation, among the reformed churches themselves—far less between any one of them and the Church of Rome. The thing with which we are faced is not only the fact but the temper of isolation.

In the summing up of this course ... my first point is this. In all our churches, there is too little movement, and too much circumspection.

I have had to do with discussions on Christian unity between leading representatives of the Church of England and of other churches for over 30 years. In many I have been an active assistant, of all a close student. I have no hesitation in saying that there is one striking result common to all. There is a new spirit as between the leaders of these churches, a new charity and a new friendship. And here is the whole Ecumenical Movement, which is "the great new fact of our time."[25] These things are of first-rate importance. But when it comes to the expression of that spirit in the more concrete form of Church relations, there is little, if any, advance at all.

In spite of a certain *rapprochement des coeurs* in the case of individuals, the dogmatic breach between the Roman Catholic Church and the rest of Christendom has grown wider. The partnership of the Orthodox Church in the Ecumenical Movement is a most cheering event and ... has sometimes been very active. But, as Bishop Cassianos Besobrasoff also said, "For an Orthodox there can be no unity without inter-communion, and nevertheless no form of inter-communion is possible within the realm of the Ecumenical Movement."

Again, it is true that agreements have been reached between the Church of England and the Old Catholic Churches, and between the Church of England and the Churches of Sweden and Finland: but there have been none between the Church of England and the great Reformed non-episcopal Churches of the Continent. And here

---

[25] Editorial note: The remark is generally attributed to William Temple's sermon at his enthronement as the archbishop of Canterbury in 1942. More precisely, it was the worldwide Christian fellowship that Temple stated to be that "great new fact."

in England, with regard to the Free Churches, a few welcome steps have been taken by the Convocations in the matter of interchange of preachers, and permission to receive Communion in certain circumstances. But so far as the achievement of a visible unity is concerned, or the new outlook and new measures to which the Lambeth Appeal summoned all Christian people, we are no further forward in 1951 than we were in 1920. Indeed, in some ways, the reports of earlier conferences went further and were more hopeful than their successors. The conclusion of the latest report on *Church Relations in England*, after 30 years of conversation, says most plainly:

> The scandal of our age-long divisions will not be lightly or easily removed.
> Traditions harden, customs become fixed, and honest opinions are tenaciously held.

Yes, the pace is slow in the older historic churches. But there has been one outstanding event in this century's record of Christian Reunion. It happened in the mission field, and affected the younger churches: I mean the inauguration of the Church of South India. There the movement began with the Indian Christians, for whom the spreading of Christianity in a non-Christian territory with millions of Hindus was a matter of great urgency. Their conferences covered almost exactly the same 30 years as the conferences in England! But how different was the result! And, in spite of the problems that remain, what a lesson this union teaches!

I am persuaded that, just as it was the overwhelmingly powerful motive of the evangelisation of India that constrained Anglicans, Presbyterians and Methodists to unite in South India, it is the want of such a motive, as powerfully held, that is the real reason for our slowness at home. We have no over-mastering passion to preach the gospel to a non-Christian world.

I believe that it is in facing all those who call themselves Christians with those who are not Christians, or are lapsed Christians, that the most fruitful approach to Christian unity will be found. Let me therefore invite you to consider the Church in relation to the gospel from this point of view.

The Church in the New Testament is the new redeemed people of God. It is "the whole company of those who share in the regenerate life." As the Report of the Archbishops' Commission on Christian Doctrine put it in 1938—"When the Church is so conceived, its unity is comparable to that of a race of people, which, while it may be divided as regards the outward organizations which condition its life, yet it has a real and concrete unity underlying these divisions. . . . in the unity of God himself."[26]

I cannot speak for the Anglican Episcopate as a whole. But I would call attention to the statement made in the Report [of the 1938 Archbishops' Commission] . . . about the meaning of schism.

> The term "schism" has historically been used with some fluctuation of meaning. It should, however, be recognized that "schism," is, in fact, a division within the Christian Body. That Body is not to be thought of as consisting of a single true Church, or group of Churches, with a number of "schismatic" bodies gathered about it, but as a whole which is in a state of division or "schism." The various denominations may and do differ in respect to the degree in which they approximate either to orthodoxy of doctrine or to fulness of organized life; but, just in so far as their very existence as separate organizations constitutes a real division within Christendom, it becomes true to affirm that if any are in schism, all are in schism, so long as the breaches remain unhealed, and are affected by its consequences, at least in the sense that each in its own degree suffers the loss or defect involved in schism; and this irrespective of the question on which side rests the major responsibility for the schism.

I would also recall the two declarations in harmony with this, made nearly 30 years ago by the same two Archbishops and 12 leading Bishops of the time, one in 1922, allowing that some non-episcopal churches are parts of the visible Church, though defective, the other in 1923, acknowledging the ministries of such churches to be "real ministries of Christ's Word and Sacraments in the Universal Church," though again in varying degrees defective.

---

[26] Editorial note: Bell's next two paragraphs argue for the real difference between the church as the Christian people united in Christ and the church as the Christian people united in the world; he recalls the 1938 archbishops' report, *Doctrine in the Church of England* (London: SPCK 1938), listing the wide range of Anglican thinkers involved, and its bearing on the meaning of *schism*.

There are, I know, many in the Church of England who resist these statements. But the main trend of Anglican thought from Hooker to Temple is with the declarations and not against them. . . . What is wanted, however, to give such declarations decisive effect in the realm of action, is a common overmastering passion compelling Christians of these separated parts to preach the gospel to a non-Christian world as the Body of Christ. And to do this with the greatest effect there must be not uniformity but unity and the sacrifices which unity involves. I emphasize the need of sacrifice, as well as the need of a renewed vision of the Body of Christ, because, if there is no spirit of sacrifice, there will be no visible unity. It is true . . . that the advocates of reunion are only pioneers; and that the next problem is the education of the laity and clergy of every one of the separated communions. But is not this lack of concern due in very large part to a failure to grasp the titanic character of the task which the Church is set in the modern world? Is not the isolationism of individual denominations and congregations, and their concentration on themselves, and their traditions, the result of blindness to the needs of the world?

As others have pointed out, the Anglican and Free Church representatives in the most recent discussions have formally pronounced themselves agreed on fundamentals. "All acknowledge the apostolic faith as contained in the Scriptures and expressed in the Apostles' and Nicene creeds." But to draw them together into a visible unity a unity in the ministry is required. And it is generally agreed, in view of the fact that the Episcopate was from early times and for many centuries accepted, and by the greater part of the Church is still accepted, as the means whereby the authority of the whole body is given, that it ought to be accepted as such for the United Church of the future; without, however, disowning past ministries of Word and Sacrament otherwise received, or requiring the acceptance of the claim that episcopal ordination is the true and only guarantee of sacramental grace and right doctrine. Various methods have been proposed for the working out of this acceptance.

The Archbishop of Canterbury has recommended the process of assimilation, through the taking of episcopacy into the Free Churches' own systems, as a step towards full communion.

The Lambeth Conference of 1948, while not unsympathetic to this, preferred schemes for the achievement of organic union; noting in careful language that "the unification of the ministry in a form satisfactory to all the bodies concerned . . . is likely to be a prerequisite to success in all future proposals for the reunion of the Church."

I know many of the difficulties from the Free Church point of view. They are written large in the Free Church Federal Council's Reply of 1941. But the difficulties are not all on one side: for I know them only too well within the Church of England!

But can we, with a good conscience, remain satisfied with things as they are? Because we cannot have perfection from our own point of view—and do we really think we have perfection in our own churches now?—are we to refuse to suffer irregularities and anomalies for a while? Dare we sit down and do nothing?[27]

So finally, conscious of the privilege which I have been allowed in concluding this course of sermons on the Approach to Christian Unity, I plead both for the cooperation of all Christians on the non-dogmatic level, and for your work and your prayers for the realization of visible unity and the fulfilment of the Saviour's prayer that all may be one.

"Christ the Hope of the World"

In 1954, the second assembly of the WCC took place in Evanston, Illinois, under the theme "Christ the Hope of the World." To mark the occasion, Bell wrote his book The Kingship of Christ *and dedicated it to the members of the Central Committee, of which he had been chairman since the first assembly in 1948. It is one of his last books to be published and is in large part a survey, remarkably comprehensive in so small a compass, of the ecumenical journey from Edinburgh 1910 onward. The final chapter takes up the assembly theme with its title, "Christ the Hope of the World." Here his ecumenical spirit finds natural expression—for example, in citing both his martyred Lutheran friend, Bonhoeffer, and Pope Pius XI. Bell not only shares his vision but also bares his personal faith and hope and his love for the ecumenical fellowship more openly than in anything he had*

---

[27] Editorial note: Two paragraphs follow on the development of the WCC and possibilities for cooperation with the Roman Catholic Church.

*written before. Four years before his death, it is a fitting last will
and testament for the movement he served so tirelessly.*

George Bell, "Christ the Hope of the World," in *The Kingship
of Christ: The Story of the World Council of Churches* (London:
Penguin, 1954), 169–175

FALSE HOPES

When the Central Committee chose this theme, it was well aware
that the world was full of false hopes. These hopes may be variously
described. There are some who believe that the spread of a democracy without God, that is a democracy inspired by purely humanist
ideals, will at long last achieve the perfect society. Such men holding the ideals of equality, freedom, and justice, but without belief in
God, take little account of the frailty of the human factor. They also
assume far too easily that in societies committed to the democratic
way of life, none of these ideals is denied in practice. But inequality,
discrimination, injustice, reliance on naked power, exploitation, and
aggression are not absent from democracies.

Others believe that scientific humanism holds the key to the future
prosperity of man. The ground of the scientific humanist's hope lies
in man's past achievement. See, he says, with what astonishing success
man has subdued nature! How marvellously he has developed his own
mental powers, and created a specifically *human* world in the midst of
nature—that is, a civilized society! All honour to the scientists, whose
labour for the achievement of truth and the advancement of man is an
inspiration to all. But civilization is the sheet-anchor of the scientific
humanist's hope. If it disappears, then hope goes with it.

Others find the way to the perfect world in Marxism, with its appeal
to the disinherited and to those who long to help the oppressed, to
the more prosperous worker who feels frustrated in his work, and to the
scientist and politician impatient for a new day. Marxism teaches that
man has no fixed nature, but is continually being made and remade
in history, which in turn by social action he helps to make. It is not
only an analysis of history, but also a metaphysic and a religion. It
shows history as a class struggle, which the workers, deprived of
property, country, and family life, taught and led by a Communist
Party, and united across national frontiers can alone bring to an end

by means of a revolution. Then (it is claimed) the golden age will come. Nature will cease to be man's enemy. There will be no more social classes, no class struggle, no coercive government, no cause for violence. All the wealth that mankind has amassed through the years will be made available for all.

These and similar prophecies have an undoubted attraction. Nor must the Church fail to confess its share in the sins which have helped to open the way for the Communist campaign. But there is another side to the picture—the methods employed by Communist leaders to seize and hold power in the name of the proletariat, and the explicit Communist teaching that any means required to break the hold of class enemies are justified. In practice, moreover, the Communist doctrine of the dictatorship of the proletariat has led in most cases to totalitarian dictatorship, in which the freedom of man is in fact denied. But more fundamental is the flaw in the Marxist creed itself: the rejection of God and his sovereignty, the unfitness of the actual proletarian as a Messianic figure, and the falsity of the expectation that sinful man as we know him can achieve, by mere stripping away of economic disabilities, a genuine resolution of historic strife.

THE CHRISTIAN HOPE

It is in contrast with this despair and with these false hopes that the World Council of Churches proclaims "Christ the Hope of the World." The Christian hope is not "a strong desire" for something which may be possible but is not certain. It is the product in us of God's acts in history, and above all of his act in raising Jesus Christ from the dead. Everything for the Christian centres on Jesus Christ. In Christ God fulfilled the hope of earlier times, and transformed it, in Jesus of Nazareth.

On the basis of the Bible, the Christian hope for the world can be seen to have two aspects. On the one hand, it calls men to acknowledge the ever-present rule of God, which means that man and the world have a definite purpose, that there are principles and standards for human society, rooted in God's everlasting will, for which man can work. There is something greater than the greatest of man's achievements, or even of his dreams, and the individual is not merely the product of his own efforts or of the discoveries of minds profounder than his own or of some impersonal process, but lives always as a son of God. For, in Christ, every man may know and work with the will of the Father, and be guided in all his efforts by the personal inspiration of the Holy Spirit.

On the other hand, there is nothing Utopian about the Christian hope. If the Church is not the Kingdom, no more is any human social order, however perfectly infused by the teachings of the Gospel. For God's Kingdom embraces the entire universe, and it involves, in the language of the New Testament, a new creation, a new world. It is always to this that the Christian faith points, and the Church surely and confidently preaches the ultimate realization of God's Kingdom in all its fullness because of its belief in the person and the work of Christ. In Him, the sting of evil in the world as it is now was drawn, the existing world-rulers of every kind were brought under God's rule, and there can be no reversal of this victory. In the future, men's highest hopes and profoundest schemes for society may come to grief as they have so often in the past. But this will not mean that they have been in vain, for it is to the establishment of God's Kingdom that they are directed, and this will at the last be achieved in God's own purpose.

We may now look a little more closely at these two aspects of the Christian hope, as they apply to the conditions of the world today.

Here and Now

God's acts in history are not confined to the past. The Power of the Kingdom which was at work in Jesus Christ continued in his people. Here and now, we believe, within the fellowship of his Church, is the beginning of the world to come, the first fruits of the new age, the transfigured heaven and earth. And there is not only a power given, but a duty laid upon us through the Kingdom that now is. The Christian hope is a hope of our earthly calling. The difference between the Christian hope of resurrection and a mythological hope is that the Christian hope sends a man back to his life on earth in a wholly new way which is even more sharply defined than it is in the Old Testament. The Christian, unlike the devotees of the salvation myths, does not need a last refuge in the eternal from earthly tasks and difficulties. But like Christ himself ("My God, my God, why hast thou forsaken me?") he must drink the earthly cup to the lees, and only in his doing that is the crucified and risen Lord with him, and he crucified and risen with Christ.[28] The Christian hope bids men work for human brotherhood and justice, for racial equality and the peace of nations, for the fait distribution of food and shelter, for freedom from fear and want, from ignorance and disease. To accept Christ as the Hope of the World is to follow Christ's way in the world. To recognize Christ as King is to accept his rule for oneself and for society, and to be active in obedience to his will.

The Church as the pilgrim people of God is called to proclaim this Kingship, and to strive to be true to it in its own life. In the words of the Encyclical Letter of Pope Pius XI (*Quas Primus*), "when once men recognise, both in private and public life, that Christ is King, society will at last receive the great blessings of real liberty, well-ordered discipline, peace, and harmony. If princes and magnates duly elected are filled with the persuasion that they rule, not by their own right, but by the mandate and in place of the Divine King, they will exercise their authority piously and wisely, they will make laws and administer them having in view the common good and also the human dignity of their subjects. The result will be order, peace, and tranquillity, for there will be no longer any cause of discontent.... If the kingdom of Christ, then, receives, as it should, all nations under its sway, there seems no reason why we should despair of seeing that peace which the King of Peace came to bring on earth—he who came to reconcile all things, who came not to be ministered unto but to minister, who, though Lord of all, gave himself to us as a model of humility, and with his principal law united the precept of charity; who said also: 'My yoke is sweet and my burden light.'"

THE NEW WORLD

But the Christian hope points to a future at the end of history. The Kingdom that now is moves towards its full realisation of God's through all creation. What we hope for is the fullness of what we already possess in him. What we possess has its meaning only in the hope of his Coming. The character of the new age cannot be expressed in the language of ordinary prose. But the believer is quite sure that God's promises will be fulfilled, that the purpose of God revealed in Christ crucified will be seen, with a clarity that even

---

[28] Dietrich Bonhoeffer, *Letters and Papers from Prison.*

the blindest cannot miss, as everywhere triumphant, and that "the new life" in Christ will be fulfilled at the end of history. The New Testament uses the language of symbols, images, and pictures in describing the fulfilment; and the images used by New Testament writers have been all too often developed in fantastic ways. Images which are very revealing to some minds, or in some ages, may seem fanciful or even grotesque to other minds or in other ages. But the truth is greater than the form in which it is presented; and the truth is that the future lies with Jesus Christ. "The kingdoms of this world are become the Kingdoms of our Lord, and of His Christ: and He shall reign for ever and ever." (Revelation 15.)

All we can be certain of is that as the past is Jesus Christ, and the present is Jesus Christ, so the future is Jesus Christ. He is the same yesterday, today, and for ever. He who is both the beginning and the end, in whom all is to be consummated, is the One who meets us now and every day and invites us to commit everything to him. We do not know what are the limits to human achievement, of our own personal history, or of the history of the race. We do not know what possibilities are in store for us or what time is before us. We do know, however, that there is a limit, for we must all die. If we do not know Christ, death is the only limit we know. But with Christ death is transcended. He who has died for us, and is alive for us, confronts us with a totally new reality, a new limit, a new boundary to our existence. With him and in him the new world has begun!

CONCLUSION

A Lasting Legacy?

There can be no doubt that J. H. Oldham and George Bell shaped the ecumenical life and thought of their generation, roughly the half century from 1910 to 1960. Their stature is well attested on their memorial tablets in Geneva and Chichester, respectively; in the unconditional affirmation of their significance by Willem A. Visser't Hooft and others; and in their biographies. But another half century and more has elapsed since both of them departed this earthly scene, and huge changes have taken place in the churches, the ecumenical movement, and the world at large. Granted that they left a legacy, it has to be asked if it is an enduring one. Oldham, for one, would not be afraid of that question and indeed was asking it himself, as his younger collaborator Kathleen Bliss discovered when one day, she found him loading a bonfire with quantities of his papers and correspondence on the grounds that the next generation would have more important concerns than his biography.[29] Fortunately, she was able to salvage much of the material.

To Oldham is largely due the following: the 1910 World Missionary Conference in Edinburgh, giving birth to a permanent international and ecumenical missionary structure, the first of its kind; the insistence on serious study within the ecumenical movement; the early prophetic discernment that mission means the transformative engagement of the gospel with social issues, above all with race; the defining event of the 1937 Oxford conference on "Church, Community, and State" and its aftermath in working out a theology that could confront the totalitarian secularisms of the hour; the emphasis on the central role of the laity; the careful preparations for forming the World Council of Churches (WCC), incorporating the existing ecumenical organizations; the concept of the "responsible society" that guided the post–World War II social thinking of the WCC for the next twenty years; and much else. To Bell belongs

---

[29] Clements, *Faith on the Frontier*, xiii.

the credit for prompting the 1925 Life and Work conference in Stockholm to initiate a more lasting body, and then ensuring that the movement in the 1920s neither perished with the death of its founder, Nathan Söderblom, nor remained a largely effete series of assemblies passing idealistic resolutions on the state of the world. Thus it became a more cohesive, thematically focused body ready for use (by Oldham, especially) as the means for ecumenical study with the 1937 Oxford conference and beyond. Above all, it was through Bell's leadership of Life and Work during the German Church Struggle that set the ecumenical fellowship on the path of discerning the truth in situations of conflict and oppression, of taking a stand against politicized evil, and of standing in solidarity with those struggling in faithful witness. Equally, it was in his relationships with members of the German church scene during and after World War II, particularly with Dietrich Bonhoeffer at Sigtuna in 1942 and with the German church leaders at Stuttgart in 1945, that Bell set an enduring example of truthful fellowship and reconciliation. As chairman of the central committee of the infant WCC, he put his reputation to the best possible use in guiding the organization through its difficult early years. Both Oldham and Bell took the prophetic and often costly stand of loyalty to the universal church, which transcends all national boundaries, and to the supremacy of God's kingdom above all else. Both were indelibly British, but both knew where their higher responsibility lay as servants of the *oikoumene*. Thus Oldham led criticism of unjust coercive British policies in Africa, and Bell protested against the Allied obliteration bombing of Germany, confounding the assumed expectations of a bishop of the established church at a time of national danger. They were, above all, pioneers in grounding the ecumenical quest for unity in concern for the life of the *world*. Their stance reiterated the prophet Jeremiah's message to the exiles in Babylon: "Seek the welfare of the city where I have sent you into exile, and pray to the Lord on its behalf, for in its welfare you will find your welfare" (Jer 29:7). Both of them manifested that prophetic commitment, if in rather different ways. Bell gave voice to the challenge of God's kingdom on the public platform, or from the pulpit, or from the benches of the House of Lords. Oldham was not often a speaker in that sense, due partly to his affliction of deafness. But the prophet is also one who *sees*—literally, the *seer* in the Hebrew Scriptures—where God's kingdom is astir in the world. One can be a prophet at the desk no less than on the platform.

Appreciative biography, of pioneers especially, always runs the risk of slipping into hagiography. That ill does not serve the subjects concerned because it distorts them beyond human reality. Nor does it foster a proper understanding of the movements that owe so much to them. The haloes bestowed on the already illustrious figures cast a splendor on the story of which they are part, encouraging an exaggerated reverence toward the organizations they served, a protection against all questioning and criticism. As far as their human reality is concerned, it can be said quite straightforwardly that Oldham and Bell, even among their admirers, were not beyond criticism. In the preparations for the 1937 Oxford conference, Oldham upset his American colleagues with his determined predilection for a narrow range of continental theologians and caused resentment with his tight rein on the study program and the conference itself. He could be single-minded to the point of an interfering possessiveness in trying to recruit promising younger people like Lesslie Newbigin and Leslie Hunter to assist in his projects.[30] William Paton, who worked with Oldham in London from 1927, becoming the London-based WCC associate general secretary in 1938, was increasingly irked by what he judged to be Oldham's exaggerated view of his ability to deal with people and by being excluded from Oldham's Moot. With the passing years, Oldham's repeated calls to recruit the "best minds" into ecumenical thinking came across to some of the younger generation as a paternalistic indulgence. For his part, Bell, who has been accorded virtual sainthood—at least within the Anglican communion—was found by some to be somewhat *too* saintly in his solemn emphasis on the moral dimension of every issue at every level of life. Hensley Henson, the idiosyncratically outspoken bishop of Durham, wrote to Bell in 1940, having just read *Christianity and World Order*, teasing him for behaving as "an ecclesiastical Ishmael, whose hand is against every man, and everyman's hand against him" and having "lived too much in the heated atmosphere of committees, conferences, congresses and the like debased outcrops of modern democracy."[31] The leading Anglican layman and missionary diplomat Kenneth Grubb,

---

[30] See Clements, 311, 355–58.
[31] Jasper, *George Bell*, 248.

chairman of the WCC Commission on International Affairs 1946–68, found Bell "by no means easy to work with," as he was determined to get his own way—and if necessary, to go it alone. Grubb states, "It often seemed to me that this truly great man over-argued his case."[32]

Such judgments on Oldham and Bell can be accepted as reactions to thoroughly human personalities by persons no less human themselves. In the context of appreciating ecumenical history, it is more important to note again what has been recorded in this study of the critical questions Oldham and Bell addressed to the movement and its organizations in which they not only took part and supported but even had major roles in creating. We have seen how Oldham, far from regarding the 1910 Edinburgh missionary conference into which he had put so much thought and energy as an unqualified success, was soon querying its productiveness as a resource for new missionary insights and, during the 1914–18 war, was questioning its very assumptions about the fitness of Western Christianity (at least in its British form) to evangelize the non-Christian world. Having in 1921 established the International Missionary Council (IMC), he was soon restive about the tameness of the conventional agendas of the mission boards represented on it and wished to place social justice and racial issues as central concerns of mission. By 1933–34, he was seeing more possibilities in Life and Work than in the IMC for facing the new challenges of global society and acted accordingly. Having during 1936–38 deftly steered the ecumenical organizations toward forming the WCC, he began to voice anxieties about what kind of body the WCC would become, fearing the growth of a centralizing, bureaucratic structure taking on innumerable roles for itself (such as what, in his eyes, came with the formation of the Commission on International Affairs in 1946) at the expense of fostering and coordinating activity among the churches. When Bell took on the leadership of Life and Work in 1932, he did so not with any intention of paying lip service to its stated ideals but with a determination to focus more realistically on the new challenges to justice and peace and, moreover, attempt to deal with its remoteness from the life of the churches at the national and local levels. At the same time (1940)

---

[32] Kenneth Grubb, cited by G. Besier, "'Intimately Associated for Many Years': The Common Life-Work of George Bell and Willem A. Visser't Hooft in the Service of the Universal Church," in Chandler, *Church and Humanity*, 172.

as he was welcoming the formation of the WCC and calling for its support, he was recognizing its potential limitations and proposing an ecumenical consultative enterprise on a wider basis involving the Roman Catholic Church—indeed, being chaired by the pope. Nor did he really need Bishop Henson's strictures on conferences and reports, since as always, he saw ecumenism and Christianity as two parts of a shared *life*. To question and criticize aspects of the ecumenical story, therefore, is not to dismiss it or betray the legacy of its pioneers; it is to embrace a vital element in the outlook of those self-same pioneers, who are rightly regarded as the prophets of their time. The tradition is not itself sacrosanct.

Bell died in 1958, Oldham in 1969. History, including ecumenical history, moved on.[33] Bell had dedicated his 1954 book, *The Kingship of Christ*, to the members of the WCC Central Committee, the chairmanship of which he was relinquishing on the occasion of the second assembly of the WCC at Evanston. The theme of that assembly, "Christ—the Hope of the World" (equally with the title of Bell's book), conveys well the ecumenical ethos of that time: a confident, affirmative, Christocentric faith addressing the challenges besetting the world. That outlook was expressed also in the theme of the third assembly at New Delhi in 1961, "Jesus Christ—the Light of the World." But new themes were now requiring attention, not least relations with other world religions, and the 1960s saw a change of mood entering into the social discussion. The "responsible society" was still an idea to be reckoned with at the 1966 World Conference on Church and Society in Geneva, but the agenda of issues was markedly different from that of the 1948 Amsterdam assembly. Then, it had largely been the East-West European and United States–led capitalist versus Soviet Communist divides that had provided the parameters of debate. By Geneva 1966, the Cold War still very much held sway, but the dominant issue was now rapid social change, especially in the developing countries and the newly (or soon to be) independent countries of Asia, Africa, and Latin America, together with the dramatic impact of modern technology. There was an insistence by some

---

[33] For an excellent overview of changes in ecumenical life and theology since the 1960s, see Michael Kinnamon, "A Theology for Today?," in *Unity as Prophetic Witness: W. A. Visser't Hooft and the Shaping of Ecumenical Theology* (Minneapolis: Fortress Press, 2018), chap. 4.

speakers that "the churches should be more active in promoting a world-wide revolutionary opposition to the capitalist political and economic system being imposed on the new nations by the Western industrial countries, which was leading to new types of colonialism and oppression."[34] The idea of the responsible society had been based on assumptions of consensus that could be achieved in largely homogeneous and relatively stable societies, particularly as found in Europe and North America. But many communities were now voicing their protest at being effectively excluded from those societies that might claim to be responsible but were, in fact, based on debarring large sections of people from the very possibility of being responsible by virtue of race or economic status or gender, apartheid South Africa being the prime example. The fifth WCC assembly at Uppsala in 1968, under the theme "Behold, I Make All Things New" and meeting just days after the assassination of Martin Luther King Jr., marked a watershed and was the most activist yet. A major outcome was the Programme to Combat Racism, out of which was created a special fund of assistance to liberation movements in Southern Africa and elsewhere, the most daring if controversial step the WCC had taken. Instead of the responsible society, the emphasis now (1976–79) was on "A Just, Participatory, and Sustainable Society."

All this activism might already have seemed a far cry from the age of Oldham and Bell, the discussions on a responsible society, and the necessary balancing of the affirmation of freedom and the requirements of community. "Cry justice!" was now the order of the day. One should not, however, assume that the new prophets were rejecting those of the previous generation. Philip Potter, for example, who was the WCC general secretary from 1972 to 1984 and deeply involved in leading the transition toward activist campaigning for justice, is unequivocal in his praise of Oldham—the debt he owed to him and all his major writings on Africa and race, above all *Christianity and the Race Problem*.[35] The Programme to Combat Racism can be seen as the tree that grew from the seed of Oldham's 1924 book and its call for a crusade against all that is manifestly opposed to the kingdom of God in human relationships. Indeed, there are a number of

---

[34] P. Abrecht, "Society," in N. Lossky et al., *Dictionary of the Ecumenical Movement*, 1051.

[35] Philip Potter, foreword to Clements, *Faith on the Frontier*, xi–xii.

surprises in store for those who assume that Oldham's legacy was spent long ago. Latin American liberation theology took center stage on the world scene in the 1970s, radically challenging traditional theologies with its claim that it is in the struggle of the poor and their base communities for justice that God is to be met. This might seem a very different context from the 1937 Oxford conference and Oldham's presentation to it. But it was a leading liberation theologian, the Argentinian José Míguez Bonino, who wrote one of the most appreciative and concise accounts of Oldham's "middle axioms" as a means of the church's discernment of the signs of the time and in each crisis of history fulfilling its appointed task. Middle axioms, says Bonino, are like the compasses and anchors required for successful navigation: "Compasses help those at sea to get their bearings and anchors help to minimize drift in troubled waters."[36] The technology of navigation may change over time and place, but the basics do not.

In the case of Bell, his (and others') vision of the universal church pointing to the divine purpose of reconciliation for the whole human community, and therewith his holistic understanding of ecumenism, has certainly been a persistent theme in ecumenical theology, as seen in Faith and Order studies on the subject of the "Unity of the Church and the Renewal of Human Community."[37] But it is above all his personal embodiment of integrity and courageous witness to the overriding claims of the truth of God in society and the universal fellowship of the *oikoumene* that his legacy has consisted. Challenges still issue from the example of his ecumenical leadership in relation to the German Church Struggle, his friendship with Bonhoeffer and other members of the German resistance, his stand against the obliteration bombing of Germany, his ceaseless care for refugees, his ministry of postwar reconciliation, his constant placing of what he believed to be the call of truth and righteousness above the apparent interests of his own country—"It is not the Church's function to say *ditto* to the State"[38]—these have proved constant, unflickering lights

---

[36] José Míguez Bonino, "Middle Axioms," in N. Lossky et al., *Dictionary of the Ecumenical Movement*, 761.

[37] See, for example, Thomas Best, ed., *Church and World*, Faith and Order Paper No. 151 (Geneva: WCC, 1990).

[38] Bell, *Christianity and World Order*, 87.

for the ecumenical movement and, indeed, beyond. Many will echo the judgment of the historian Adrian Hastings that Bell was "the outstanding English Christian of the Second World War, as Dietrich Bonhoeffer was the German."[39] In calling for sacrifice in Christian and ecumenical commitment, the one who in 1944 incurred wrath, and probably the loss of the highest preferment, knew what he was talking about. The esteem in which Bell has continued to be held became evident when in 2015, the Church of England issued a press release stating that the church had paid a sum of money and issued an apology to a person who alleged that as a child, she had been sexually abused by Bell in the early 1950s. The resulting shock at this news, which was accompanied by the church and some civic authorities seeking to remove from public view Bell's memorials and portraits, was matched only by the widespread anger and disbelief that broke out when it became clear that the allegation had not been investigated in any serious or legally competent way. After more than a year of public pressure by groups and concerned individuals—including journalists, lawyers, historians, politicians, and theologians—the church commissioned an independent review by a leading barrister and member of the House of Lords, Lord Alex Carlile. His extensive and detailed review, prepared over many months, covering all aspects of how the case was handled, found the process severely flawed and amounted to a dismissal of the allegations.[40] Particularly objectionable to many people was that Bell, who in his lifetime campaigned so vigorously for victims of injustice, was himself in death denied any semblance of justice. His public reputation, however, so carelessly yet so seriously impugned, quite literally stands again: work on a statue intended for Canterbury Cathedral, suspended when the allegations became public, has been resumed.[41]

Examples can be cited of how Oldham and Bell viewed from afar issues that are now contemporary to the ecumenical witness

---

[39] Adrian Hastings, *A History of English Christianity, 1920–1985* (London: Collins, 1986), 399.

[40] Alex Carlile, "Bishop George Bell: The Independent Review," October 2017, https://www.churchofengland.org/sites/default/files/2017-12/Bishop%20George%20Bell%20-%20The%20Independent%20Review.pdf.

[41] In fact, on November 17, 2021 in a public statement the archbishop of Canterbury Justin Welby apologised for having said, following the Carlile Review, that a "significant cloud" remained over Bell's reputation.

today. There is Oldham's remarkably prescient call—a full forty years before the ecumenical program for Justice, Peace, and the Integrity of Creation was set up—for a new, faith-based reverence for the earth to counter the thoughtless technological exploitation of natural resources inflicted by growth for growth's sake.[42] Moreover, it is hard to see how—in a world once more beset by growing nationalisms and competing communal identities, many of them violent and racially or religiously energized—Oldham's and Bell's arguments, which recognize the realities of communal existence but always within the perspective of the ultimate loyalty to God and the universal fellowship of the body of Christ, can be said to have lost their relevance. One can, of course, try to squeeze every conceivable drop of relevance out of historic figures. Feminist theology and the call to recognize women as equal members of the community of the church have transformed the ecumenical scene over the past forty years, and it would be a gross distortion to portray either Oldham or Bell as protofeminists. At the same time, I well remember the Methodist theologian Pauline Webb, a champion of women in church and society and the first woman vice moderator of the WCC Central Committee (1968–75), pointing out with glee to a largely male clerical audience that Bell, in his much-loved hymn "Christ Is the King, O Friends Rejoice!" begins the fourth verse by reversing the conventional male-first order of speech with "O Christian women, Christian men, / all the world over, seek again." In his studies, writing, and editing, Oldham sought and valued collaboration with women, first and foremost with his wife, Mary, and such as Betty Gibson, Eleonora Iredale, Georgina Gollock, and Marjorie Perham. In later life, he looked to Marjorie Reeves. Above all, Kathleen Bliss, who became his most important ecumenical protégée, taking over the editorship of the *Christian News-Letter* in 1945, was a main speaker at the Amsterdam assembly and served on the governing bodies of the WCC. It was, in fact, Bliss who occasioned one of the few heated personal rifts between Oldham and Visser't Hooft. In 1951, Visser't Hooft invited Bliss to consider moving to Geneva as an associate secretary with oversight of the WCC women's and youth departments. In a spirited exchange of letters, Oldham objected to the very idea of his right-hand worker in Britain being transferred to Geneva and urged that the best service

---

[42] See pages 53–54 in this volume.

the WCC could do in relation to women would be not to create a "women's desk" but to set an example by appointing a woman to do the same kind of work as was done by a man.[43]

There is, however, a further and far-reaching question about the fitness of the legacy of Oldham and Bell, as also with others of their generation. This is the challenge of the *postcolonial* world and the advocacy of postcolonial theology and mission and, indeed, a post-colonial critique of ecumenism. Postcolonial theology views colonization as not just the political, economic, and cultural conquest of Africa, Asia, and Latin America by the European powers, a process that ended with the political independence gained in the twentieth century, but the mindset that determined such dominance and control and still persists in the relations of the former colonizers to non-Europeans. Indeed, it leaves its impression among the colonized too. The Western missionary project shared in this colonizing of the mind as much as of the land: "By and large, missionizing was seen as a civilizing effort, at converting the natives of every conquered land, homogenizing these subjects and turning them into Christians shaped in the image of their western tutors and masters."[44] This not only was a matter of outward practice but was born out of a fundamental feature of Western theology that undergirded the missionary effort: the belief that there is only *one* valid form of Christian belief, traceable to the earliest Christians in quest of a unified faith. Further,

> Western Christian missionaries consequently saw their mission in the world as getting all people everywhere to believe and practice the faith of their tutors as a whole. Deviations from this "one true faith" were punished as heretical.
>
> Western-missionized Christians in the colonies, like their tutors, were not trained or given tools to handle diversity or difference in any other way than through "conversion," persuasion, conquest, or suppression. Present-day churches across the globe, steeped in the dualistic, adversarial and conquest mentality of western missionary Christianity likewise seem particularly

---

[43] See Clements, *Faith on the Frontier*, 447.

[44] Emmanuel Y. Lartey, "Borrowed Clothes Will Never Keep You Warm," in *Postcolonial Practice of Ministry: Leadership, Liturgy, and Interfaith Engagement*, ed. Kwok Pui-lan and Stephen Burns (Lanham, MD: Lexington, 2016), 21.

unprepared to deal with diversity in a way in keeping with the love ethic of their Christian faith.[45]

This is a severe indictment not just of the missionary enterprise itself but, by implication, of the ecumenical movement that traces its birth to the 1910 Edinburgh missionary conference, and the charge will accordingly be extended: whether seen as the search for visible, structural church unity or the coordinated effort toward a Christian-inspired order of society, Western-led ecumenism manifests the typical imperialist or colonizing "top-down" imposition of unity on diverse people and communities. In contrast, postcolonial Christianity recognizes and celebrates diversity in which people and groups are allowed to speak for themselves, to express their faith and freedom in the way they relate to and engage with others, and to challenge unjust structures. It can be debated how historically accurate or fair such an indictment of the missionary enterprise and modern ecumenism is. Some may also question whether postcolonialism is not itself posing yet another binary distinction and adversarial opposition of the kind it claims to reject. These questions cannot be explored further here but must become part of the ecumenical agenda of discussion. To a degree, it has been on the table, but not so named, for some time. In 1971, the German ecumenical theologian and missiologist Ernst Lange warned against the claims of the churches to work for both their own unity and the unity of humankind: "Stored up in the realities of (world social) interdependence is a potential for conflict of such grotesque dimensions that any large claims for the church simply die on our lips."[46]

What role might Oldham and Bell play in such a discussion? At first sight, hardly any, if they are to be dismissed simply as products of the colonial age and its top-down ways of thought: Oldham was literally a child of the British Empire in India and a "friend of Africa," but even when combating colonial injustices, he was accused by his critics of working paternalistically within the supposedly benign imperial framework. In his study projects in London, he was also elitist in his search for "the best minds." Bell was the bishop of the established national church who spoke out politically but from his

---

[45] Lartey, 22.

[46] Cited in Abrecht, "Society," 1053.

privileged bench in the House of Lords. He also chose for his last book a title that implies the top-down approach of wishing to impose an order on the world: *The Kingship of Christ*. Not many would care or dare to use such a title today, whether in Britain or the wider world, where kingship is out of favor and pluralism reigns. On the other hand, and more positively, if what postcolonialism values is diversity, especially of voices otherwise unheard in the official counsels of the church, then both Oldham and Bell can offer interesting case studies, especially if we adjust the lens from the big picture to the smaller and more local scene. Oldham's Moot was a highly eclectic group of people from within and without the church who, Oldham believed, should be heard and allowed to interact. His core belief, inspired by Martin Buber and Eberhard Grisebach, was that it is precisely in the often unsought, unexpected, unpredictable, and uncontrollable encounters that new insights and perspectives emerge. His emphasis on the laity, who in their daily lives experienced the pressures that were shaping society for good or ill, was likewise a means to amplify the voices of those outside the official channels of leadership. His *Christian News-Letter* was, for its time, a vital means of enabling such people to share their views, as was the Christian Frontier. Bell, taking his cue from Oldham, saw the future of Christian community and witness in small, often spontaneous cells of people forming at the local level. The selections from the writings of Oldham and Bell in this book offer many instances of their welcome of diversity and rejection of any imposed uniformity.

Moreover, at times, they exemplified divergence between themselves. For example, Oldham disagrees with Bell on the matter of interreligious relations. In late 1943, Bell presided over a meeting of the World Congress of Faiths. In his presidential address, he called for representatives of the great world religions to come together after the war to take counsel on how they might strengthen the will of people everywhere for peace. He followed this up with a speech in the House of Lords, expressing similar hopes and concerns and suggesting the formation of an association of those who worship a sovereign creator. He was not advocating any kind of amalgamation of faiths; rather, he wished to formulate a common commitment to justice and love. He envisaged a common code of rules agreed to by the religions and an international organization, in addition to the World Congress of Faiths, of representatives of the religions that would have authority when questions of international morality were involved. All this, of course, sounds very prescient of more recent concerns for interreligious dialogue and advocacy—for example, Hans Küng's call for a "world ethic" to be compiled by the world religions.[47] Oldham, with exemplary politeness, was grateful for the good intentions behind Bell's proposals but extremely skeptical about their feasibility.[48] As for the religions, Oldham argued that if they met together at the world level, then the most proper matter for their deliberations would be their *differences*, and if they gathered to discuss social cooperation, there would be a sense of unreality because those differences would be sidelined and the misleading impression given that all faiths are the same. Surely, Oldham argued, the real need was not for the religions qua religions corporately to agree on social and international action but for people of whatever faith or none to cooperate, not as representatives of religions, but as citizens of their particular countries. Furthermore, any "code" agreed to by the world religions would receive scant attention and would have negligible influence if offered to governments from without. Only if it reflected the sincere intentions already held by governments as the basis of their actions would it count for anything. Such moral agreement was not even remotely in sight in the world at the moment. Oldham then moved to one of his most typical and long-running perceptions: the difficulty of applying any moral code to a situation from the outside. In the first place, very often in politics and statecraft, it is a matter of not one but *two or more* principles claiming priority or even being in conflict; and even if the overriding principle is clear, the question for the statesperson to crack is how, given the actual circumstances and the limited choices available, ideas become effective when embodied in national tradition and practice, and the priority for British Christians must be to reinvigorate the strength of the Christian tradition in the nation's life such that it guides national and international policy more effectively.

This was a cautionary word against wishing to start with the big picture and then seeking to impose it on particular situations, and therefore at least an implicit recognition of diversity. But neither was Bell, for his part, afraid of letting voices from outside the usual

---

[47] Hans Küng, *Global Responsibility: In Search of a New World Ethic* (London: SCM Press, 1991).
[48] *Christian News-Letter* 197, December 15, 1941.

boundaries of the church make their contribution. Indeed, he invited them. His enthusiasm for bringing the performing arts into the cathedrals of Canterbury and Chichester (somewhat controversial at the time) was not just a cultural indulgence; it was born out of a desire to see and hear what would not normally be heard from figures as diverse as John Masefield, T. S. Eliot, and Gustav Holst—orthodox Christians or not, but in Bell's own words, "auxiliaries of the gospel," with their own insights on what it means to believe, to doubt, and to be human.

This book, I hope, discourages any easy categorization of Oldham and Bell that would deny them a voice in our continuing journey. We may even hope that it is precisely from the postcolonial perspective, and interrogation of them from the Global South, that we may see in these pioneers significant elements of their thinking that we have not noticed before. I, for one, am sure they would have welcomed this encounter. As pioneers, they were not given to standing still in a place of safety. *Adventure*, we have noted, was a key word for Oldham, as was *sacrifice* for Bell. While having to be seen as people of their time and place, these terms indicate how they wished to challenge and transcend their context. In shaping the ecumenical life and thought of their time, they opened new pathways for the future, not all of which we have finished exploring today—and for which adventure and sacrifice are needed no less than yesterday.

SELECTED BIBLIOGRAPHY

SELECTED LIST OF J. H. OLDHAM'S PUBLISHED WORKS

(Ed.) *The World Missionary Conference, Edinburgh, 1910.* Vols. 1–9. London: Oliphant, Anderson & Ferrier, 1910.

The World and the Gospel. London: United Council for Missionary Education, 1916.

Christianity and the Race Problem. London: SCM Press, 1924.

A Devotional Diary. 1st ed. London: SCM Press, 1925.

What Is at Stake in East Africa. London: Edinburgh House, 1929.

White and Black in Africa: A Critical Examination of the Rhodes Lectures of General Smuts. London: Longmans, Green, 1930.

(With B. D. Gibson) *The Remaking of Man in Africa.* Oxford: Oxford University Press, 1931.

Church, Community and State: A World Issue. With a preface by William Adams Brown and an introduction by George Bell. London: SCM Press, 1935.

(With Willem A. Visser't Hooft) *The Church and Its Function in Society.* Church, Community and State 1. London: Allen & Unwin, 1937.

(Ed.) *The Churches Survey Their Task: The Report of the Conference at Oxford, July 1937, on Church, Community and State.* London: Allen & Unwin, 1937.

The Resurrection of Christendom. Christian News-Letter Books 1. London: Sheldon, 1940.

The Roots of Our Troubles. London: SCM Press, 1941.

(With H. A. Hodges and P. Mairet) *Real Life Is Meeting.* Christian News-Letter Books 14. London: Sheldon, 1942.

"A Responsible Society." In *The Church and the Disorder of Society: An Ecumenical Study Prepared under the Auspices of the World Council of Churches,* ed. World Council of Churches, 120–154. London: SCM Press, 1948.

"Technics and Civilisation." In *The Church and the Disorder of Society: An Ecumenical Study Prepared under the Auspices of the World Council of Churches,* 29–49. London: SCM Press, 1948.

Florence Allshorn and the Story of St Julian's. London: SCM Press, 1951.

Life Is Commitment. London: SCM Press, 1953.

SELECTED LIST OF PUBLISHED SECONDARY LITERATURE ON J. H. OLDHAM

Bliss, Kathleen. "Oldham, Joseph Houldsworth." In *Dictionary of the Ecumenical Movement,* edited by N. Lossky et al., 746–747. Geneva: WCC, 2002.

Cell, J. W., ed. *By Kenya Possessed: The Correspondence of Norman Leys and J. H. Oldham, 1918–1926.* Chicago: University of Chicago Press, 1976.

Clements, Keith. *Faith on the Frontier: A Life of J. H. Oldham.* Edinburgh: T&T Clark, 1999.

SELECTED LIST OF GEORGE BELL'S PUBLISHED WORKS

(Ed.) *The War and the Kingdom of God.* London: Longmans, Green, 1915.

(Ed.) *Documents on Christian Unity, 1920–24.* Oxford: Oxford University Press, 1924.

"The Church and the Theologian." In *Mysterium Christi: Christological Studies by British and German Theologians,* edited by George Bell and Gustav A. Deissmann, 277–284. London: Longmans, Green, 1930.

(Ed.) *Documents on Christian Unity.* 2nd ed. Oxford: Oxford University Press, 1930.

Randall Davidson, Archbishop of Canterbury. Oxford: Oxford University Press, 1935.

Christianity and World Order. London: Penguin, 1940.

The Church and Humanity, 1939–1946. London: Longmans, Green, 1946.

Christian Unity: The Anglican Position. Olaus Petri Lectures at Uppsala University, October 1946. London: Hodder & Stoughton, 1948.

(Ed.) *Documents on Christian Unity.* 3rd ed. Oxford: Oxford University Press, 1948.

"The Approach to Christian Unity." In *The Approach to Christian Unity: Sermons Preached before the University of Cambridge, 1951,* by University of Cambridge Select Preachers' Syndicate, 57–63. Cambridge: W. Heffer & Sons, 1951.

The Kingship of Christ: The Story of the World Council of Churches. London: Penguin, 1954.

(Ed.) *Documents on Christian Unity.* 4th ed. Oxford: Oxford University Press, 1958.

SELECTED LIST OF PUBLISHED SECONDARY LITERATURE ON GEORGE BELL

Chandler, Andrew. *Brethren in Adversity: Bishop George Bell, the Church of England, and the Crisis of German Protestantism.* Woodbridge, England: Boydell & Brewer, 1997.

———, ed. *The Church and Humanity: The Life and Work of George Bell, 1883–1958.* Farnham, England: Ashgate, 2012.

———. *George Bell, Bishop of Chichester: Church, State, and Resistance in the Age of Dictatorship.* Grand Rapids, MI: William B. Eerdmans, 2016.

Jasper, Ronald C. D. *George Bell: Bishop of Chichester.* Oxford: Oxford University Press, 1967.

Robertson, Edwin. *Unshakeable Friend: George Bell and the German Churches.* London: CCBI, 1995.

Rupp, Gordon. *I Seek My Brethren: Bishop George Bell and the German Churches.* London: Epworth Press, 1975.

Rusama, Jaakko. *Unity and Compassion: Moral Issue in the Life and Thought of George K. A. Bell.* Helsinki: Finnish Society for Missiology and Ecumenics, 1986.

SELECTED SECONDARY LITERATURE RELEVANT TO THE HISTORICAL BACKGROUND AND ENGAGEMENTS OF OLDHAM AND BELL IN THEIR CONTEXT

Bethge, Eberhard. *Dietrich Bonhoeffer: A Biography*. Revised ed. Minneapolis: Fortress Press, 2000.

Bonhoeffer, Dietrich. *Dietrich Bonhoeffer Works*. English ed. 16 vols. Edited by Victoria J. Barnett and Barbara Wojhoski. Minneapolis: Fortress Press, 1996–2013.

Clements, Keith. *Dietrich Bonhoeffer's Ecumenical Quest*. Geneva: WCC, 2015.

——, ed. *The Moot Papers: Freedom and Society 1938–1947*. London: T&T Clark, 2010.

Fey, Harold, ed. *A History of the Ecumenical Movement*. Vol. 2, *1948–1968*. Geneva: WCC, 1986.

Hastings, Adrian. *A History of English Christianity, 1920–1985*. London: Collins, 1987.

Hogg, W. R. *Ecumenical Foundations: A History of the International Missionary Council and Its Nineteenth-Century Background*. New York: Harper & Brothers, 1952.

Jackson, Eleanor. *Red Tape and the Gospel: A Study of the Significance of the Ecumenical Missionary Struggle of William Paton (1886–1943)*. Birmingham: Phlogiston Press and Selly Oak Colleges, 1980.

Kinnamon, Michael. *Unity as Prophetic Witness: W. A. Visser't Hooft and the Shaping of Ecumenical Theology*. Minneapolis: Fortress Press, 2018.

Methuen, Charlotte. "The Anglo-German Theological Conferences 1927–1931: Some Preliminary Findings." *Kirchliche Zeitgeshichte* 20 (2007): 418–449.

Newbigin, Lesslie. *Unfinished Agenda: An Updated Autobiography*. Edinburgh: St Andrew Press, 1985.

Reeves, Marjorie, ed. *Christian Thinking and Social Order*. London: Cassell, 1999.

Rouse, Ruth, and Stephen Neill, eds. *A History of the Ecumenical Movement*. Vol 1, *1517–1948*. London: SPCK, 1967.

Scholder, Klaus. *The Churches and the Third Reich*. Vol. 1, *1918–1934*. London: SCM Press, 1977.

——. *The Churches and the Third Reich*. Vol. 2, *The Year of Disillusionment: 1934 Barmen and Rome*. London: SCM Press, 1988.

Visser't Hooft, Willem A. *Memoirs*. Geneva: WCC, 1987.

Wood, John Carter. *This Is Your Hour: Christian Intellectuals and the Crisis of Europe, 1937–49*. Manchester: Manchester University Press, 2019.

INDEX

Africa: education and missions, 27–30; Hilton Young Commission, 31; Oldham on enforced labor, 27, 215; paramountcy of African interests, 29–30; South Africa, 29, 30, 219

arts, role of, 2, 120, 164, 194

Azariah, V. S. (Samuel), vii, 13, 153

Barmen, Theological Declaration of, 38, 127, 160, 165

Barmen synod, 127, 129, 165

Barth, Karl, 32, 36, 127, 160

Bell, George, in relation to Oldham, 36, 38, 39, 45

Berggrav, Eivind, 132, 141, 145

Bliss, Kathleen, 3, 4, 5, 22, 49, 53, 54, 55, 146, 156

bombing of Germany, 139–41, 156, 161–64, 176, 215

Bonhoeffer, Dietrich, 16, 42, 46, 117, 118, 119, 121, 122, 124, 125, 126–27, 128, 129, 137–38, 140, 142–43, 151, 153, 159–61, 165, 212, 215, 220, 221

Bonino, José Míguez, 220

Brunner, Emil, 32, 36, 38, 41, 85

Buber, Martin, 13, 33, 48, 106, 107, 225

Chakko, Sarah, 155

Chandler, Andrew, 4, 129, 150, 154

Chandran, Russell, 153

Christianity and the Race Problem, 28–29, 72–83, 119, 219

Christian News-Letter, 3, 47, 48, 49, 53, 57, 136, 141, 156

church: centrality of, 189–90; role in society, 60–62, 83–95; a universal fellowship, 44, 96, 187, 189–90

Churchill, Winston, 141

Cold War, 97, 102, 218. *See also* totalitarianism

communism/Marxism, 100–103, 197

Confessing Church, German, 1, 5, 37, 38, 127, 128, 129–31, 133, 143, 151, 152, 159, 160, 165

Datta, S. K., 12, 27

Davidson, Archbishop Randall, 23, 114–15, 116, 120

earth and nature, reverence for, 53–54, 221–22

Edinburgh World Missionary Conference (1910), vii, 13, 15–17, 18, 21, 31, 114, 115, 154, 157, 214, 217, 224

European postwar reconstruction, 141–42, 162–63, 176

evangelical(ism), 9–11, 16

Faith and Order, vii, 25, 36, 38, 44, 45–46, 121, 131, 155, 157, 195, 220

Fanø conference (1934), 1–2, 35, 38, 127–29, 156

First World War: as challenging Western missionary assumptions, 19, 59; church reactions to, 114–15; effect on missions, 19–21; treatment of German missions during, 22–23

Fisher, Archbishop Geoffrey, 141–42, 145–46

friendship in ecumenism, 12, 36, 48–49, 150, 151–52, 220

Gandhi, Mohandas K., 153

German Christian movement, 37, 123, 162, 165